A. J. BERGER and NANCY BRUNING

LADY LUCK'S COMPANION

How to play...How to enjoy...How to bet...How to win

Harper & Row, Publishers   New York/Hagerstown/San Francisco/London

It is not the editors', authors', or publisher's intention to either encourage or discourage gambling. We recognize that gambling is becoming an entertaining hobby and an exciting fact of life for an increasingly large number of people. Legalization appears to be a certainty. The statements and suggestions you will find in this book represent the judgement and research of the editors, authors, and gambling experts. But we cannot guarantee results; a gamble is, after all, still a gamble. Except for the mysterious, elusive thing called luck, a well-informed gambler definitely has a better chance of winning than his less knowledgeable fellow wagerer. So, all we can add is . . . Good luck!

All original photography, unless otherwise credited, by Sally Andersen-Bruce.

Section opening illustrations by David Murray.

Designer: Madelyn W. Lesure

 created by Media Projects Incorporated

LADY LUCK'S COMPANION. Copyright © 1979 by Media Projects Incorporated. All rights reserved. Printed in the United States of America. No part of this book may be used or reproduced in any manner whatsoever without written permission except in the case of brief quotations embodied in critical articles and reviews. For information address Harper & Row, Publishers, Inc., 10 East 53rd Street, New York, N.Y. 10022. Published simultaneously in Canada by Fitzhenry & Whiteside Limited, Toronto.

FIRST EDITION

ISBN: 0-06-014696-6

LIBRARY OF CONGRESS CATALOG CARD NUMBER: 79-1693

79 80 81 82 83 10 9 8 7 6 5 4 3 2 1

ACKNOWLEDGMENTS

The authors would like to thank the following for their help in writing, researching, and checking this book:

Jack Friedman, Donald P. Kelly, Vicki E. Lindner, Dorothy M. MacKinnon, James M. Martin, Joseph Powell, Shelley Fogel, Mark Tanner, Alvin Roth (Mayfair Club), Bruce Robbins (Bridge World Magazine), Edith Simon, Philip Guptil (American Contract Bridge League), and Joel Rudinger (from his manuscript, History of American Bingo).

For supplying numerous photographs used in the book, special thanks are given to the Gambling Unit of the FBI Laboratory, and particularly to Special Agent Phil Harker for his many helpful suggestions.

CONTENTS

One

PRESENTING LADY LUCK AND HER FRIENDS

FOR LOVE OR MONEY? 2
GAMBLING THROUGH THE AGES 10
TYPES OF GAMES 20
PROBABILITY, ODDS, AND LUCK 22
FROM THE RIDICULOUS TO THE SUBLIME 29
GAMBLER'S HALL OF FAME 34

Two

NEIGHBORHOOD GAMES

FOR FUN AND PROFIT 46
ROLL THE BONES 48
ALL MEN ON BOARD 60
FRIDAY NIGHT POKER 70
BLACKJACK OR BUST 100
A TOAST TO GIN 110
B*I*N*G*O 121
BRIGHT LIGHTS AND BOOBY PRIZES 125

Three

THE PAPER PLAYERS

GREAT EXPECTATIONS 132
THE STATE OF THE LOTTERY 133
SWEEPSTAKES—THE CROWD PLEASERS 146
THE NUMBERS RACKET 151
PLAYING THE STOCK MARKET 160

Four

HORSE RACING—A RUN FOR YOUR MONEY

NOT FOR KINGS ONLY 168
AT THE TRACK 178
A BEGINNER'S GUIDE IN HANDICAPPING 183
PLACE YOUR BETS 199
IN THE HOMESTRETCH 209

Five

A SPORTING CHANCE

MEET YOUR MATCH **214**
FOOTBALL—THE SUPER SPORT **220**
ON THE REBOUND **230**
PLAY BALL! **233**
IN THE RING **237**
ON THE ICE **239**

Six

**CASINOS—
IN THE BIG TIME**

ALL THAT GLITTERS **244**
ANYONE FOR TWENTY ONE? **248**
BANK CRAPS—CALL THE ROLL **253**
BANK ON BACCARAT **257**
PLAYING THE SLOTS **261**
ROULETTE—ROUND SHE GOES **263**
KENO—JUST THE TICKET **268**

SUGGESTED READING **273**
INDEX **277**

LADY LUCK'S COMPANION

PRESENTING LADY LUCK AND HER FRIENDS

FOR LOVE OR MONEY?

"Thou wouldst have no divine power if we were prudent." So wrote the Roman poet Juvenal of the original Lady Luck, Fortuna. This Roman goddess was thought so powerful that greater deities feared her whim. The Romans paid her great reverence, and held festivals in her honor. They even erected several temples for her, including one called "Felicitas," meaning good fortune.

If you visit the Vatican Museum, take a look at the magnificent statue of Fortuna, which shows her with a rudder in one hand and a cornucopia in the other. The rudder symbolizes her power to guide the affairs of the world; the symbolism of the horn of plenty needs no explanation. Other representations show her holding a sphere, said to indicate how slippery and unsteady fortune really is.

Over the centuries, Fortuna fell into much disfavor. Andrew Steinmetz, a nineteenth-century historian, tells this apocryphal story about her: "Fortuna, a selfish creature who could be placated only by cards, counters, and dice, gave birth to a 'misfigured child' known as 'Gaming.' Then Gaming herself gave birth to hideous twins. They were called Duelling and Suicide, and they became Gaming's constant companions."

Those of you who enjoyed flipping baseball cards as children . . .

Gambling is taking any kind of risk in order to gain something. So, broadly speaking, you're all gamblers—and have been ever since you were kids. If you once played marbles for keeps, or flipped baseball cards, you gambled. In those halcyon days the stake may not have been the legal tender that motivates the older gambler. Perhaps you couldn't put a price on having a complete collection, or being known as "the best." Nevertheless, those payoffs were substantial. And it was the gamble—the risk—to get that payoff that made those games more exciting and challenging. Chances are you're still some sort of gamester, or you wouldn't be reading this now. And those "friendly games" you have with your adult playmates now—the routine or occasional game of cards, golf, darts, or bowling—usually begin with someone asking "What'll we play for?"

A closer look at those who gamble by risking money to win money, usually on the outcome of some game, could take a lifetime of study. There are plenty of them. According to one recent survey, two out of every three Americans aged eighteen and over gamble—legally or illegally. Count yourself among these real gamblers if you play the horses, numbers, or casinos; attend afternoon card parties, weekly poker games, "Las Vegas Nights," or church bingo games; enter magazine sweepstakes or the drawing at the high school's annual bazaar; enter the office World Series pool; or buy state lottery tickets.

But gambling penetrates more than just such leisure–time activities. Some gamble in more subtle ways, such as speculating on stocks or commodities. You're a gambler too if you own insurance. Insurance is supposed to be the antithesis of risk-

taking—a safeguard—but scratch its respectable surface and underneath you'll find that the entire industry is based on figuring the odds against the occurrence of accidents, disasters, and the like, and then "betting" accordingly. Marriage, lifestyle changes, career changes, a move to a new home, are all high-stakes gambles that most of you have taken, or will take in the future. Even daily life is full of hidden little gambles. Every time you leave your umbrella home when there's a "chance of rain," you gamble. Of course not all gambles involve substantial risks, or result in outcomes that will affect the gambler directly. Yet the gambling spirit is there. Few, for instance, can resist the temptation to predict the outcome of future events. Who will the office Casanova approach next? Who'll get married? Who'll split up? Will your pregnant neighbor have a boy or girl? Which actors will win

Oscars? If you recognize yourself here then you've got that gambling spirit. And chances are you'll find you enjoy gambling for money. You'll discover that occasional and moderate gambling is simply a hobby—an intoxicating form of pure entertainment. Within the financial limits you should establish, it's fun; it's exciting; for skillful players, it's a healthy challenge. And there is always the chance of latching on to some "free" money. Although your daydreams may include saving the life of some eternally grateful millionaire, you don't really believe that such dreams will come true. But the dream of winning the big payoff, jackpot, daily double or grand prize could come true—if only you're willing to take the gamble.

So, put your fate into the hand of Lady Luck. Maybe next time she'll single you out from all the rest. After all, *someone* has to win.

The Gambling Mania

No person who has not felt it can appreciate the absorbing passion, the fierce lust for gain that seizes upon the victim of the gambling mania. At first he skirts only the outer edge of the whirlpool, trying to capture here and there a little fish, the silvery sheen of whose scales entices him. Grown bolder with success, and quite confident of his ability to withdraw at will, he steps in a little deeper, and then a little deeper, to obtain a larger fish. Bye and bye the swift, circling, inexorable current seizes him. His feet lose their hold. He ceases to struggle, or even to wish to struggle. He abandons everything to the fierce passion of the swirl. Conscience is stifled. The calls of honor fall upon deafened ears. The pleas of wife and children are unheeded. The demon of greed has him in its dire, relentless clutch, and at last he is pushed into the vortex whose bottom is the fires of hell!

(*Harry Browlaski, from* Easy Money.)

. . . now find similar pleasure in "real" gambling, by risking money to win money, usually on the outcome of some game. When affordable limits are set, it's fun . . .

Gambling is . . .

Gambling can be more than simply taking risks on uncertain events. It's also been said to be . . .

. . . a principle inherent in human nature. It belongs to us all. (*Edmund Burke*)

. . . a revolt against boredom. (*Stuart Chase*)

. . . a form of robbery. (*Moses Maimonides*)

. . . [that which] promises the poor what property performs for the rich—something for nothing. (*George Bernard Shaw*)

. . . the surest way of getting nothing for something. (*Wilson Mizner*)

. . . an activity you recall when and where but not why. (*Anonymous*)

The IRS Wants YOU

Gambling winnings—from cards, horse races, lotteries, TV game shows, or any game of chance—are reportable to the IRS as income and, therefore, taxable. Your losses for the year, however, are only deductible up to the amount of your winnings, and only if you itemize your deductions. And you must back up your claim for losses with documents. The gambler should record all successes and failures (just as records of business expenses are kept for itemized deductions). Keep a diary of trips to the tracks and bets made, and keep betting tickets, sweepstakes stubs, postage receipts, etc. If any traveling is involved, keep hotel bills or gasoline credit records to help substantiate your wagering activity and your claim.

. . . and there's always the chance that you'll win.

WHO GAMBLES?

In 1976, the Commission on the Review of the National Policy toward Gambling announced the findings of a survey conducted in 1974 by researchers at the University of Michigan. Perhaps the most surprising of their discoveries is that 98 million American adults gamble to some degree or other, some even making it their profession. And consider that number in light of the fact that many won't admit to gambling. (One reason for that is the tax laws.) Here are some more of their findings:

Twelve million people reported they only bet with friends—on card games, sporting events, political elections, and backgammon. Some 11 percent owned up to placing illegal bets with bookies; these bets totaled $5.1 billion a year.

Many are quite young. Of all people aged eighteen through twenty-four, 73 percent gamble. As they get older, people gamble less: The survey found that fewer than one person in four in the over-sixty-five age group gambles.

The average gambler is well heeled and well schooled: the higher the income and education, the more likely he is to gamble.

Gamblers tend to be suburban more than urban and urban more than rural. Eighty percent of adults living in the Northeast are gamblers, 66 percent in the North Central states, 65 percent in the West, and 40 percent in the South.

On an average, about 80 percent of all money bet is returned as winnings: after deducting the winnings from the entire amount of money bet in 1974, the net loss to bettors was $4.4 billion—or about $80 per adult (the equivalent of what the average American spent on tobacco, newspapers, and magazines for that year).

Interestingly enough, it was discovered that when the government sanctions gambling both legal and illegal gambling operations tend to benefit. When the state organizes a lottery, or when it sets up gambling parlors, citizens not only flock to these legal operations, but to bookies and numbers runners as well. (This is often a prime argument against legalizing gambling.)

However, some feel the economic benefits that result from the legalization of gambling have been vastly overrated. Even if all states legalized

Roll Over, Apple Pie

According to Clarence Darrow, gambling is as American as cowboys and Indians—or apple pie. He believed we love gambling so much because all our lives we hear that our nation was founded by people who took all kinds of chances. Our ancestors risked their lives getting to Pike's Peak or bust, fighting the Indians; they took their chances with vigilantes, hired gunslingers, land sharks, cold and calculating bankers, and lawyers "deadlier than rattlesnakes." They gambled that they would find water and survive crossing Death Valley, and that they would find gold during the Gold Rush. So gambling is part of the old American "get-up-and-go"; a part of everyone's dream of holding four aces, or rolling a 7 six times in a row.

lotteries, about $8.3 billion would be gained in revenues from this source. But that is only 4 percent of the $200 billion we contribute annually in state and local taxes.

Psychologists too have studied gamblers and many divergent theories have resulted from such research. Some see gambling as a regression to childhood. Others say gambling activates a "latent rebellion" against such things as logic and moderation. Some have argued that gambling is the acting out of an urge to live dangerously (i.e., masochistically). Some say gamblers sublimate Oedipal aggression. In all probability though, part of the reason psychologists have so much trouble deciding upon a single theory is because there is no single type of gambler.

Four out of every six Americans gamble.

Mixing Betting with Business

Here is an interesting sidelight of the legalized off-track betting situation from a large New York corporation. They ran a computer check on outgoing phone calls, and discovered the the most frequently dialed number belonged to the New York OTB betting office. So that's where their salaries go!

HOW MUCH WAGERED PER YEAR PER WAGERER

$1094.60

$665

$273

$273

$26

NATIONAL AVERAGE (ALL TYPES OF BETS)

LOTTERY TICKET BUYER

NUMBERS BETTOR

NEVADA CASINO GAMBLER

NEW YORK OTB BETTOR

The 1974 survey cited showed that each American gambler spent an average of $273 a year on all types of wagers—from 50¢ lottery tickets, to $21.05 New York off-track horse race bets.

The Sexual Side of Gambling

Sigmund Freud studied how gambling relates to sex and concluded that it serves as a kind of substitute. He interpreted Dostoevsky's pathological wagering as as expression of the writer's inner conflict over masturbation.

Theodore Reik stressed the obsessional character of gamblers, and wrote that the wagerer is plagued by the uncertainty of whether he will be punished or forgiven for sexual "sins."

Others, including Edmund Bergler, author of a seminal book on the subject, view compulsive gambling as a manifestation of the Oedipal conflict. Bergler believed that the gambler is actually a psychic masochist, who unconsciously wants to lose to punish himself for incestuous desires.

Rene Laforgue theorized that, for the gambler, fear and orgasm inwardly become identical. The gambler wagers to experience first fear and forepleasure, then punishment and orgasm.

Some psychoanalytic writers have cited evidence that compulsive gamblers are, to a degree, products of arrested character development. They point out, for example, that smoking, eating and drinking greatly increase during gambling.

Still, the average gambler shouldn't worry that he is laying his psyche on the table along with his cards. Bear in mind that Freud also said, "Sometimes a cigar is just a cigar."

TYPES OF GAMBLERS

Todd Coleman

Each one of the five people on this imaginary line at a Las Vegas cashier's window represents one of the five broad categories that most gamblers fall into: the recreational gambler, the serious amateur, the professional gambler, the compulsive gambler, and the cheat.

The first guy on line is the *recreational gambler*—recognizable by his stack of ten one-dollar bills. He usually plays penny–a–point gin rummy, or bingo at the church social. He may even get out to the racetrack occasionally, but sticks to the two-dollar bets on favorites. If he's ahead for the day, he just might risk an attractive longshot. He's quite partial to lottery tickets, and

can't resist a short Las Vegas stopover on his way to a California vacation. He figures that he can afford to lose a few dollars and take in a show besides.

The business suit is one clue to the *serious amateur*. Though he often bets on professional sports, either among friends or with his bookie, he also enjoys poker now and then. He's glad he decided to come to Las Vegas—he hasn't been here for years. But this line is making him a little impatient and he's checking his watch to make sure there will be time to get to a phone before the business day ends back home. He wants to call his broker, and check up on his favorite form of gambling—playing the stock market.

The patient guy at the end of the line—the one with wads of money—is the *professional gambler.* He'll get enough chips to keep him busy day and night, for gambling is his living, and his life. For him, gambling is a science and, more than anyone else in the line, he knows the truth in "Titanic" Thompson's dictum that "smart is better than lucky." Typically, he specializes in one game only, nearly always one that involves as much skill as chance. He has little or no regard for money, as it is only a means to an end for him—winning! His most valuable assets are a thorough knowledge of his game and its odds and percentages, his unflagging steadfastness, and his understanding of psychology.

Want to bet that the man reading the racing form and clutching the piggy bank is the *compulsive gambler?* He would rather gamble than do just about anything else. He's done some pretty unbelievable things to satisfy his gambling fever; his kids' piggy bank will be staking him today. He's not alone though: surveys show that 1 percent of all Americans who gamble are compulsive about it and can't control it. Some distinguished people have shared this same disease.

The slick-looking character who's left is the *hustler,* or cheat. For rogues like him, everything is a sure shot. His methods range from slipping a pair of loaded dice into the corner crap game to super swindles, like the time three Australians bribed a warehouse clerk to slip some doctored roulette balls into the Las Vegas casino-bound shipments. He might lead an extremely interesting life, but it's also one with a pretty high mortality rate. As the saying in Vegas goes, "Old cheats never die; they just disappear."

Gamblers Anonymous

One day in 1957 two gamblers met, and engaged in a marathon confession session that lasted five hours. A few months later they founded Gamblers Anonymous. Today, Gamblers Anonymous has a national membership of over 4,000 people in some 200 chapters across the country. Gamblers Anonymous keeps a low profile, refrains from promotion, rejects outside contributions, does not collect dues from members, and avoids debates on the morality of gambling. They will help the gambler determine if he is indeed a compulsive gambler (about 1 percent of the gamblers in America are compulsive wagerers)—and if so, they will help him cope with his illness.

GAMBLING THROUGH THE AGES

The level of popularity that gambling enjoys today is not unique to your lifetime, for the love of gambling is timeless and universal. Whether or not the urge to gamble is an integral part of human nature, we've been doing it so long that it might as well be. For example, archaeologists believe that cave men not only beat their wives, they wagered them as well.

It could be argued that man's love of gambling influenced a large part of history, for the world leaders, explorers, and inventors who got their names in the history books were all gamblers. They took a chance that they had a better idea. They risked their reputations, their lives, and their money. Those who won became the greats; those who lost have no claim to fame, but they

Bronze mirror case, 4th century B.C., depicting Aphrodite dicing with Pan. (Reproduced by Courtesy of the Trustees of the British Museum.)

probably lowered the odds for others. In this broad sense, the history of gamblers and gambles could fill libraries. But even in a literal sense, gambling history could fill volumes, because, for as long as we know, man has been inventing, adapting, discarding, and reinventing ways of testing Lady Luck. Here's but a sampling:

The Egyptian pharaohs had gambling devices buried right along with them. Among the finds unearthed in the tomb of Tutankhamen was an ivory gaming board. Gambling, it seems, was more than a part of their lives—it was part of their afterlives too. (Apparently, you *can* take it with you.)

Life during Biblical times did not escape the vagaries of chance, since all manner of events were deter-

Heads I Win, Ears You Lose

From China comes the story of two compulsive gamblers who had no money left. So they decided to bet their ears on which side of a leaf would be on top when it fell to the ground. The loser immediately made good his bet, cut off his ears and gave them to the winner.

These 15th century card players were immortalized in tapestry. The original can be seen in the Historical Museum in Basel, Switzerland. (Das Historisches Museum Basel.)

Cards used to be packaged in paper wrappers. This one is an 18th century French card wrapper.

CARTESTRESFINESFAITES
A L'UNION ROYALE

mined by lot. It was by lot that goats were chosen to be offered to Aaron, and by lot that Saul was selected to receive the Hebrew kingdom.

The Olympian gods, as well as their ancient Greek worshippers, played dice at their leisure. This 4th century B.C. mirror case depicts a dice game between the goddess of love and the god of the shepherds. Excavations have revealed that horse racing was a part of all their athletic events, including the early Olympic games. A Greek named Kleoitas invented the starting gate for horse races.

The Romans loved gambling at least as much as the Greeks. They invented the lottery as we know it today, and the Roman spectators at the chariot races were always ready to wager. The Emperor Nero was addicted to chariot racing, which proved to be the downfall of his marriage. One day his wife reprimanded him when he came home late from the races, and he kicked her—fatally. It's known that the game of *par impar*, which involved guessing the number of nuts or beans held in a fist, was popular among schoolboys in ancient Rome and Pompeii. But the large scale gambling seems mainly to have involved dice. Augustus was a confirmed dice gambler, as was the Emperor Claudius. In fact Claudius was found playing dice on the day of his sister's funeral. Such was his dedication to the game that Claudius is said to have written a book on the subject. Whether or not he did, however, is only even money, for it has never been found.

Sources reveal that gambling was widespread even in ancient India. Rajas played for days and days, until ". . . the wretched loser had been deprived of everything he possessed and was reduced to the condition of an exile or a slave." Such turns of events, however, were attributed to one's karma, rather than luck.

In 400 B.C., the Persian queen Parysatis gambled at dice against the king. The stake? The life of a slave. Unfortunately (for the slave) the queen won the toss and ordered the slave's execution.

Throughout the ages, gambling has caused wars to be lost and kingdoms to topple. During the reign of Charles V of France, the Prince of Orange gambled away the money entrusted to him to pay the French army. France's King Henry IV had a "grovelling passion" for wagering, according to the memoirs of the Duc de Sully. It is rumored that Henry lost enough money in a single evening's play to enable the winners to purchase Amiens (then held by the Spanish).

Playing cards, as we know them today, were used in France as early as the fourteenth century. (The earliest playing cards were Chinese, and were derived from Korean playing sticks.) They were used for fortune-telling, and for portraying a pictorial history of the times, as well as for diversion. Though a fourteenth century decree prohibited the people from playing at "tennis, bowls, dice, cards or ninepins, on working days," card games were popular among the noblemen, and the records of many a royal treasury in-

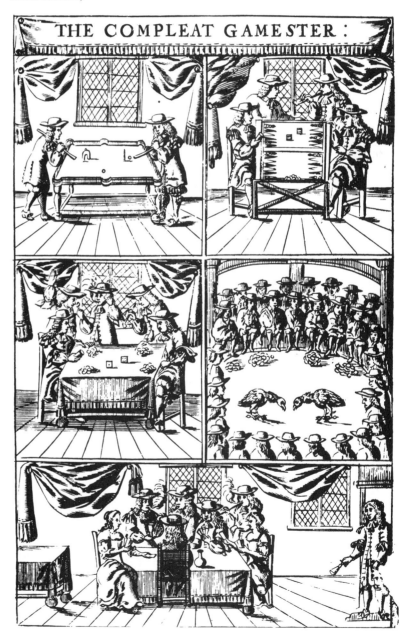

Frontispiece from The Compleat Gamester. (Reproduced by Courtesy of the Trustees of the British Museum.)

It's in the Cards

Lovers of the occult, the supernatural, and witchcraft may not realize that the ancient 78–card tarot deck, which was used for games as well as fortune-telling, is the ancestor of today's 52–card deck.

The tarot deck consisted of 56 cards divided into 4 suits, and 22 atouts. Each suit consisted of 14 cards—numbered cards from 1 to 10, a King, Queen, Cavalier, and Page. The atouts were numbered I to XXI, with one unnumbered card called Le Mat (or The Fool). Piquet (a card game of knights and chivalry) was supposedly invented in the fifteenth century by a French knight, and the old tarot suits of Épées (Swords), Coupes (Cups), Deniers (Coins), and Bâtons (Scepters) were respectfully changed to Piques, Coeurs, Carreaux, and Trèfles. These later became Spades, Hearts, Diamonds, and Clubs. Over the centuries, the Cavalier and the Page were combined into the Jack, and all but one atout—Le Mat—were dropped. Le Mat became the Joker.

The expressions of these 18th century English gambling-house players tell all—some gloat and count their winnings; some brawl amongst themselves; others quietly or dramatically bemoan their losses.

19th century French "vampire" ate francs with relish!

cluded monies spent for game cards. Louis XV used a pack made out of silver.

England's King Henry VIII was as notorious for gambling as he was for wining, dining, and wenching. In fact, one authority on gambling history called him "a gamester of the most unscrupulous sort." Strangely enough, at one point of his reign, this very same gamester banned card playing—except at Christmas. In the seventeenth century, the gambling fever caught on in England and spread like wildfire. Books like *Mr. Hoyle's Games* and *The Compleat Gamester* were popular, laws were written to settle gambling disputes, the fashionable hired tutors (Gaming Masters) to round out the education of their young, and gaming houses were established and thrived in spite of protests. (Essays, stories, poems, and plays of the time satirized the dispute.) In the late eighteenth century, England's loss of the American colonies (as well as the high divorce rate and other "horrors") were blamed on the widespread English addiction to casino gambling.

The history of gambling in the United States, though relatively short, is a colorful one. The American invention of poker, which immediately became the rage on Mississippi riverboats and in the Wild West, is a prime example. The late H. L. Hunt won his first productive oil well in a poker game. And several American presidents have been avid wagerers—according to Earl Mazo, Richard Nixon's biographer, the future president gave his poker face a good workout while stationed in the South Pacific during World War II.

It wasn't irrigation of non–arable desert, but the legalization of casino gambling that put Las Vegas on the map, and made this little American city as world-famous as Monte Carlo. Actually, gambling was legal in Nevada during the days of the gold rush but reforms swept the state in 1910. Then, in 1931, the issue of legalized casino gambling became a hotly-debated subject in the legislature. It must be remembered that at this time Las Vegas was nothing but a desert town, a trading center with a population of about 5,000 in a resource-poor state. Casino gambling alone made Las Vegas a household word, swelled the population, and poured enormous revenues into the state treasury. In 1946, the mobster Benjamin "Bugsy" Siegel opened the Flamingo Hotel. About six months later, Bugsy was murdered, but the "Glitter Gulch"—a strip of super–neon lights, extravagant casino–hotels, opulent entertainment, high living, and, of course, gambling—was just being born.

Ladbroke's

"If you can bet on it, we'll give you odds and hold your money"—that's what Ladbroke's motto should be. Although 95 percent of their business is from those who play the ponies, this English bookmaking firm—whose real motto is "Bookmakers to the Establishment"—has offered odds and accepted wagers on just about everything imaginable since 1895. They've even accepted bets on the selection of the Visiting Professor of Poetry at Oxford: in 1968, they put their money on Yevgeny Yevtushenko, but the Russian rhymer lost out to critic–poet Roy Fuller. The loss to Ladbroke's? About £1,000 sterling, or (at that time) $2,800. If the Loch Ness Monster is proven extinct, Ladbroke's must shell out $5,000 to one wagerer. And they lost a fortune in 1974, when Richard Nixon resigned from the Presidency before his second term was up. Ladbroke's had offered 3 to 1 odds against this outcome. One would-be wagerer, John Fairfax, successfully rowed across the Atlantic and wanted to bet on his safe return. But the only bet that Ladbroke's won't take is one concerning a matter of life or death.

Ladbroke's can see profits of $1.49 million in a relatively good year.

GAMBLING IN AMERICA'S WILD WEST

Along with monte, roulette, blackjack, and poker, faro (also called "The Tiger") was popular in the Wild West gambling establishments. To the honest gambler's relief—it was easy to be duped in this game—faro has died out.

In 1848, *everyone* was heading "out west" for a chance of finding instant fortune. Gambling was the grand amusement, one aspect of the American get-rich-quick dream. Gambling houses—often crooked and anxious to turn a quick profit before the gold mine ran dry—appeared in towns that literally sprang up overnight.

Actually, the term gambling house is a misnomer, for many were actually makeshift tents that could be pulled up and moved at a moment's notice to the next bit of action. Proprietors usually hired suave, male French croupiers with plenty of sang-froid and psychological know-how. They manipulated their customers as deftly as they did the cards in order to reap the most reward. There were exceptions, as the illustrious careers of Poker Alice, Madame Moustache, Madame Vestal, and Calamity Jane will attest. In a world populated largely by other men, rough-and-ready guys easily fell prey to their womanly charms, and supposedly hardly minded losing at all.

San Francisco was without a doubt the gambling capital of the West. By 1850 there were 1,000 gambling establishments in this city of 25,000 people. The El Dorado was the most famous of all—a huge tent that rented for $40,000 a year. The *handle* (total amount bet) was usually over $200,000; bets of $5,000 to $20,000 on a single hand were not uncommon. And everything was terribly expensive, even by today's inflationary standards: a bottle of whiskey cost $30; a hard-boiled egg went for $5.

In the plains, the situation was much the same—except the crowds were wilder and whiskey-logged. In Dodge City, which ran a close second in gambling activities to San Francisco, the whiskey was a concoction known variously as red-eye, skull-cracker, p'izon, forty-rod, or panther piss. (The base was raw distilled alcohol mixed with tobacco juice and pepper, and a few other ingredients better left unnamed.) Cheating was rampant, and many a gambler died violently over a card table. The obituary of one fellow caught cheating at poker reads: "Played five aces. Now playing the harp."

A room with a desert view was all that could be offered the 1930s Las Vegas tourist. (Las Vegas News Bureau.)

Today, the Las Vegas gambler can bet on practically anything, at any hour of the day. (Las Vegas News Bureau.)

In 1977, New Jersey voters went to the polls and legalized casino gambling in Atlantic City. Although strongly opposed by many voters, the proponents of legalized casino gambling argued that it would pump new life, jobs, and money into the decaying resort city. Resorts International, the first Atlantic City casino (and the first legal casino in the United States outside Nevada) had gross winnings of $16 million in its first month of operation. Spurred by similar dreams of economic booms, a dozen other states began to seek their voters' sanction for legalized casino gambling. Meanwhile, more and more states are getting their share of the action through lotteries. Some diehards insist that today's gambling craze is just a phase that, hopefully, will pass. But, gambling—under the protective umbrella of state government, inspired by the huge purses offered by national competitions and tournaments, and supported by the "bettor" class of people—is everywhere. If we can learn anything from history, it's that gambling is here to stay.

The First Gambling Laws

The first gambling legislation in the United States was passed on March 22, 1630, in Boston, Massachusetts. It ordered that "all persons whatsoever that have cards, dice, or tables in their houses shall make away with them before the next court under pain of punishment."

The first blue law for the regulation of gambling in America was passed in 1624 by the Virginia Assembly. It specified that "Mynisters shall not give themselves to excesse in drinking or yette spend their tyme idelie by day or by night, playing dice, cards, or any unlawful game."

Who's the Dishonest Man?

George Devol, the famed Mississippi riverboat gambler, saw the sucker who plays monte as a con man, whose intentions are just as dishonest as the monte thrower's. Says Devol: "When a sucker sees a corner turned up, or a little spot on a card in three-card monte, he does not know that it was done for the purpose of making him think he has the advantage. He thinks, of course, the player does not see it, and he is in such a hurry to get out his money that he often cuts or tears his clothes. He feels like he is going to steal the money from a blind man, but he does not care. He will win it, and say nothing about how he did it. After they have put up their money and turned the card, they see that the mark was put there for a purpose. Then they are mad, because they are beat at their own game. They begin to kick and want their money back. . . . They expected to rob a blind man, and got left. I never had any sympathy for them and I would fight before I would give them back one cent. It is a good lesson for a dishonest man to be caught by some trick, and I always did like to teach it."

(*George Devol, from* Forty Years a Gambler on the Mississippi.)

MISSISSIPPI RIVERBOAT GAMBLERS

Passenger boats that steamed up and down the Mississippi River in the 1800s were the scene of the hardest, fastest, and most dishonest gambling in American history. Passengers from diverse backgrounds used the riverboats for transportation but it was the Southern planters and merchants, traveling to and from trading and business trips, that were the main suckers. Playing cards and other gambling games was a popular way to fill the free time and relieve the boredom of a trip that could last several weeks. A well-equipped Mississippi riverboat gambler provided the passengers with varied entertainment: slot machines, bird cages, squeeze spindles, eight dice, shell games, monte, countdown, craps, faro, roulette, keno, and the ever-popular poker. They used every conceivable trick to set up the unsuspecting passenger for a fleecing. Getting the suckers drunk was standard practice, as was the use of marked cards, reflectors, loaded dice, hold-outs, and other cheating paraphernalia.

George Devol, perhaps the most famous Mississippi gambler, who vowed at an early age to "live off fools and suckers," said, "It [the hold-out] requires a great deal of cheek and gall and I was always endowed with both." Such gamblers had to be good if they wanted to collect their winnings peaceably and continue their performance to the last port. Large amounts of money were often involved but debts were also settled with mules, cotton, jewelry, or, if the gambler's performance was less than convincing, with guns. Cheats who were caught were dealt with by the captain or

The hold-out (*also called a* bug) *was a device carried in the vest pocket and used to conceal desirable cards until they would be useful.*

Steamboat races, though dangerous, were encouraged by passengers, crew, and the betting public. A race between the "Robert E. Lee" and the "Natchez," between New Orleans and Saint Louis, was won by the "Lee" in a record breaking 90 hours and 14 minutes.

sometimes by the passengers themselves. If nothing else, the cheats were turned in at the next port or stranded at the first possible landing place. But for years no amount of law enforcement could put a crimp in the riverboat gamblers' violent and colorful trade. Only the decline of steamboat travel itself could put the riverboat gamblers out of business.

Today, a few Mississippi steamboats still exist, but people ride them mostly out of nostalgia, not necessity. While sailing on the river, the boats are under federal jurisdiction—which allows gambling. As soon as they dock, though, they fall under state jurisdiction and a state that considers gambling illegal can confiscate any gambling equipment on board. But you may still run into a shell game now and then, or even Bondine Jackson Balasco, the "Last of the Riverboat Gamblers," an entertainer who recreates the dress and behavior of the flashy figure of the past.

Gentleman Jim

Jim Bowie enjoyed beating crooked gamblers at their own games. One oft-told story relates how he boarded a steamboat that was also carrying a young planter, with his bride and $50,000. The usual hoard of card sharps descended upon the innocent young man, and proceeded to separate him from his money. Bowie, who had been a silent observer, talked the despondent planter out of killing himself, and then proceeded to go work on the culprits. Near the end of the game, when the pot held about $70,000, Bowie was dealt a winning hand. The one opposing player had, of course, cleverly hidden a winning card up his sleeve. As he reached to retrieve it, Bowie whipped out his famous namesake. The cheat disappeared, leaving Bowie to claim the pot. He returned the $50,000 to the wide-eyed planter, and collected a kiss on the cheek from the grateful bride.

TYPES OF GAMES

The names of the games gambled upon throughout the ages may have changed, but the types of games haven't. In a more perfect world, there would be three types of games to bet on: games of pure skill, games of pure chance, and games that combine both skill *and* chance. In this world, however, we must settle for the last two.

Games of pure skill, where the bettor has total control and his ability—and nothing else—determines the outcome, just don't exist. While it's true that a game's winning strategy can be analyzed and even mastered, it's still:

Skill: 100
Luck: 0

only under unrealistically controlled playing conditions. There never was a game played where some chance factors didn't affect the outcome, or a bet on the outcome, to some degree or other: the screams of the hometown football fans, or the unexpected delay that caused you to get to the pari–mutuel window too late to bet on a 100 to 1 shot that came in. An element of uncertainty—no matter how small—exists when it comes to predicting what will happen in the future. Even a judge's indigestion could affect an outcome. Any winner shares the victory to some extent with Lady Luck.

But there *are* games of pure chance. Tossing coins, sweepstakes, lotteries, wheels of fortune, bingo, roulette, and others of their ilk give Lady Luck complete control. These games have no complex rules and variations to understand, no skills to master, no complicated mathematical strategies. Once you've decided to "take a chance" on them, little you do, or don't do, will affect the outcome. Compulsive gamblers like such games because they are fast and provide the opportunity for repeat bets. Some people wouldn't even call this gambling, since the chances of winning can be so small, but the millions of people who do bet on such games will attest that they are exciting and fun—if only for a moment.

Most games, though, fit into the category that combines both skill and chance. And it's this dual challenge that makes horse racing and sports wagering, card games and dice games, so immensely popular. Take poker, for instance. It's Lady Luck who deals the cards to you, but it's your knowledge of the game's strategies, the odds of drawing needed cards, and your opponents' vulnerabilities that make it such a good gambling game. Backgammon, basically just a simple dice game, is also immensely popular with gamblers because of the combination of skill and luck. You make the moves and control the stakes, but it's Lady Luck who controls the dice and, therefore, to a great extent, the outcome of the game. (One amateur backgammon champion attributed his $180,400 winning purse to 75 percent luck.)

The type of game that combines luck and skill attracts the smart gambler because he can control some

The Only Game in Town

One of the most famous gambling stories concerns William Jones (Canada Bill), who was stranded in a southern town. Inverterate gambler that he was, he set out to look for a card game. As soon as he found one, he sat down to play. A friend of his warned him that the game was crooked. "I know," said Bill, "but it's the only game in town."

TV GAME SHOWS

Perhaps the most public form of gambling takes place on TV game shows, where one person's wins and losses are broadcast to millions of homes. Contestants bet that their brains, memories or wacky costumes will be sufficient to win cash or merchandise prizes. It's possible to win thousands of dollars by appearing on one of these extravaganzas.

Since many producers pick contestants from the studio audience, your first step on the road to riches and fame is to get tickets to the show of your choice. Almost all of NBC's shows originate on the West Coast; write to NBC Tickets, 3000 West Alameda, Burbank, CA 90515. For CBS shows that are taped on the East Coast, write to CBS Ticket Bureau, 524 West 57th Street, New York, NY 10019. For their West Coast shows: CBS Television City, 7800 Beverly Boulevard, Hollywood CA 90036. For tickets to ABC shows, write to ABC Guest Relations, 38 West 66th Street, New York, NY 10023.

If you should be chosen to be tested, remember that producers are looking for contestants who are excitable, good-looking, and bright—usually in that order. If you can easily get worked up over an instamatic camera, twelve cases of dog food, or a trash compactor, you're practically home free. Some of the more serious shows also keep an eye out for contestants who can ad-lib entertainingly or come up with rib-tickling repartee.

Bear in mind, though, that prizes won are not strictly "free." Even merchandise is considered taxable "income."

(© 1978 American Broadcasting Companies, Inc.)

factors. And where consistent winning is concerned, there is no substitute for superior knowledge brought to a game that requires some degree of skill. And a large part of the skill needed—no matter what the game—is an understanding of probability and odds.

PROBABILITY, ODDS, AND LUCK

Your chances of winning any wager can be reduced to a matter of mathematical probability. And, if you fail to learn at least the principles of probability theory, you will never win consistently.

Basically, probability theory is a set of principles used to predict the outcome of future chance events. The most important principle to remember is that probability theory states what is *expected* to happen, not what is *inevitable*. There are no specific guarantees.

The second principle to remember is that each and every chance event occurs independently, without any relation to previous events. If you have tossed a coin thirty times, and it has landed heads up each time, you still cannot assume that the next toss will be heads too. Nor can you assume that the next toss has to be tails, simply because "it's about time."

Each and every time you toss a coin, the chances are even that it will come up either heads or tails—even if the last million throws were, miraculously, heads. Whoever coined the old sayings, "The dice have no memory," and "Poker chips have no home," understood the principle of independent events.

This principle singlehandedly repeals what most people call "the law of averages." Also known as "the maturity of chances" and "the gambler's fallacy," this misguided notion promises the gambler that if he rides out a losing streak, his bad luck will change to good. Or, if he is winning, he assumes that the law of averages dictates that his good luck must inevitably turn to bad. Both notions ignore the principle of independent events.

Probability theory also states that if you are flipping coins with a friend, in the long run you have as good a chance as he does to win—even if you insist on calling heads every time you toss the coin. You might have to flip the coin an infinite number of times to realize this, but in the long run heads will tend to even up with tails. This should not, however, be interpreted as meaning that winnings must exactly even up in the end. Probability theory deals with the general and large numbers, not with the specific. Heads will turn up *about* half the time in the long run, but heads will not necessarily turn up exactly an equal number of times as tails.

"Once, twice, three . . . shoot!" Probability theory states that each chance event is independent of what occurred before. In this choosing game, each player's chances of winning remain the same no matter how many times they play, and no matter what the outcomes were in previous games.

Since probability theory cannot provide guaranteed information about specific events yet to happen, there is still some uncertainty in any future happening. Statisticians label this uncertainty in mathematical terms, but the gambler calls it luck.

Luck is the biggest trap, and the folly of every gambler since gambling began. Some skeptics point out, quite rationally, that the chances of winning don't change for "lucky" or "unlucky" gamblers. What *does* change from player to player is their skill and knowledge of the game. And yet, no one can prove that Lady Luck doesn't exist—and no one can give a better explanation for the occasions when the theory of probability seems to go haywire.

Imagine that a raffle was held and you bought 1999 out of the 2000 tickets sold. When the winning ticket was picked, it turned out to be the 2000th ticket—the one you didn't buy. The chances of your winning were very good. Your winning was a probable (expected) outcome but not a sure (inevitable) outcome. There was the chance—though slim—that that one other ticket could be chosen. The outcome of any event is uncertain, but when the less probable outcome does occur, it's attributed to luck.

"It's the mark of an inexperienced man not to believe in luck," wrote Joseph Conrad. You may believe in it, but don't depend on it. It is not luck that improves the memory of the dice or guides the poker chips home, so much as it is the thorough knowledge of the games you play and an understanding of how to increase your probability of winning.

"The lucky couple!"

Probability theory states what is expected to happen, not the inevitable. But there are no guarantees. When the unexpected does occur, we call it luck.

PIONEERS OF PROBABILITY

It was inveterate gamblers who first interested scientists in the study of probability. The foundation was laid by Galileo Galilei who, at the behest of his friend and benefactor, the Grand Duke of Tuscany, became intrigued by a problem posed by the tossing of dice. The duke, an avid gambler wanted to know why, when three dice are used, the number 10 is thrown more often than the number 9.

Galileo computed the probabilities and ultimately published a treatise, *Thoughts about Dice Games.* In it he said that there is a very obvious reason why certain numbers in a dice game are more advantageous than others—some numbers are more easily and more frequently made than others. The frequency depends on the number of various combinations with which any one number can be made. He explained that since one die can land in six different ways, three dice can fall in 216 ways (6 x 6 x 6 = 216). Some totals, or combinations, occur more often than others, and so are more likely. For example, with three dice, a 3 can be thrown in only one way: 1–1–1. A 9, on the other hand, can be obtained in 25 ways, and a 10 can be thrown in a total of 27 ways. Those two extra combinations give the number 10 a slight edge over 9, and so 10 will come up more often.

Galileo Galilei.

Blaise Pascal.

The next important scientist concerned with odds and probabilities was Blaise Pascal, whose 1654 meeting with another gambler, the Chevalier de Méré, resulted in Pascal's theory of probability. When betting even money that the number 6 would come up at least once in every four rolls of a single die, the Chevalier, a bit of a sharper, won handsome sums. Then, on the assumption that if two dice were used, double-6's would come up at least once in every 24 rolls, he lost a bundle. He asked Pascal to find out why.

With the one-die bet, Pascal determined, the Chevalier had better than a 3.5 percent advantage at even money, but the two-die bet was advantageous only with 24.6 or more rolls—an impossible even-money wager unless the Chevalier could figure out some way to roll fractions. If the Chevalier were to have the advantage with two-die rolls, he'd have to roll at least 25 times. With 24 rolls, he was at a better than 1.2 percent disadvantage.

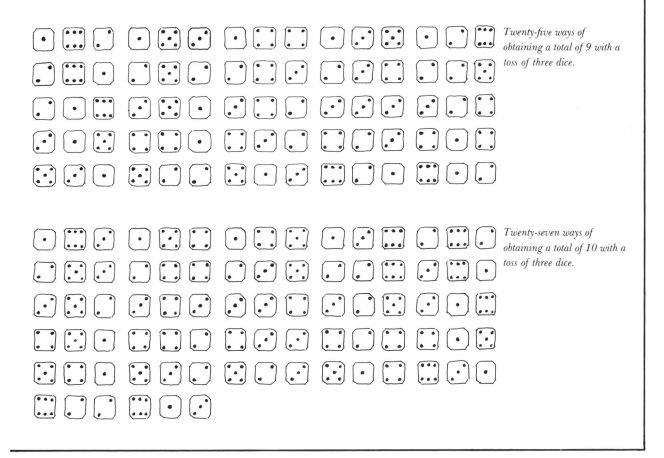

Twenty-five ways of obtaining a total of 9 with a toss of three dice.

Twenty-seven ways of obtaining a total of 10 with a toss of three dice.

THE WIZARD OF ODDS

There's really no great mystery shrouding the methods for computing odds, though as one pro admitted, "for those who understand, it's easy; for those who don't, it's tough." But an understanding of how the odds are figured, and what they mean in terms of money bets, is an indispensable aid to intelligent betting. You'll understand, for example, why betting favorites won't make you instantly rich, and know when an opponent, such as a gambling casino or bookie, is slanting things in his favor by paying winners at incorrect odds.

As a start to this understanding, you must be able to express probability in mathematical terms. When the outcome of some event is impossible, the probability is 0; when it is sure to happen, the probability is 1. Most events fall somewhere between 0 and 1, so the probability is expressed as a fraction. The fraction is obtained by using this formula: The probability of any particular outcome occurring is equal to the number of desirable outcomes possible, divided by the total number of outcomes possible. Let's say you have entered into a little coin-tossing proposition. You want heads and your friend wants tails. There are a total of two possible outcomes for each toss (heads or tails), but there is only one desirable outcome for you (heads). So the probability fraction would be ½. Or you can say you have a 50 percent chance (probability) of getting heads. Or that the probability of getting heads is 1 in 2, or 1 out of 2.

The numbers derived from mathematical expressions of probability for and odds against mean exactly the same thing.

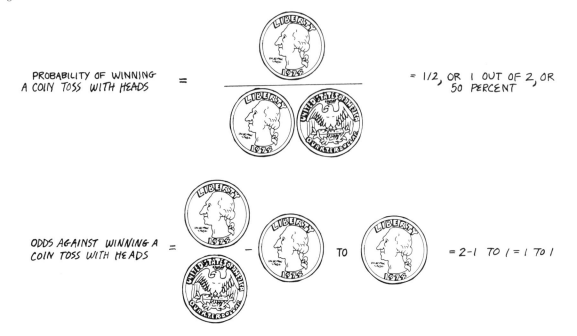

PROBABILITY OF WINNING A COIN TOSS WITH HEADS = _____ = 1/2, OR 1 OUT OF 2, OR 50 PERCENT

ODDS AGAINST WINNING A COIN TOSS WITH HEADS = ___ − ___ TO ___ = 2−1 TO 1 = 1 TO 1

For betting purposes, the mathematical probability is most often converted to the *odds against* something happening, which is also expressed in mathematical terms. The odds are the number of undesirable outcomes (total number of possible outcomes minus the number of desirable outcomes), against the number of desirable outcomes. When the probability of getting heads on a single toss is ½, the odds against it happening are 1 (2 minus 1) to 1. These particular odds have a funny ring to them. It's one type of *even-up proposition*, or *even-money bet*, where each possible outcome has the same probability of occurring, and you stand to win the same payoff no matter which outcome you bet on. If you bet one dollar on heads or tails you stand to win one dollar. You also get back the original dollar you bet, so the *payoff* would be two dollars. However, 1 to 1 odds rarely occur in gambling situations because usually one outcome will be favored (more likely to occur) over the other.

Calculating the odds and payoffs is a simple operation when dealing with two sides of a coin. Now apply this same reasoning to the roulette wheel. Let's say you bet one dollar on number 18. There are 38 pockets into which the ball can fall, and number 18 is one of them. So, your chance of winning (probability) is 1/38, 1 in 38, or 2.63 percent. There are 37 pockets other than the number 18 so the odds *against* your winning are 37 (38 minus 1) to 1.

(Another way of putting it is that in the long run, for every 38 spins of the wheel, you can expect your number, 18, to come up once. Bear in mind, however, that this is not inevitable. Each spin of the wheel is an independent event, and you could play 100 times and never win.) To figure out how much money you would stand to win, use this formula:

$$\text{the first odds-against number} \times \frac{\text{the amount bet}}{\text{the second odds-against number}} = \text{amount to be won}$$

With 37 to 1 odds, a $1 wager on number 18 would win you $37 (37 × $1/1 = $37) and your payoff would be $38 ($37 plus your original bet).

Belief in luck and in probability theory are not mutually exclusive. Probability and odds calculations "work" because they deal with large numbers. However, the unexpected can occur in any individual event. Therefore, though your chances of winning a jackpot, for example, may be slim, they do not preclude the possibility that you will be lucky enough to win.

Is Nothing Sacred?

Even the papacy is not immune to the odds-makers' wizardry. In 1978, at least one odds-maker succumbed to the temptation of predicting the outcome of the next papal election. Italian cardinals Sebastiano Baggio and Segio Pignedoli were predictable favorites at 8 to 1; non–Italians Johannes Willibrands and Aloisio Lorcheider were pegged at 16 to 1 and 25 to 1 respectively. The winner, Albino Luciani, was such a surprise that no one had bothered to give him any odds at all. All this should perhaps have been taken as a sign from above. As you may recall, the new Pope died a mere month after his election.

Taking this a few steps further with cards, the chance of drawing the king of hearts from a deck of 52 cards is 1 in 52; and the odds against drawing that particular card are 51 to 1. But if you need *any* king, the probability of drawing one is 4/52, or 1/13 or 1 out of 13; the odds against drawing any king are 48 (52 minus 4) to 4, or 12 to 1. If any picture card will do—jacks, queens or kings—the odds against drawing one are reduced to 40 to 12, or 10 to 3. In any particular situation, the odds against a desirable outcome happening (i.e., drawing the card[s] you need) decrease, and the chances of it happening increase, as you increase the total number of possible desirable outcomes. The converse is also true.

When betting on a particular outcome, the smaller the odds against it happening, the less you'll win if the outcome does occur. Such "safe" bets don't return much money, because there's not much of a risk. That's why betting on the favorite doesn't pay off much more than your original bet. Riskier bets—bets on an outcome with greater odds against it happening—will pay off more. That's why winning bets on longshots offer higher payoffs. The choice is yours.

If you understand this concept, you will also be able to understand how casino owners or bookies can assure themselves of a profit with the house percentage or edge they give themselves. This edge is based on giving less than correct odds on bets. By lowering the odds, they assume a bet is "safer" (or more probable to occur) than the correct odds say it is, and so they lower the payoff they give to winners. They pay off at lower odds, even though the actual odds are higher, so the gambler is taking a greater risk than is fair.

Betting on horse races and sports will be discussed more fully in later sections. Both are more complicated than games of chance because horses and athletes are not inanimate objects like cards. There are more variables that can affect the outcome, and those factors must be analyzed and weighed. Both, however, do utilize odds and, as in other games of chance, the odds help you determine whether a bet is a good one, and whether the payoff is worth the risk.

The science of genetics is often explained to the layman in terms of probability theory. The probability of a single birth being a boy (or girl) is, like the head (or tail) outcome of a single flip of a coin, 1 in 2. Similarly, the boy-girl arrangement of a family of four children and the head-tail arrangement for four flips of a coin are mathematically equivalent events. The probability of this all-girl arrangement for a family of four children is 1 in 16. (The probability of an all-boy arrangement for a family of four children is also 1 in 16, so the chances are 2 in 16 of getting a 4:0 ratio.) The probability of a fifth child also being a girl remains at 1 in 2, regardless of the outcome of previous births.

FROM THE RIDICULOUS TO THE SUBLIME

Mathematical formulas won't, however, provide *all* the answers. Even gamblers who bet wisely have tried to find ways to control the uncertainty that exists. All sorts of superstitions have resulted from this quest.

Nothing better illustrates the power superstition holds over gamblers than the riches-to-rags story of George Bryan (Beau) Brummell, the wealthy Englishman more famous for his *haute couture* than his gaming habits. At times extremely lucky, he nevertheless died in poverty and insane, in Caen, in 1840.

Brummell was walking through Berkeley Square one day in 1813 when he chanced upon a shining object lying in the road. He picked it up and, seeing it to be a crooked sixpence, said to his companion, "Here is a harbinger of good luck!" That night, he punched a hole through the coin and attached it to his watch chain.

The talisman did prove fortunate, for during the next two years, Brummell realized casino and track winnings of almost £30,000. Then one day, by accident, he gave the "lucky" coin to a hackney-coachman, and a streak of ruinous bad luck followed until at last poor Brummell was forced into exile to escape his creditors.

Brummell's faith in his coin is really not so unique. Many who gamble appear to have at least one superstition they believe can control those "mysterious forces" that influence the outcome of future events. These superstitions are found among all cultures the world over. The Christian believes the number thirteen unlucky because Jesus was the thirteenth man at the Last Supper, and Greek mathematicians thought it to be an "imperfect" number. Modern day American urbanites are hard pressed to find a 13th floor in high-rise structures—or an airport with a Gate 13. The Chinese won't discuss gambling while they eat. In some European countries, gamblers carry mandrake roots with them. They are said to bring good luck, as are—as legend has it—the thumbs of hanged men.

Beau Brummell, the 19th century dandy, blamed the loss of his fortune on the loss of a good luck charm.

Must be his lucky day.

In Germany, wagerers used to write this rhyme on a piece of parchment and keep it in their pocket for good luck: "Lirum, larum, broomsticks hot; Aged women eat a lot." During the late nineteenth century, tiny pigs made of porcelain or silver were considered lucky. Sunday is said to be the luckiest day. And there are those who will never play longshots on Fridays.

Card players seem to have their own peculiar hang-ups. Some refuse to gamble with their backs to the

THE LABOUCHERE SYSTEM

"Rouge et Noir," whose real name was Charles William Heckethorn, was a self-confessed reformed gambler who wrote a learned if preachy treatise on "hazard and speculation" titled *The Gambling World*. In it, he told of a magazine editor named Labouchere who boasted of taking the waters at the spas of Hamburg each year, invariably paying his vacation expenses out of winnings at the gambling tables. Labouchere, it seems, had an "infallible" system.

Labouchere's system is so quaint that we can't resist passing it on, taking no responsibility, of course, for any lives ruined or fortunes lost as a result of its practical application. Although Labouchere employed the system at the *trente et quarante* tables, you may, if you wish, see what good comes of trying it at craps, roulette, or any casino game.

First, write on a slip of paper the following sequence of numbers:

3
4
5
6
7

moon. Others, remembering the fate of the Wild West's Bill Hickok, won't play poker with their backs to a window. Some Texas poker players insist that there's no surer way to lose than to let someone's foot touch your chair during a hand of play. A team of bridge players will often insist on sitting at the table in the same relative direction (for example east-west) as the bathtub in the house. Lending money while playing supposedly brings bad luck; borrowing, the opposite.

The usual charms used to overcome unfavorable odds include horseshoes, four-leaf clovers, orange peels, rabbit's feet, newly-found heads-up pennies, and ladybugs. One of the weirdest charms is the touch of a hunchback—especially if you can rub a coin against him without his perceiving it.

The hardest way to win any gamble must surely be the one that's based on superstition—even on your lucky day.

Wild Bill Hickok

Although no stretch of the imagination could consider this legendary western hero a good card player, he was nevertheless an avid one. Wild Bill Hickok joined in whenever there was a game, and loved to drink while playing. He died not only with his boots on, but with his cards in his hand. Here's how it happened: During a game in a Deadwood saloon in 1876, a young, would-be gunslinger named Jack McCall sneaked up behind Wild Bill. Then, for no apparent reason save to establish his own reputation, he shot Wild Bill in the back. As Hickok collapsed, dead, to the floor, his poker hand was exposed: a pair of aces, a pair of 8's, and a queen. This hand, so unlucky for Wild Bill, has come to be known as "the Dead Man's Hand."

Your stake will always consist of the top and bottom numbers added together. If you win, scratch out the two figures; if you lose, write the amount of the stake you've lost at the bottom, then add the bottom and top figures again for your next wager. Go on in this way until you have scratched out all of the figures on your sheet.

Let's say, for example, you're playing roulette. You've played $10 on the red and it comes up black. You write the number of your loss, 10, at the bottom of the list, under the number 7. Now you add the bottom number and the top, or 10 and 3, and bet $13. Let's say you play even and the ball stops in an even-numbered pocket. Simply cross out or erase the top and bottom numbers (3 and 10) and bet the next two top and bottom (4 and 7, or $11).

"The basis of the system was this," Labouchere wrote, "Before reaching the maximum I could play a series of even chances for about two hours, and if during these two hours I won one-quarter as many times as the bank, plus five, all my figures were erased. During these two hours an even chance would be produced 200 times. If, therefore, I won 55 times, and the bank won 145 times, I was the winner of 25 napoleons, florins, or whatever was my unit."

Labouchere admits, however, that he might simply have been lucky. Concludes the dubious Heckethorn, "It was luck and nothing else."

A SAMPLING OF SYSTEMS

Let Them Sell Vegetables!

"He's a very nice man with a clear mind and strong nerves, but he wins too much!" With that observation, Dr. Richard Jareki was banned from the roulette tables in a casino in San Remo, Italy in 1969. The man had developed a system based on the fact that some roulette wheels have slight defects that cause some numbers to come up more frequently than they should. The Heidelberg University researcher simply observed the wheel and noted which numbers the ball was most attracted to. He then fed the data into a computer, which discerned a pattern. In the years prior to his banishment, he reportedly won over $1 million, but he maintained that the reports of his winnings had been exaggerated and that they didn't take his heavy losses into account. Pointing out that gambling, roulette, and academia just don't mix, he shunned the publicity surrounding him and his computer as much as he could. His parting comment was, "If casino managers don't like to lose, they should sell vegetables."

"Show me a New Yorker with a sure-fire system and plenty of hard cash to bet on it, and I'll send a taxicab to pick him up." So goes an old saying, attributed to the pit boss of a popular casino on the Las Vegas strip. They *love* system-players in Vegas because systems just don't work. To begin with, they completely disregard the principle of independent events. As you may recall, this means that any chance event occurs independently, without being influenced by any previous event. So, the outcome of any wager you make is in no way related to any previous wager that you, or anyone else, has made.

Some systems are based on the old Martingale System, whereby the bettor progressively doubles bets in a vain attempt to recoup losses. The Martingale System and its legion of imitators consistently fail because an eventual win will only recoup a player's losses plus his original basic bet, and he'll be back where he started from. And, only a few successive losses can wipe him out. Even if the Martingale player did have the cash to double up from here to eternity, it couldn't be done, because all casinos have house limits on the amount of the highest acceptable wager. Eventually, the Martingale player would be forced to quit while behind.

Another type of system player bets according to streaks of good or bad luck. He increases his wagers when he's hot and winning, but cuts back on the amounts he bets when he's cold and losing. Again, he flouts the principle of independent events. Besides, a streak is only a streak in retrospect. You can't recognize a prolonged series of wins until after they occur. You never know what the next outcome of the dice will be until it has happened. There is always the possibility that your next roll will be a loss—and that will be the end of your winning streak.

Horse racing fans and sports fans utilize a myriad of handicapping systems to pick winners—all rated as sure-fire by the people who use them. One of the newest systems ideas is based on biorhythms. Biorhythms are the natural cycles (determined by one's date of birth) that regulate physical, mental and emotional highs and lows. Sigmund Freud suspected their existence, and scientists have investigated them thoroughly, finding at least some validity in the principle. It has been found, for example, that 60 to 80 percent of accidents occur on just 20 percent of the days of our lives. Marilyn Monroe and Judy Garland both committed suicide on their "critical days," and Clark Gable suffered a fatal heart attack on one of his critical days. And a famous tennis star, riding high on two of her three cycles, won a championship match.

Biorhythm theory has been applied to sports and sports wagering with some degree of success. All you have to know about a player, or a jockey, is the day of his birth, which

A. WILSON

Biorhythm theory is not a new idea. As far back as 420 B.C., Hippocrates was aware of the "rhythms of life" in man. The biorhythmic devices sold today trace *a person's emotional, physical, and intellectual highs and lows in cycles beginning at birth and continuing until death. Emotional cycles run for 28 days (from point A to point C), physical cycles 23 days, intellectual cycles 33 days. Critical times occur when one is changing from a high, or positive, period to a negative period and vice versa. Some gamblers use biorhythms to predict peaks and, therefore, potential wins for athletes or teams, and also to forecast their own lucky days.*

is easily accessible. Odds-makers predicted a win by the Washington Redskins over the lower–rated New England Patriots, but biorhythmic bettors predicted an upset and won. Some people even claim that they've predicted the biorhythmic winner by charting all of the horses in a race. But biorhythms ought perhaps to be taken with a grain of salt. When you come right down to it, it's smart to remember that nothing in life is really sure, aside from death and taxes.

GAMBLER'S HALL OF FAME

You may find the stories of these candidates for the Gambler's Hall of Fame roguish, comical, outrageous, or even tragic. You may cast a doubtful eye at some of the "facts" in their life stories. And indeed you should. But in a world where bravado and braggadocio are a means of dealing with constant danger and insecurity, a bit of exaggeration is to be expected.

Nicholas Andrea Dandolos (Nick the Greek)

In the pantheon of the gambling world, Nick Dandolos, known as "Nick the Greek," reigns supreme. A legend in his own time, and respected by his peers, he gambled for high stakes with a joy and passion that were surpassed only by his consummate skill, shrewdness, analytical ability, and unimpeachable integrity. A natural linguist, poet, philosopher, and all-around incredible guy, he managed to accommodate such diverse elements in his life as extreme poverty, extreme wealth, underworld gangsters, and the Oval Office. His acquaintances included Al Capone, Dutch Schultz, Legs Diamond, Bugsy Siegel, the Prince of Wales, Mayor Jimmy Walker, Jack Dempsey, Ava Gardner, President John F. Kennedy, Albert Einstein, and the Kings of Spain and Greece. He won as much as $50 million in a

single night, and went from rags to riches and back again 73 times.

Born in 1893 on the island of Crete, he emigrated to the United States at the age of 18. But it was in Montreal, Canada that he began to bet the horses, theoretically to relieve his overriding grief over the death of his fiancée. He bet blindly, wildly, and won just as wildly. After several months he had parlayed his $150 into over $1 million—enough to convince him that his true calling lay in gambling.

He returned to the United States, where he promptly lost all his money playing craps. Thus chastised, he set out to learn not only how to play craps properly, but faro and poker too. And he learned these games so well that at the height of his career other players would leave their own games just to watch Nick practice his craft. To this maestro, gambling *was* indeed a craft that had very little to do with winning money. This revealing remark sums up his philosophy: "Win money, lose money. Have, don't have. Who cares?" For him, gambling games represented the eternal cosmic struggle between the individual and the world. Material goods held so little sway, in fact, that all his earthly possessions could supposedly fit inside a shoebox. The only possession that gave him any real pleasure was his gambling skill and spirit.

Giacomo Jacopo Casanova de Seingalt

It should come as no surprise that this famous romantic figure loved more than women. A gambler—at faro mostly—throughout his lifetime, he won and lost huge sums of money. (Friends and lovers always provided his stake money when his luck wore out.)

At the height of his "career," in the mid 1700s, Casanova came up with a legitimate scheme designed to line his pockets painlessly. He convinced the King of France to run a lottery to raise money to build a military academy. Casanova would supervise the lottery and deduct a percentage of the money taken in as a fee. The scheme proved to be very successful—they sold 2 million francs worth of tickets on the very first day. The King was happy, the populace was happy—and so was Casanova.

During his 60–odd years as a gambler, Nick the Greek won and lost more than $500 million. But gambling enjoyed no monopoly over his time and liquid assets. He also put 29 of the children of friends through college, paid 1,000 hospital bills, gave 300 non–interest loans to small businesses, and donated $5 million to charity. He died, poor of purse but rich in spirit, on Christmas Day, 1966.

Sarah Bernhardt was able to conquer a gambling compulsion; Edgar Allan Poe never did.

John W. "Bet-a-Million" Gates

Gates has justifiably been dubbed one of the greatest gamblers the world has ever seen. He had a love of gambling, a *joie de vivre*, a "devil–may–care" attitude that exemplifies our image of the carefree gambler. He'd bet any amount on anything at any time: $10,000 on the toss of a coin, $1,000 on the speed of a rain-drop on a windowpane, $1,000 on whether the next approaching train would be eastward or westward bound.

He began this illustrious career with poker, which he learned from railway workers near his farm home on the outskirts of Chicago. He quickly noticed that these card players were prey to certain give-aways, like relighting their pipes or biting their lips, which indicated the strength of their hands. Gates put this information to work, and usually won. It is estimated, however, that over the course of his lifetime, he lost $1 million at the poker table.

Gates left the farm and utilized his sharp wits selling barbed wire. By the time he was 39 he headed two of the largest steel companies in the world. But he missed the thrill of gambling, and invested his money in the stock market. He invested so wisely that he became a millionaire several times over.

His great new wealth gave him freedom to indulge extensively in casino gambling and horse racing (to which he owes his fame and nick-name). He often lost large sums of money, but his shrewdness and abil-ity to calculate the odds enabled him to win big on occasion too. He once won $600,000 on a single race . . . and lost $400,000 in a single day. In fact, he was so successful at the track that eventually he was asked to limit his bets to $10,000 per horse.

While he gambled, he continued his career in the legitimate business world, and helped to establish the U.S. Steel Corporation. He also con-tinued to live lavishly until the day he died in Paris, in 1911.

Bizarre Bet

John W. ("Bet-a-Million") Gates, famed "high roller" of his day, was once himself a chip in a crap game. Gates was as big a tipper as he was a gambler, and the waiter who served him regularly at a resort in Palm Beach, Florida, was the envy of all the others. One day, Gates saw him working in another section of the dining room. He called him over and asked what happened. "Well," the waiter glumly explained, "last night we had a little crap game. I just kept losing and losing until finally I had no money left. So I put you up . . . but I lost you too!"

John W. "Bet-a-Million" Gates.

George Devol

He called himself "the most daring gambler in the world" and he certainly was the most famous, though atypical, of the great Mississippi riverboat gamblers of his day. He was also the only one of his ilk to write an autobiography, *Forty Years A Gambler on the Mississippi,* which is packed with gambling stories, advice, philosophy, and adventures—many of which are daring indeed.

His long and fascinating career began at the tender age of 15, when he and his cousin became gamblers on a Rio Grande boat. From then on, it was full-speed ahead—from boat to boat, game to game, and sucker to sucker. Although he was an adequate three-card monte man (a hustle as old as the hills, but for which there is still no shortage of dupes), he was an expert at "ringing in" newly-stacked decks of cards. If there was little money on board, he was not above gambling for chickens, or even alligators. The prime motivation, however, was money, and Devol claims to have cheated his fellow passengers out of a total of $2 million. But, as is typical of professionals, he seemed equally unable to resist Lady Luck's beguiling possibilities, and lost it all in the big cities, playing faro.

The life of a riverboat card sharp was not all fun and games, and needless to say sometimes the suckers found out they had been cheated. He carried a gun, "Betty Jane" by name, but supposedly never used it. Instead, Devol, who weighed 200 pounds, preferred to use his head—literally. He was known to butt his adversary senseless with his huge, hard skull. Or he would effect dare-devil escapes, such as diving into the water, trailed by bullets, or flee the scene in a clever disguise.

Devol was more than willing to put his skill and knowledge to uses other than filling his pockets, such as teaching someone a lesson. One of his favorite forms of entertainment was tricking ministers into betting against him. They lost, of course, and Devol would give them their money back, accompanied by the following advice: "Go and sin no more."

George Devol.

FORTY YEARS

A GAMBLER

ON THE

MISSISSIPPI

BY

GEORGE H. DEVOL.

A CABIN BOY IN 1839; COULD STEAL CARDS AND CHEAT THE BOYS AT ELEVEN; STOCK A DECK AT FOURTEEN; BESTED SOLDIERS ON THE RIO GRANDE DURING THE MEXICAN WAR; WON HUNDREDS OF THOUSANDS FROM PAYMASTERS, COTTON BUYERS, DEFAULTERS, AND THIEVES; FOUGHT MORE ROUGH-AND-TUMBLE FIGHTS THAN ANY MAN IN AMERICA, AND WAS THE MOST DARING GAMBLER IN THE WORLD.

ILLUSTRATED.

SECOND EDITION.

NEW YORK:

GEORGE H. DEVOL.

1892.

*Title page from Devol's
1892 autobiography.*

Bodine Jackson Balasco. (<u>Gambling Times</u>, 839 North Highland Avenue, Hollywood, CA 90038.)

Bodine Jackson Balasco

The heydays of the Mississippi riverboat gambler are over, but step onto one of the few remaining steam boats today, and you stand a good chance of running into Bodine Jackson Balasco, their modern-day equivalent. "The last of the riverboat gamblers" is mostly a showman and entertainer, but he occasionally accommodates fellows who want to play his specialties (three-card monte, faro, and the shell game) for money. His "character's" dress and behavior are based on thorough research of George Devol and other river gamblers. Balasco chose to represent this particular piece of American history because he feels the riverboat gambler "is a bon vivant, the beau ideal. He is a cultured gentleman, well-mannered and well-bred, but with a raucous, footloose, fancy-free side to his personality."

Francois Blanc

A man of humble origin, Francois Blanc learned the ropes while working as a waiter in European gambling clubs. At an early age, he cleverly—and unethically—made a lot of money in the stock market. Unfortunately, he was not clever enough to escape detection, and was imprisoned for fraud and bribery. Upon his release he took his ill-gotten money and opened a casino in Luxembourg, which was so successful that he was asked to develop a casino in Baden-Baden, Germany. But the curative effect of the waters did nothing to assuage the miseries of the heavy losers, and rumors sprung up that many of Blanc's customers were committing suicide. The ensuing scandal prompted his move to Monaco and he took over operation of Monte Carlo, a high-class gambling joint that four previous operators had failed to make successful. There was only one problem: northern Italy was contemplating the legalization of gambling, which would compete with Monte Carlo. So Blanc surreptitiously stirred up the anti-gambling sentiment of the public and the Italian government banned the construction of future casinos. But, once again, rumors of suicide plagued Blanc. This time, he put a stop to them by employing men to stuff the pockets of suicide victims with cash, to make the deaths seem unrelated to gambling losses. Another example of his genius was the way he handled the complaints of Monaco's citizens, who protested that they were unable to enjoy any benefits from the casino. Not only were they forbidden to enter the gambling hall, but the visiting gamesters didn't bother to shop in town. Blanc's solution? The abolition of income taxes for residents of Monaco. Needless to say, Monte Carlo continued to flourish, and Blanc died, in 1877, a very rich man.

Monte Carlo's Game Room (Salle de Jeu) in Blanc's time.

Rudolph Walter Wanderone, Jr. (The Fat Man, Minnesota Fats)

Minnesota Fats.

Bizarre Bet

The members of the White's Club in London would bet on almost anything, including life and death. A beggar, who had collapsed outside the club, was brought in and laid on the dice table. Bets were made as to whether he would survive until the doctor arrived. One version has it that the bet was whether he was alive or dead already—and that no first aid could be given because it would affect the fairness of the outcome.

Rudolph Walter Wanderone, Jr., "The Fat Man," was the giant of pool hustlers—in more ways than one. Extravagant in every sense of the word, he loved to talk, eat, play pool, spend money, and promote himself and his game. He called himself the greatest athlete in the world, and this 200-plus pound man with the 51-inch waist came awfully close to proving it. For in spite of his bulk, he moved around the pool table gracefully, his somewhat ominous appearance softened by a kind of gentleness. His endurance, too, was extraordinary, and he managed to stay awake for days playing pool. Perhaps it was the whole chickens and hams, the 30 quails consumed in one sitting, the occasional 8 gallons of ice cream, the buckets of Coca–Cola, or the daily doses of $100 worth of candy that kept him going through such ordeals.

The wealth he accrued from his pool hustling supplied him with another kind of sustenance—material possessions. He sported silk suits, with matching alligator, lizard, crocodile, and python shoes and cue cases. He owned, at one time or another, Pierce Arrows, Packards, La Salles, and Duesenbergs complete with side tires and fluted horns.

He was his own biggest fan, and insisted he "ain't never had any experience" in losing. The closest he ever came to it was when he fell through a creaky floor just as he was completing a decisive shot. Just before making this dramatic exit, he managed to see that his shot was successful, and on the way down he knew he had won the game. The biggest game he ever played was for a quarter of a million dollars. It was played against Arthur Thurnblad, the three–cushion billiards world champion; most people placed their bets on him because Fats' reputation was based on pool, not billiards. Fats won anyway, he says, because his opponent was afraid, and The Fat Man was *never* afraid.

Rudolph Wanderone, born in 1913, began his gambling career as a boy. He learned to play one-handed pool by the age of four; at six he was playing for medium stakes; and at ten, for serious cash. By 14 he'd left home to further his education on the streets of New York and the Midwest, studying with the "Grand Masters of the Game." He played for money in games all over the country, and was able to support himself well even through the Depression. After World War II all forms of gambling took a nosedive. The Fat Man had been in retirement quite a while when the film, "The Hustler," was released in 1961. He thought the character in the film, Minnesota Fats, resembled him too closely and threatened to sue. The film–makers, in turn, denied the film was based on The Fat Man's life. But then a weird thing happened. The man who had been known up to then only as The Fat Man or New York Fats began to be called Minnesota Fats; he enjoyed the renewed notoriety and the game of pool enjoyed a new respectability.

Edmond Hoyle

Although he wasn't a famous gambler, this section would be incomplete if Edmond Hoyle were left unheralded. For he was the first man to write serious books on indoor games, and thereby the first to set up standard rules of play. He became such a well-known authority in his own lifetime that he has had bestowed upon him a kind of immortality. Since 1746, when his first book appeared, the term "Hoyle" has been used to signify a rule book of card games. Only five games were included in that first work, but all of the hundreds that now exist use the same standard deck of cards and many follow the original patterns.

Hughie Rowan

Hughie Rowan is not exactly a household word, but many consider this outrageous Australian to be the most spectacular gambling figure that ever dazzled the British racing world. Most Edwardian Englishmen earned between £1 and £5 a week; Rowan spent £30,000 ($75,000) a year. His ignorance of horses was legend, but that didn't stop him from wagering £100,000 ($250,000) in a single day. His unbelievable success lasted for years, but he finally began to lose more than he won. He fell heavily in debt and gradually faded away into obscurity. But his death, in 1947, was as chancy as his life had been. Feeble and penniless, the 80-year-old man sat in his hotel room, preparing a noose to hasten his death. But Lady Luck had her last fling with Hughie Rowan—a heart attack took his life before he could slip the rope around his neck.

Feodor Dostoevsky

This famous Russian writer's addiction to gambling began in 1863, when he casually stopped off at a casino in Wiesbaden, Germany. On his first day at the roulette wheel he won heavily; the second day he lost half his winnings. But the second day's losses didn't matter—he was hooked. For the next nine years his life was a nightmare of ever-increasing gambling debts and constant borrowing. His wife and family were forced to live in poverty, while Dostoevsky sold his literary works outright to raise stake money. After one final spree, for which his more than understanding wife gave him the money, and during which he tormented himself with guilt, he decided never again to play roulette. Out of this sad mess only one thing endures: a short story, *The Gambler,* written by someone who knew his subject at first hand.

F. M. Dostoevsky.

Anna Dostoevsky wrote of her famous husband's gambling binges in *Reminiscences of F. M. Dostoevsky.* After satisfying his craving he would return home, calmed in the realization of the futility of his hopes of winning. During these calm periods he had renewed strength to write, and in a couple of weeks would make good his losses.

Alice Ivers (Poker Alice)

Alice Ivers claimed to have the best poker sense of anyone in the West, man or woman. Born in England in 1850, this very proper young lady received her education in a special finishing school. The death of her husband led her to gambling, and she became a notorious professional

It's in the Bag

Titanic Thompson once bet a man that he could throw any walnut from the bag of them he was eating, over a building. "Impossible," the sucker said, and theoretically he was right—no one could have accomplished the feat honestly. But Titanic had filled one walnut with lead and it sailed over the building with ease. Titanic collected $100 from the bewildered chump.

who worked the cards while smoking long black cigars and spoke with an upper-class English accent. Nevertheless, she remained a woman of high moral principles: she never drank or gambled on Sunday. During the course of her colorful lifetime, she went through three husbands, was in great demand in the famous gambling houses of the day, and was arrested for running a gambling house and a brothel, for selling whiskey, and for killing a soldier. In spite of all this, she managed to live to a ripe old age.

Alvin Clarence Thomas (Titanic Thompson)

Ty Thompson was not only the king of the proposition bet (a seemingly sure-fire thing to the poor innocent sucker who accepts it), he was an expert marksman, craps player, and card player as well. During the early 1930s, he shared top billing with Nick the Greek as the most cunning gambler in the United States.

Raised in the South in poverty, he soon learned to amuse himself by gambling. All his male relatives wagered on their ability to shoot at targets, throw rocks, and play card games, checkers, and dominoes. Ty learned these country games so well, in fact, that his ability soon surpassed that of his fellow wagerers, who refused to gamble with him after a while. He began to think of gambling as a way out of his back-

woods existence. So, for the next few years, Ty sharpened his talent for performing such tricks as pitching coins and jumping long distances—thus setting the stage for the proposition bets for which he would become famous. He also learned early and thoroughly the value of the maxim, "smart is better than lucky." And although he had real intelligence and ability (he memorized the correct odds for many gambling games), he was not above utilizing a little hanky-panky now and then to make sure he had the advantage in every betting situation.

So astounding and consistent was his ability to win seemingly impossible bets (such as jumping over a 10-foot pool table without touching it), that one side bettor once remarked to another, "He must be Titanic. He sinks everybody," and the nickname stuck.

Ty once went to Chicago for the express purpose of meeting Nick the Greek. Ty and Nick thought they could do "a little business together" and left for San Francisco. There they played high-stakes poker as partners, splitting the take at the end of each day. The little business proposition paid off: eighteen months later, Ty was two cars and $1 million richer. The pair traipsed off to New York soon after their poker coup, where Ty lost all his winnings—and then some—playing the horses. But he always recouped his losses by playing craps, golf, or card games, and was seldom broke for long.

Good Luck!   (Roosevelt Raceway.)

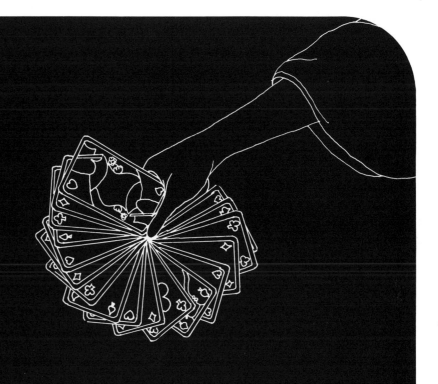

NEIGHBORHOOD
GAMES

FOR FUN AND PROFIT

The thrill of gambling and the fun of socializing need not be mutually exclusive, and the proof can probably be found in your own neighborhood. The school carnival, the local bingo parlor, and those weekly card or dice games at home all attest to the fact that playing for money need not ruin friendships, marriages, or bank accounts. It does foster competition, but who can argue against a trait that's as American as baseball?

A game of gin rummy or backgammon "just for fun" can offer a pleasant diversion from the daily grind. But playing for money adds to the character of the game, and makes all the difference in the challenge it offers. Winning by 100 points is satisfying, but satisfaction becomes excitement when money is involved.

Naturally, there are no tangible statistics, but those who ought to know suspect that neighborhood games are so popular that they account for more money changing hands than any other form of wagering. They don't offer spacious, statue-studded lobbies or elaborate gaming facilities, but on the other hand, there's no experienced "house" to compete against and to pay a percentage of your winnings to. You're competing only against the other players, and every player gets an even break, at least theoretically. Also, if all players agree, any rule can be revised, or bent a little to fit the occasion, or the kind of game you want.

An ideal game will be played with enough understanding of the procedures to make it interesting and to test one's skill, and with enough stakes to make the losses have some impact. All players should enter the game with the understanding that everyone is playing for fun *and* to win. However, draw the line and limit the stakes so that an evening's losses never exceed a comfortable amount.

The games described here are the ones that are most often gambled on among friends or in the community. Remember that the game rules given in this chapter, along with the accepted rules of conduct, do vary. So make sure these are stated clearly, and agreed upon before the play begins.

"The Card Players."

A friendly private game is gambling at its most pleasant, but serious and competitive nonetheless.

The odds on your winning it big in these neighborhood games may be nothing to write home about. In fact, a beginner should expect to lose. Just consider your losses as the price paid for a lively and challenging evening's entertainment. With enough practice and ability, though, you may find yourself playing for both fun *and* profit.

ROLL THE BONES

Craps, like other games involving dice, combines elements of luck and skill and is, therefore, a good gambling game. Luck controls the outcomes of the rolls of the dice and there is nothing you can do to influence those outcomes. Skill enters the picture in the bets that are made on those outcomes. Since in the long run the occurrence of any total on two dice can be expressed in terms of mathematical expectations, you can be a winner if you play intelligently. First, learn the basics of the play. Then, by arming yourself with a knowledge of the proper odds against the occurrence of all possible outcomes, bet accordingly. The tempo of the game is fast, but aside from memorizing the odds, there is no other skill involved.

Although a high-class form of craps, called bank craps, is found in casinos, you can play privately—anywhere there's a flat surface and a pair of dice.

An emotional game of hazard, the ancestor of modern day craps.

HOW TO PLAY

Any number can play. All you need to play craps are two dice and a smooth playing surface on which to roll them. If you can, try to have a wall or some kind of backboard touching one side of the playing surface, as the dice should preferably hit this before coming to rest. Before each series of rolls, each player bets on the outcome—the total number of dots that will appear on the top surfaces of the dice. Certain totals are winning outcomes; others are losers.

To begin the game, determine the first *shooter* (the person who rolls the dice) by having each player roll the dice once. The highest total determines the first shooter. (In large games, the first shooter is usually the one who picks up the dice and offers the first bet.) As the game progresses, the dice pass to players in turn so that each one will have an opportunity to be the shooter.

Before rolling the dice, the shooter places a bet (called the *center bet*) by putting up a *stake* in the center of the playing surface. (The stake, or amount of the bet, can be any amount, but most private games establish minimum and maximum limits.) The shooter is betting that he will win. The other players then *fade* that bet by matching—or covering—all or part of the center bet. These bets are placed in front of each player. Each player who fades is betting that the shooter will lose. After any uncovered portion of

the center bet is removed by the shooter, he is ready to make the first roll. This first roll (the *come out*) has three possible outcomes:

• If the come out totals 7 or 11, called a *natural,* the shooter wins the roll, and collects all the money that had been bet by the other players. The dice can then be passed to the next player on the shooter's left. Or, the first shooter can continue to roll, in which case he may *drag down* (collect part of his winnings and leave the rest as his stake on the next roll) or *let it ride* (bet his winnings—including his original center bet—on the next roll). Each of the other players fade, and the dice are rolled again.

• If the come out totals 2, 3, or 12, called *craps,* the shooter loses the roll and pays each player the amount of his bet. Again, the shooter may pass the dice to the player on his left or continue to roll.

• If the come out totals 4, 5, 6, 8, 9, or 10, the number becomes the shooter's *point,* and the dice must be rolled again before a winner can be determined. The shooter continues to roll the dice until a 7 or his point number appears again. If the shooter rolls a 7 before his point number appears again, he has missed (*crapped out,* or *sevened out*). He's lost the roll, and must pay each player, and pass the dice to the next player on his left.

The best throw at the dice is to throw them away.

(Austin O'Malley)

Crap-ese

Next time you shoot craps with your friends, try impressing them with these:

• The total of 2—*Snake Eyes.*

• Total of 2, 3, or 12—*Craps.*

• Total of 4—*Little Dick, Little Joe, Little Joe from Kokomo, Little Joe from Baltimore.*

• Total of 5—*Phoebe, Little Phoebe, Fee-Bee, Fever.*

• Total of 6—*Sixty Days.*

• Seven on the come-out throw—*Natural.*

• Seven after the first roll—*Seven Out.*

• Total of 8—*Ada Ross, The Stable Hoss, Decatur, Ada from Decatur, Eighter from Decatur.*

• Total of 9—*Carolina Nine, Ninety Days, Nina.*

• Total of 10—*Big Dick, Big Dick from Boston.*

• Total of 11—*Natural.*

• Total of 12—*Box Cars.*

• If he rolls his point number (*makes his point*, or *passes*) before a 7 appears, he has won the roll and all the money that has been bet. (If a shooter's point number is 5, it does not matter whether he passes with 1-4 or 3-2. It's the total that counts.) The shooter may pass the dice to the next player or continue to roll.

Side Bets

When the shooter establishes a point, the players (including the shooter) often make additional bets before the dice are rolled again. These are called *side bets* and are placed to one side of the playing surface. A player who bets that the shooter will pass (win) is called a *right bettor*. One who bets on a shooter to lose is a *wrong bettor*. Two of the most popular side bets are *point bets* and *hard way bets*. Here is where a knowledge of the proper odds comes into play. This knowledge determines how to bet—which bets are good ones, and which ones are not. The correct odds for these bets are shown in the Tables of Point Numbers. Note that a right bet on point 4 or 10—the points with the greatest odds against them—will pay the greatest payoff.

Point Bets / After a shooter's *come out* (first roll), wrong bettors *lay odds* that he won't make his point. Right bettors *take odds* that he will.

Hard Way Bets / There are four points that can be made by throwing doubles: 4(2-2), 6(3-3), 8(4-4), and 10(5-5). This is called making a point the *hard way*, and the odds against this happening are greater (so the payoff is greater). Wrong bettors may lay odds that a shooter won't make his point the hard way; right bettors take odds that he will. The hard way number can be bet any time.

TABLE OF POINT NUMBERS

The point number	Odds against passing number	If you bet	What you win if the point appears
4 or 10	6 to 3, or 2 to 1	$1.00	$2.00 + original bet
5 or 9	6 to 4, or 3 to 2	$1.00	$1.50 + original bet
6 or 8	6 to 5	$1.00	$1.20 + original bet
4 the hard way	8 to 1	$1.00	$8.00 + original bet
6 the hard way	10 to 1	$1.00	$10.00 + original bet
8 the hard way	10 to 1	$1.00	$10.00 + original bet
10 the hard way	8 to 1	$1.00	$8.00 + original bet

Proposition Bets / There are many other types of bets on what specific numbers or combinations of numbers will appear, either on the shooter's point or on the come out throw. These are often suggested by someone who either offers incorrect odds or knows that even the correct odds are highly in his favor. In any case, these bets are at best unfair. If one is offered, it's time to leave the game.

The Hottest Game in Town

The much-maligned bovine lantern-kicker may not have been responsible for the great Chicago fire of 1871 after all. A different account lays the blame on Mrs. O'Leary's crapshooting son and his friends. It seems they were enjoying a lively game in the famous barn the night the fire broke out. In all the excitement one of the shooters knocked over the lantern that started the fire.

USING ODDS

Winning at craps is simply a matter of having the correct odds against any roll at your fingertips, and then making right or wrong bets accordingly.

In order to understand the odds in craps, you must accept the fact that any one face on each six-faced die is as likely to appear as any other. There is a 1 in 6 chance that any specific number will appear on a single die; the odds are 5 to 1 against. When you throw two dice, as in craps, there are thirty-six (six times six) possible two-die combinations. Any total from 2 to 12 may appear within the thirty-six combinations. Some of these total numbers are, however, more likely to appear than others in the long run, because they can be made with more combinations.

For example, there is only one way to roll a 2 (1-1); there are thirty-five ways not to. The odds are 35 to 1 against throwing a 2. On the other hand, there are six ways to throw a 7 (4-3, 3-4, 6-1, 1-6, 5-2, 2-5) and thirty ways not to. The odds against throwing a 7 are considerably less than throwing a 2: 30 to 6, or 5 to 1. Odds for all numbers are shown in the Table of Rolls. To help you remember, notice that the number of ways to roll the sequential numbers 2 through 12 increase one at a time up to six (number of ways to roll a 7)

and then decrease one at a time. ($1+2+3+4+5+6+5+4+3+2+1=$ 36.) The odds against rolling the sequential numbers 2 through 12 decrease from 35 to 1 (odds against rolling a 2) to 5 to 1 (odds against rolling a 7); then increase again up to 35 to 1 (odds against rolling a 12).

The next step is to use this information to determine the correct odds against passing on any of the possible point numbers. To do this, the number of ways the point can be made is figured against the six ways a 7 can be made. Let's say the point is 4. This number can be made in three ways, so the odds against its appearing before a 7 appears are 6 to 3, or 2 to 1. If you bet one dollar that the shooter makes his point, you stand to win two dollars (plus your original bet). The Table of Point Numbers shows the correct odds and what this means in dollars and cents for all point numbers.

Notice that the odds are always *against* the shooter making his point. In the long run, the wrong bettor—one who bets the shooter will crap out before he makes his point—will win more often than the right bettor. This is the reasoning behind the saying, "All right bettors die broke." It is also the reason why hustlers are always wrong bettors, and pass the dice to the next shooter when it's their turn.

Table of Rolls.

Number   *All possible combinations and* Θ*dds against rolling*

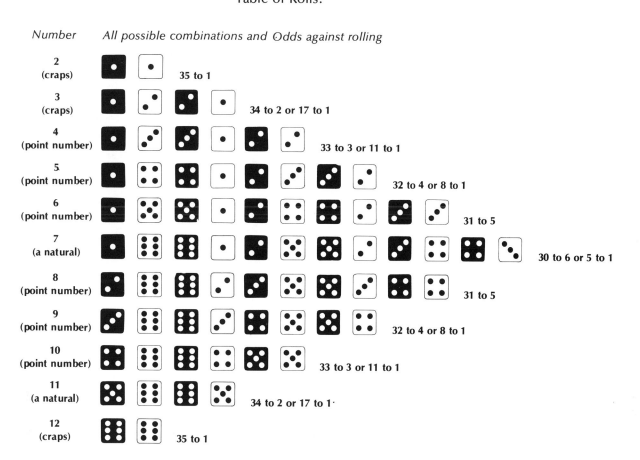

Number											Odds
2 (craps)											35 to 1
3 (craps)											34 to 2 or 17 to 1
4 (point number)											33 to 3 or 11 to 1
5 (point number)											32 to 4 or 8 to 1
6 (point number)											31 to 5
7 (a natural)											30 to 6 or 5 to 1
8 (point number)											31 to 5
9 (point number)											32 to 4 or 8 to 1
10 (point number)											33 to 3 or 11 to 1
11 (a natural)											34 to 2 or 17 to 1
12 (craps)											35 to 1

THE HISTORY OF DICE AND CRAPS

Throwing some form of dice is the oldest gambling game in the world. When you play craps, and pray for a 7—or anything but—you have much in common with prehistoric man, who prayed for a fortuitous outcome when he threw the original "bones," which came from the ankle of a sheep.

Since then, dice have been made of many substances, including wood, ivory, clay, metal, glass, amber, even jade and precious stones. Perhaps the most delightful dice of all were those made of silver or bronze in the shape of a seated figure. (They could fall in six positions: on their backs, on their stomachs, on their faces, on their left and right sides, sitting upright and sitting upside down.) Excavations have revealed that dice—occasionally loaded for cheating—were used in ancient Pompeii, Egypt, Rome, Greece, and many parts of the Orient. They are even mentioned in the Bible: soldiers at the foot of the cross rolled dice for Christ's clothing.

All in a Name

An infamous English dice cheat lent his name to our language as an all-encompassing epithet for villains and rogues of all kinds. His name: John Outlawe.

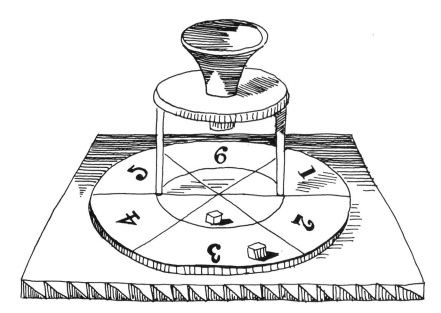

A medieval dice box.

Modern craps is an American descendant of an old game called "hazard." This high risk game was immensely popular in Europe during the Middle Ages, and it is said that entire fortunes and estates were lost on the outcome of the dice. During the 19th century, hazard came to New Orleans, where the rules were somewhat simplified. From the very moment it was introduced, the simplicity and fast pace of the game appealed to everyone, but it is especially associated with blacks, who have been responsible for many of the colloquialisms that add so much to the personality of the game. It was not uncommon for men who worked in the lumberyard camps on the Mississippi River to be paid in quarters and half-dollars to make betting easier. The games in such camps began Saturday nights and ended Monday mornings.

The game of craps was picked up by numerous riverboat gamblers, and spread like wildfire throughout the country.

Army Song

They put your name on a piece
 of paper,
Fellow over there gives you your
 pay,
Take it to the squad–room, put it
 on a blanket,
Fellow yells "CRAPS!" an' takes
 it all away.

CHEATING AT CRAPS

Many would-be craps players have a somewhat tarnished image of the game because of hustlers, who cheat at craps in three ways: using crooked dice, controlling honest dice by skillful throwing, and laying incorrect odds.

Crooked Dice

Also called *gaffed dice*, these dice have been altered to favor, disfavor, or eliminate certain numbers. (They are often introduced into the game by sleight of hand.) Some gaffs (*percentage dice*) won't roll the favored numbers all the time, maybe not even a majority of the time. They will, however, alter the long-run expectancy of the favored number. For example, in 360 throws, the number 7 is expected to come up 60 times.

The dice may be gaffed so that the number 7 will come up 70 times, and this is enough of an alteration for a crook "in the know."

Mismarked dice (*tops*) are gaffed dice on which some faces are duplicated and other omitted. A pair of dice may be marked so that 3-4-5 and 1-5-6 each appear twice on one die; it is then impossible for a 2, 3, 7, or 12 (the only losing combinations) to be rolled. Since only three faces are visible at one time from one direction, tops often remain undetected. To check a suspicious pair, first make sure opposite faces add up to 7. To check further, if the face toward you is 5 and the face on top is 6, the face to the right should be 3. Gaffed dice can also be misspotted in numerous ways: on *loaded dice*, heavy metal has been placed in the

Gaffed dice are introduced into the game by sleight of hand.

recessed spots, under the paint. The face that is loaded is, therefore, heavier than the others and causes the face opposite to land upward. To test for loaded dice, drop them repeatedly into a glass of water, changing the uppermost face each time as you drop them. If they turn over as they sink and if two or three numbers show up frequently and others never do, the dice are loaded. *Shapes* are gaffed dice whose shape has been altered so they are no longer perfect cubes. *Beveled* dice have rounded faces so they fall more often on the flat faces. To test for beveled dice, hold each face of one die against that of another. A beveled face will wobble. *Flats* are dice with one or more faces shaved down, so they fall more often on the flattened face(s). To test a pair of suspected shapes or flats, simply compare the sizes of all sides.

Don't expect most gaffed dice to be as obvious as this one.

It should be made clear that the tests for crooked dice may not detect all gaffs unless the tests are done by an experienced person. Some gaffs are so clever that a microscope is needed to detect them.

Manipulating Honest Dice

The dice cheat places the dice in his palm with the desired numbers on top, and then rattles the dice without actually shaking them. He then throws the dice in such a way that they spin but do not roll, so the desired numbers stay on top. Another move causes the dice to roll straight, end over end. The side numbers never appear, so certain combinations cannot show up. Both of these techniques are hard to detect or prove; your only protection is to insist that a backboard be used.

Laying Incorrect Odds

Private craps players are easy marks for any hustler, because so few know the correct odds against the possible rolls. They often foolishly accept side bets at incorrect odds in the wrong bettor's favor. Perhaps the most common is for the sucker to lay even money that the shooter will make a 6 or 8 point. The proper odds are really 6 to 5 that he won't, and the payoff should be $1.20 for the wrong bettor's $1, not $1 for his $1. To protect yourself from accepting incorrect odds, memorize the Table of Point Numbers.

Poker Dice

Did you know you can satisfy your urge to play poker with a roll of the dice? The game, appropriately enough, is called *poker dice,* and all you need to play is five standard dice (or special dice whose faces carry A, K, Q, J, 10, and 9, instead of dots) and a dice cup. The object of the game is to throw the best poker "hand," during your turn, which consists of up to three rolls of the dice.

The one–spot may be designated high or low. As in poker, the hands rank as follows: five of a kind (highest), then four of a kind, three of a kind, two of a kind, high card. Straights (five numbers in sequence) do not count, and there can be no flushes, since there are no suits.

To begin, each player contributes an equal amount to the ante. After the first roll, you may stand on the outcome if it's favorable. Or you can roll up to two more times (for a total of three rolls), each time setting aside whichever dice you want, and picking up and rolling the others to try to improve your hand. Players are limited to whatever number of rolls the first player takes, unless they want to take fewer.

Whoever throws the highest hand wins, and collects the ante.

HUSTLERS AND THEIR TRICKS

There are some gambling games that the player is guaranteed to lose—those played against the hustler. Anyone who plays the hustler's game is known as a sucker or pigeon, and is usually an inexperienced gambler. The hustler works by enticing the sucker into betting on the game. This must be done cleverly for the sucker must fall for the bait all the while knowing that the hustler wants him to lose. *Shills,* con men who try to convince the sucker that it's possible to win, are often employed by the hustler to help lure the sucker into the game.

Cups and Balls has been used since Greek and Egyptian times to separate fools from their money. One modern version is known as the *three-shell game.* The shell game operator hides a pea (or other small round object) under one of the three walnut-shell halves (or other small containers) and moves them around rapidly. He then asks the pigeon to wager on which shell half harbors the pea. The pigeon, who has been allowed to spot—or to think he spotted—the correct shell, makes his bet. The hustler however, has already shot the pea under another shell with the tip of his finger, or flicked it off the table. You may think that you would never fall for such an obvious trick, but the hustler manipulates his fingers so rapidly that it is impossible for the human eye to detect his maneuver. After a bet has been made, the hustler replaces the pea under a different shell with equal agility. So the sucker loses no matter what shell he had bet on.

Monte, another version of Cups and Balls using cards, has been cheating suckers since the Wild West days. A famed Mississippi riverboat gambler said of three-card monte in 1911, ". . . It would not seem possible to find anyone so densely ignorant as to make a wager on it." Yet three-card monte is widely played on street corners even today. Perhaps there *is* a sucker born every minute.

This medieval cups-and-balls spectator looks on in amazement as a shill practices his own form of "the hand is quicker than the eye" magic. (Photo Giraudon, Paris.)

The monte-hustler shuffles three cards—usually two aces and a queen—and throws them face down. In an intriguing, fast-talking come-on, he invites passers-by to wager on which card is the Queen, and promises to pay even money if the bettor wins. "Hey there," he chants, "pick the red and pocket the bread." "Find the queen and take home the green." "Turn up an ace, you lose your case." If monte were an honest game, the bettor would stand one chance in three of picking the queen—but it is never played honestly.

The monte thrower has many ways to operate his game. He may bend the edges of the queen and hire a shill to make the first bet. The shill pretends not to notice the bent card and loses the game. A typical sucker *does* spot the bent card and thinks he holds the key to the game. By the time the sucker places a bet, however, the bent queen has been palmed and substituted with a bent ace. The two-shill version of monte is even newer. One shill acts as a customer; the second shill poses as a knowledgeable gambler, tells the pigeon all about the shills who are hired to entice bettors, and explains the signals used.

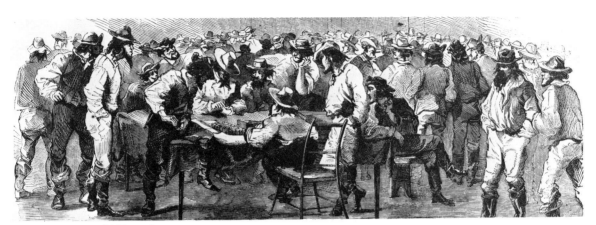

Three-card monte, Wild West style.

He urges the sucker to put his money down when he does. Of course, the sucker loses. A second shill may also watch for the police, or start a phony argument with the thrower to distract the sucker's attention. Like the shell game, monte can be an amusing theatrical performance with many variations—provided you're not silly enough to bet.

The shell game and monte are not the only hustles in town. Suckers galore have lost private betting propositions based on tossing or spinning coins—when the coins are actually double-headed or double-tailed; throwing dice—when the dice are actually gaffed, or the shooter knows how to throw them with a sleight of hand so he's always favored to win; or guessing facts or betting on feats of skill—when based on carefully worded misstatements or little known facts, or when the outcomes have been rigged. There is only one way to beat a con artist at these games—walk away as fast as possible.

Three-card monte, Coney Island style.

ALL MEN ON BOARD

Backgammon is basically a race between two players to see who can move all his men (*markers*) around a special board and then, ultimately, off the board (*bear off*). A well-played game of backgammon is fast-paced and calculating. It can be played anywhere—indoors or outdoors—for hours at a stretch. Since the outcome of a roll of two dice determines how many spaces (*points*) a player can move his markers, the results are often unpredictable. (Master players have been known to lose to novices; nonprofessionals have won tournaments.) But the game is not all luck. There are strategic moves and odds to memorize. To use them successfully takes practice, and the good players play often.

The game must be played on a backgammon board which comes supplied with thirty markers (fifteen for each player), four dice (two for each player), two dice cups (one for each player to shake up his dice in before each roll), a *doubling cube* (used for doubling the stakes, it resembles a large die with a different number on each of its sides), and a set of detailed rules. Not all rules or recommended moves are included here, but you will learn enough to see why this game has reached a near fad level of popularity.

Backgammon is one game that need not be played for a stake, or for stakes that can be doubled. None of the basics change if it isn't. Once you understand its gambling aspects, however, you'll share backgammon champ Billy Eisenberg's sentiment—"Playing backgammon without the doubling cube is like getting a plate of spaghetti without any sauce."

BACKGAMMON BASICS

Two persons—each playing for himself—face each other across the backgammon board. The board, with the markers set up to begin the game, appears on the facing page.

The markers are positioned in triangular spaces, called *points*. Players roll their dice in turn and the number of dots appearing on the top of each die determines how many points the player's markers can move. But it is the player who decides which markers to move and where. If a player rolls 3-1, for example, he can: move one marker 3 points, then 1 point; move one marker 1 point, then 3 points; move one marker 3 points, and another marker 1 point. Rolling doubles allows a player to double his moves. Rolling 3-3 for example, allows a player to make four 3-point moves. (One to four markers can be moved.)

Player A must move all his white markers clockwise onto the "inner table" in front of him; Player B must move all his black markers counterclockwise onto the inner table in front of him. As the players roll their dice in turn, each moves his markers toward his inner table. There is no limit to the number of markers a player can have on one point. And the numbers on both dice must be played if possible. A marker can move to any point other than one *covered* by an opponent (occupied by two or more of an opponent's markers). Covering points you occupy with two or more of your markers is an important part of the game, so you should always try to move men in pairs. It not only blocks your opponent from landing on a point (when a player cannot move because of blocked points, he loses the move)—it also protects you. If only one of your markers sits on a point and is *hit* by an opponent's marker landing there, your marker is removed from the board and placed on the center bar. When your turn comes again, you must roll a number that allows that marker to re-enter the board. The hit marker re-enters the board at the opponent's inner table, but cannot enter on a point covered by the opponent. And, a player whose marker is hit cannot make any other move until he first gets the hit marker back into the game. The more inner-table points covered, the less chance there is for re-entry by an opponent's hit marker. If, for example, your opponent has the first five points of his inner table covered, you cannot bring your hit marker in unless you roll a 6. And,

Out of the Mouths of Champs

Champion backgammon and bridge player Billy Eisenberg waxed philosophic about the game in an interview in *Gambling Times* magazine. "Backgammon," he said, "has a way of revealing people as they really are. [It] is a game a lot of people might think is very, very evil because people become crazy. But the truth is no game make you crazy. It just allows you to experience your craziness."

Another champion player, Paul Magriel, said, "Luck is very much overrated . . . the fascination of the game is that it's a blend of luck and skill. But the luck part is so obvious and so omnipresent—you're rolling the dice every time—and the skill part is a lot more hidden. The game is unbelievably deceptive. There is much, much, much more skill than will appear on the surface."

And Moishe (Chico) Felberbaum, who won the final round of the 1978 amateur backgammon championships, said of his success, "I was extremely lucky, and backgammon is 75 percent luck." In his case he was right—he'd never even read a book on the subject.

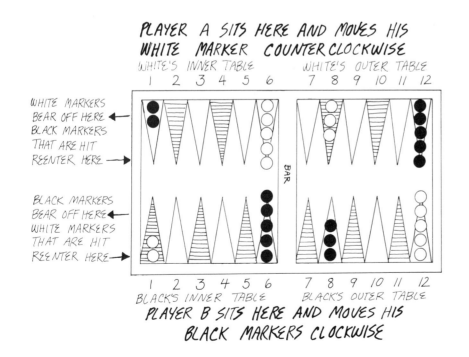

PLAYER A SITS HERE AND MOVES HIS WHITE MARKER COUNTERCLOCKWISE

WHITE'S INNER TABLE   WHITE'S OUTER TABLE
1 2 3 4 5 6   7 8 9 10 11 12

WHITE MARKERS BEAR OFF HERE
BLACK MARKERS THAT ARE HIT REENTER HERE

BLACK MARKERS BEAR OFF HERE
WHITE MARKERS THAT ARE HIT REENTER HERE

BAR

1 2 3 4 5 6   7 8 9 10 11 12
BLACK'S INNER TABLE   BLACK'S OUTER TABLE

PLAYER B SITS HERE AND MOVES HIS BLACK MARKERS CLOCKWISE

Backgammon's Background

Games that resemble backgammon have been around for centuries—in fact, the ancient Greeks and Romans played a game called tabula, which was nearly identical to the backgammon of today. The crusaders are probably responsible for bringing it to Europe where it caught on as a gambling game in several countries, under various names. In the twelfth century, Richard the Lion–Hearted forbade anyone below the rank of Knight to play the game for stakes. The medieval English nobility frequently amused themselves at "tables" as they called it. In 1925, the doubling cube was introduced. But that has been the only significant change since the ubiquitous Edmond Hoyle standardized the rules over 200 years ago.

At one time, backgammon was associated almost exclusively with the elite. Today, however, everyone plays the game. Its current resurgence of popularity is attributed to Prince Alexis Obolenski, who introduced the game to his exclusive circle of New York friends in the 1960s.

you cannot move any of your other markers either. A player who covers all six points in his inner table blocks his opponents from re-entering the game if hit (a *shutout*).

Getting all the markers to the inner table is only half the game. Once all are in, a player must *bear off* by removing each marker from the board. The outcome of a roll of the dice determines which markers can bear off. For example, a player with all of his markers in his inner table rolls 5-2. He can bear off one marker each from his second and fifth points. If he has no markers on those points, he must move markers within the inner table. If he cannot move within the inner table, he can bear off at the next lowest point. In this case he can bear off a marker from his second point and another from his third or fourth point if he has none on the fifth or sixth points. The first player to bear off all his markers wins the game.

On any turn in the game, before he rolls, a player can double the stakes originally agreed upon. The chance to double alternates between players. If an opponent refuses to double, he forfeits the game.

HOW TO PLAY

Players use their dice cups to shake and roll their dice. To begin, each player rolls one die, and high man moves first. If there is a tie (rolled doubles) the stake automatically doubles and players roll again for first move. The outcome on these two dice determines how many points the high man can move. Succeeding moves are determined by players rolling their own two dice.

In general, you can play a *running* game, where your main objective is to get your markers off the board, come hell or high water. High rolls tend to encourage this type of play. Or, you may prefer to play in a more conservative style, which consists mainly of trying to *block* your opponent's progress as you plod steadily toward your inner table. Low rolls are conducive to playing a blocking game. In a blocking game, paradise (or *prime*) is covering six points in a row, so your opponent is absolutely stuck behind you. (The prime may be lost by moving markers as you proceed toward your inner table.)

When trying to cover points, remember that some are more important and take precedence over others. In general, the best points to cover are those on your own inner table. The 5-point and the 7-point (called the bar point) are particularly effective blocks.

The opening move is an important one. A player should memorize the standard recommended moves, to make the most of an opening move when he gets the opportunity. Here are a few classic openings, all illustrated by Player A moving his white markers in the opening move:

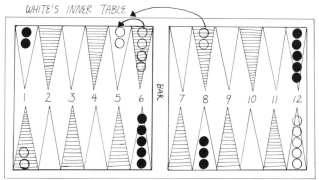

Roll 1-3: move one white marker from 6 point to 5 point (1); move one white marker from 8 point to 5 point (3). This covers white's 5 point—a good block.

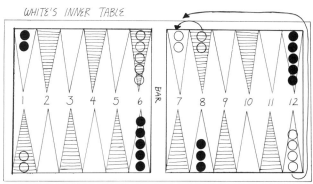

Roll 1-6: move one white marker from 8 point to 7 point (1); move one white marker from 12 point to 7 point (6). This cover's white's 7 point (bar point) and gives him three covered points in a row—a formidable block.

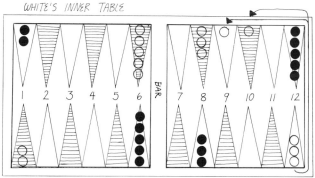

Roll 3-4 (the daring approach): move one white marker from 12 point to 10 point (3); move one white marker from 12 point to 9 point (4). This leaves two markers open to be hit, but the odds are less than 1 in 3 for either to happen.

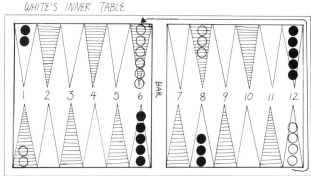

Roll 3-4 (the safe approach): move one white marker from the 12 point to the 6 point (3 + 4).

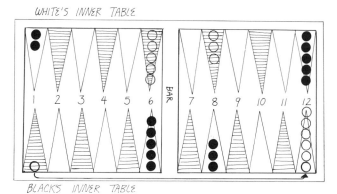

Roll 5-6 (also known as "Lover's Leap"): move one white marker from 1 point to 12 point (5 + 6).

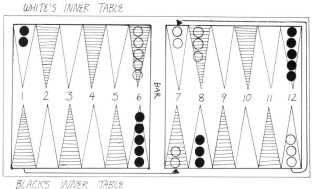

Roll 6-6: move two white markers from 12 point to 7 point (6 + 6); move two white markers from 1 point to 7 point (6 + 6). This gorgeous opening is a really lucky roll and covers two bar points.

USING ODDS

The odds of rolling specific numbers are important in backgammon. You should know how likely it is that a *blot* (a single marker on a point) will be hit by your opponent before you can cover it with another man. Knowledge of the odds will also help you plan where to set up blocks against your opponent's progress.

The odds against any one specific number coming up on the dice are shown below. The possibilities include the outcome of a single die, totals of both dice, and bonus totals from rolling doubles. (Note that including single die and doubles outcomes makes the odds different from those in craps, page 53).

Number	All possible combinations	Odds against rolling
1	1-1, 1-2, 1-3, 1-4, 1-5, 1-6, 2-1, 3-1, 4-1, 5-1, 6-1	35 to 11
2	2-1, 2-2, 2-3, 2-4, 2-5, 2-6, 1-2, 3-2, 4-2, 5-2, 6-2, 1-1	35 to 12
3	1-1, 1-3, 1-2, 2-1, 2-3, 3-1, 3-2, 3-3, 3-4, 3-5, 3-6, 4-3, 5-3, 6-3	35 to 14
4	1-1, 1-3, 1-4, 2-2, 2-4, 3-1, 3-4, 4-1, 4-2, 4-3, 4-4, 4-5, 4-6, 5-4, 6-4	35 to 15
5	1-4, 1-5, 2-3, 2-5, 3-2, 3-5, 4-1, 4-5, 5-1, 5-2, 5-3, 5-4, 5-5, 5-6, 6-5	35 to 15
6	1-5, 1-6, 2-2, 2-4, 2-6, 3-3, 3-6, 4-2, 4-6, 5-1, 5-6, 6-1, 6-2, 6-3, 6-4, 6-5, 6-6	35 to 17
7	1-6, 2-5, 3-4, 4-3, 5-2, 6-1	35 to 6
8	2-2, 2-6, 3-5, 4-4, 5-3, 6-2	35 to 6
9	3-3, 3-6, 4-5, 5-4, 6-3	35 to 5
10	4-6, 5-5, 6-4	35 to 3
11	5-6, 6-5	35 to 2
12	3-3, 4-4, 6-6	35 to 3
15 or 20	5-5	35 to 1
16	4-4	35 to 1
18 or 24	6-6	35 to 1

THE DOUBLING CUBE

The ability of either player to double the stakes at any point in the game single–handedly perked up the game of backgammon and made it the gambling game it is today.

Doubling of the stake can increase indefinitely (there is no limit to the amount of times a player can double) but there are usually not more than four or five doublings per game. A player indicates he is doubling with the doubling cube. The cube looks like an oversized die except that each of its sides is marked with one of the following numbers: 2, 4, 8, 16, 32, and 64. Each represents the number of times the amount of the original stake is multiplied.

At the beginning of the game, all players decide upon the original stake. The friendly game is played for a stake anywhere from ten cents to a dollar. Place the cube on the bar with the 64 side up. Either player can double first—whenever he feels that he has a good chance of winning. He turns the cube so the number-2 side

is facing up. His opponent can decline this double (or any other double later in the game) but, if he does, he forfeits the game and the original stake. If he accepts the double, the game continues, but at the risk of losing twice the original stake.

The right to double alternates, so no one player can double twice in a row. The next doubler turns the cube so the 4 is face up, the next 8, and so on until one player refuses to accept the double and forfeits the game and the entire stake at that point, or until one player wins. You should accept any double if your opponent has only a slight advantage. When it's a sure thing (a shutout), or seems like a sure thing (he's bearing off and you're still trying to get a hit marker back on the board), don't accept. You are better off forfeiting the game and the stake at that point, to prevent: a *gammon* (where the loser has not borne off a single marker at the end of the game), which automatically doubles the entire stake (including earlier dou-

Chouette

When three to five players want to play backgammon and there's only one board, play chouette. One player (called *the man in the box*) plays against all the other players as a group and accepts all bets.

To begin, each player rolls one die and the highest roller becomes the man in the box; second highest roller becomes the captain of the opposing team; all others become partners of the captain. The game is played as usual, except that the partners are allowed to discuss the game and advise the captain of the best way to play a roll, and whether to offer or accept a double. The captain makes the final decision, electing to take or reject his partners' advice.

If the man in the box wins, he keeps his position and the captain loses his position to the partner who had the third highest original roll (before the first game). If the man in the box loses, the captain becomes the next man in the box, the partner with the third highest original roll becomes the next captain, and the man in the box joins the group.

Ten cents doesn't sound like much of a stake, but when you use the doubling cube a ten-cent game could cost you—or win you—up to $6.40.

Keeping Score

The simplest way of keeping score is game by game. Usually, though, you play a series of games to determine the winner of a match, as is done in tournaments. Scoring is done with units called *points* (not to be confused with the triangular points on the board). If you win a game you score:

- 1 point if your opponent was able to bear off at least one of his markers.

- 2 points if your opponent was unable to bear off at least one of his markers—a gammon.

- 3 points if your opponent was unable to bear off any of his markers, and still had a hit marker off the board or in your inner table—a backgammon.

When playing for money—usually a specified amount per point—you can settle up after each game or at the end of the match. The loser pays the winner the money equivalent of the difference in their point scores. Using the doubling cube can bring this difference up to a sizable amount.

bles); or a *backgammon* (where the loser has not borne off a single marker, and has a hit marker off the board or in an opponent's inner table at the end of the game), which automatically triples the entire take (including earlier doubles).

Understanding an opponent's playing habits can help you decide whether to double or whether to ac-

cept a double. An overly cautious player, for example, tries to avoid big losses by seldom offering or accepting doubles. You should double him as often as you can until he begins to question his decisions. Some players double wildly, especially when trying to recoup losses on a losing streak. (Single games are rarely played because they go so fast.) When playing against this type, don't double until you're pretty sure of winning. Some players take crazy chances and like to play hunches. When two such players get together both high spirits lock horns—the doubling cube may even reach 64, a rare occurrence under ordinary circumstances.

Billy Eisenberg playing backgammon, with Dr. Richard Katz looking on. As well as teaming up in backgammon tournaments, the two are among the best bridge players in America. (Robert Landau.)

Collecting playing cards as a hobby began in the United States around the turn of the 20th century. These Indian-design cards date from the 1930s.

A CAVALCADE OF CARDS*

Few things in life have as colorful or mysterious a background as the humble deck of cards. Although many legends attempt to explain their origins, none can be passed on with certainty. Some scholars suggest that cards were developed in China in the 12th century, to entertain the emperor's 300 concubines who more often than not had little else to do.

Over the years, cards have been in and out of favor with church and state. The Puritans called them "The Devil's Book." Royal decrees outlawed them. In 1937 working people in Paris were denied cards along with other "vices" such as tennis and nine pins. The law may have been somewhat redundant, since early playing cards had to be colored by hand, making them too expensive for most working people.

But for those who could afford them, cards became an important means of social contact. A London newspaper in 1753 reported, "There is a new kind of tutor lately introduced into some families of fashion in this Kingdom, namely a Gaming Master, who attends his hour as regularly as the Music, Dancing, and French Master in order to instruct young misses in principles of the fashionable accomplishment of card playing."

But, then, as now, card-playing enjoyed less then universal approval. Even Benjamin Franklin was criticized for wasting time at cards. His reply: "You know that the soul is immortal; why then should you be such a niggard of a little time when you have a whole eternity before you? So, being easily convinced, and, like other respectable creatures, satisfied with a small reason when it is in favor of doing what I have a mind to, I shuffle the cards again and begin another game."

(Courtesy of the Dominion Bridge Company Ltd., Montreal, Quebec, Canada)

Chinese domino cards. In China, cards and dominoes are interchangeable, and many of the designs on dominoes appeared originally on cards. The Chinese used both cards and dominoes for fortune telling, which may account for the detailed design. Over the years, however, much of the symbolism has been lost.

Cards from India are unlike those from any other country. They were made from paper, thin wood, and sometimes even ivory. Some of the cards are just an inch in diameter, which supports a belief that round cards were once played on chess boards instead of the "men" we know today.

Despite the youthful cut to his garb, this fellow is at least 530 years old. He's Lancelot, one of the oldest surviving cards, printed from hand-carved wooden blocks in France around the 1440s.

In 1710 the British government enacted a tax on cards. The law called for a duty mark to be printed on the ace of spades in each deck. Forging a "duty-paid ace" was punishable by hanging, and the ace of spades has since been known as the card of death.

The torn card has long been a popular device for two parties wanting to identify each other at a later time by matching the two halves. Rum runners, who had good reason for making sure they had the right party, revived the idea during prohibition.

Next time you watch a saloon game in a western movie, see if the studio knew their cards. If the action is supposed to be taking place before 1865, you shouldn't see a card with a double-sided picture or numbers in the corners. Such designs didn't become standard until 1865 to 1870.

Why a bicycle for a trademark? In 1885, one United States firm brought out a new brand of cards called Tally-Ho, named after an attractive carriage very much in vogue at that time. A competitive firm chose the recently-developed high-wheeled bicycle— newer and faster than the carriages—as a stroke of corporate one-upmanship. Bicycle cards have served as a trademark for the company ever since.

FRIDAY NIGHT POKER

When it comes to gambling on card games, poker is king. Once a simple game called straight poker, or bluff, poker now has hundreds of variations and millions of fans. Some are sporadic enthusiasts, but many have made poker a part of their weekly routine.

Luck is a factor in the game, but poker is first and foremost a game of skill—the skillful player will definitely come out ahead of the poorer player in the long run. And to be a skillful player you must know when to stay in the game and when to drop out; when to match a bet and when to increase it; how to estimate the odds against improving your hand, and the hands you think your opponents hold; how to conceal what's on your mind and figure out what's on your opponents'. And a good player must be an individualist—brave and feisty enough to hold his own when another player begins to bet aggressively. There's a lot of psychology at work in any good poker game, yet the basic rules are straightforward. You can learn these basics in one sitting. After a little practice—it's the only way to learn—you'll be able to adapt the fundamentals to the two most popular poker games—draw and stud—and their variations. After that, get ready for the fancy footwork required to play some of the dealer's choice games.

POKER BASICS

Any number, up to ten, can play poker. As few as two will do in a pinch, but more players add spice and make for a bigger *pot*. (The pot comprises all bets made by all players in any one deal of the cards.) The best game consists of six to eight players. Every man plays for himself; there are no partnerships.

The standard 52–card deck is used. The ace *ranks* (or is valued) highest, then king, queen, jack, 10, 9, 8, 7, 6, 5, 4, 3, 2. The ace is sometimes ranked as both a high and low card. And sometimes, one or more cards are designated as *wild cards*, which can stand for any card that the holder signifies. The joker is sometimes added to the deck as a wild card, to make 53 cards. At other times, the deck is *stripped* (certain cards, usually low-ranking ones, are removed), so you're actually playing with less than 52 cards.

The object in any poker game is to win the pot by holding the most valuable combination of cards, called a *hand*, at the end of the game. Unless a player is bluffing, every time he bets it means that he thinks he has the most valuable hand. When the players are finished betting, they show their hands (appropriately called the *showdown*), and the most valuable hand wins the pot. But you can't bet intelligently in poker unless you know the value or rank of your hand in relation to other possible hands. The ranking of hands is based on the theory of probability: as the probability of being dealt a certain hand decreases, its rank increases, and the more likely you are to win the pot if you

In a Nutshell

Really good play in poker is psychological. It consists of the ability to analyze what your opponent has and to keep him guessing about what you have; to know who can be bluffed and who can't; to know who only plays with good hands to start with and who comes into the pot with nothing but hope and a stout heart.

(Oswald Jacoby)

The showdown—the point at which you may find the biggest surprises, and heartbroken groans mingled with self-satisfied, gleeful chuckles.

hold that hand. Knowing the rank of poker hands—that a royal flush beats all other hands, for example—is second nature to the skillful player. So, before you even think about joining other pokerphiles, memorize the various hands and their rank, beginning below. The number of ways each hand may be dealt and the probability of getting each hand with the first five cards dealt are also shown. Though these numbers can change with the type of poker you play, the rank of poker hands never changes except when a wild card (or cards) is used and a five-of-a-kind hand becomes possible. In that case, five of a kind beats all other hands.

RANK OF POKER HANDS FROM HIGHEST TO LOWEST

		Number of ways hand may be dealt	Probability of getting hand with first five cards dealt is 1 in:
Royal flush	The five highest cards in the same suit. (*Note:* When a wild card(s) is used, five of a kind ranks highest.)	4	649,740

Straight flush	Five cards in sequence, all of the same suit. If there is more than one straight flush at the showdown, the hand with the highest-ranking high card wins: the hand shown wins over 8(H), 7(H), 6(H), 5(H), 4(H). Aces may rank high: A, K, Q, J, 10, or low: 5, 4, 3, 2, A.	36	72,193

Four of a kind	Four cards of the same rank, and one odd card. If there is more than one four-of-a-kind hand at the showdown, the hand with the four highest-ranking cards wins: the hand shown wins over 7(C), 7(H), 7(D), 7(S), Q(H). The highest-ranking four-of-a-kind hand is four aces. (*Note:* When several wild cards are used it becomes possible to have a tie between two four-of-a-kind hands. In that case, the higher-ranking odd card determines the winner.)	624	4,165

Full house

Three cards of the same rank (three of a kind or *triplet*) and two cards of the same rank (a pair). This combination is also called a *full hand,* and is sometimes identified by its triplet, as in *king full,* shown here. If there is more than one full house at the showdown, the hand with the highest–ranking triplet wins: the one shown beats J(H), J(D), J(S), A(C), A(H).

(*Note:* The rank of the pairs does not count in determining a winner between two full houses unless the triplets are of the same rank, as can happen when wild cards are used. In that case, the higher–ranking pair determines the winner.)

3,744   694

Flush

Five cards all of the same suit, but not in sequence. If there is more than one flush at the showdown, the hand with the highest–ranking high card wins: the hand shown wins over J(S), 7(S), 5(S), 3(S), 2(S). If high cards tie, the hand with the highest–ranking second-high card determines the winner: K(C), Q(C), 6(C), 5(C), 3(C) wins over the hand shown. Ace is always ranked high.

5,108   509

Straight

Five cards in sequence, but not of the same suit. In case of ties at the showdown, the hand with the highest–ranking high card determines the winner: the hand shown wins over J(H), 10(S), 9(C), 8(C), 7(H). The highest straight, A, K, Q, J, 10, is called an *ace-high straight,* or sometimes a *Broadway.* The lowest straight is 6, 5, 4, 3, 2.

10,200   255

(continued)

RANK OF POKER HANDS FROM HIGHEST TO LOWEST

		Number of ways hand may be dealt	Probability of getting hand with first five cards dealt is 1 in:
Three of a kind (*triplet*)	Three cards of the same rank, and two odd cards. If there is more than one triplet at the showdown, the hand with the highest–ranking triplet wins: the hand shown wins over 10(S), 10(C), 10(D), 5(H), 3(C). (*Note:* When several wild cards are used, it becomes possible to have a tie between two triplet hands. In that case, the highest–ranking odd card determines the winner. If the odd cards tie too, the second odd card from each hand determines the winner.)	54,912	47
Two pair	Two sets of two cards of the same rank, and one odd card. If there is more than one two-pair hand at the showdown, the hand with the highest pair wins. If the highest pairs are tied, the hand with the highest–ranking second pair determines the winner: K(H), K(C), 10(D), 10(C), 5(S) wins over the hand shown. If both pairs tie, the highest-ranking odd card determines the winner.	123,552	21
Two of a kind (*a pair*)	One set of two cards of the same rank, and three odd cards. If there is more than one two-of-a-kind hand at the showdown, the hand with the highest–ranking pair wins; if both pair are tied, the hand with the highest–ranking odd card wins; if they tie, the highest–ranking second-high odd card determines the winner, and so on. The hand shown wins over Q(D), Q(S), 7(S), 5(C), 2(H).	1,098,240	2.36
High card (*no pair*)	No matches or combinations at all—all cards are of mixed suits and ranks. If two such "nothing hands" should make it to the showdown, the highest–ranking card determines the winner. Ace is highest card, then K, Q, J, 10, and so on. If players tie for highest–ranking card, the second highest–ranking card is considered, then the third–highest, and so on. The hand shown wins over A(C), J(S), 6(S), 5(D), 2(H).	1,302,540	2

HOW TO PLAY

The game begins with choosing the dealer. This can be done by drawing for the highest–ranking card, in which case the cards are spread face down and each player *draws* (or pulls) one card. The dealer can also be chosen by having one player shuffle the cards then deal them, face up, one at a time going clockwise, beginning with the player on his left. The first player to be dealt a specified card (usually a jack or an ace) is the dealer.

Before the dealer distributes any cards, each player is required to start the pot with an initial bet called an *ante*. The ante is usually small—one or two chips. (Most social games are played with real money, which drives home the point that that's exactly what's at stake if you lose—real money. But in this discussion, referring to bets in chips will keep things simple.) In some social games, the dealer antes for everyone. This saves time, and also avoids the possibility of a player inadvertently forgetting to ante. Since the deal rotates, no one dealer antes up more money than another.

The dealer shuffles the cards, and anyone except the dealer cuts them (usually it's the player to the dealer's right). The dealer then distributes the cards, one at a time, clockwise, beginning with the player to his left. (The number of cards dealt, and their face-up or face-down position depends on the type of poker being played.) Each player looks at his cards, and the betting begins.

The essence of poker is the bet-

ting that takes place in the *rounds* (or betting intervals) between deals. Any round begins when the first bet is made (the rules of the particular type of poker being played determine who the first bettor will be) and ends with the last bettor. For all rounds, the first bettor must either:

• *Open the pot*, by making a bet and putting those chips into the pot; or
• *Check*, by making a bet of "nothing." Checking allows a player to stay in the game without putting in any money.

After the first bettor has either bet or checked, the turn to bet moves around the group, beginning at the first bettor's left. Each player in turn, and *only* when it's his turn to bet, must do one of the following:

• *Drop* or *fold*, by putting no chips into the pot, and discarding his hand by placing it face down. A player folds when his hand is weak and the

Fifty dollars in chips (where one white chip represents a dollar) and money.

In the Chips

Bets may be in the form of pennies, nickels, dimes, quarters, dollar bills, or poker chips that represent money. Most poker players like the feel of real money, but some prefer to use chips because they're neater. If you use them, one person must be designated as banker, to keep stock of chips and to keep tabs on the number that have been issued to each player. Players should have no private transactions or exchanges among themselves; a player with surplus chips may return them to the banker and receive credit for them, while a player requiring more chips should obtain them only from the banker. For a game of seven or more players, there should be a supply of at least 200 chips. White chips are worth one unit (whatever is the minimum bet), a red chip is worth five whites, a blue chip is worth ten whites or two reds. If the limit in the game is 5 chips, there should be 100 whites and 100 reds. If the limit is 10, there should be 100 whites, 50 reds, and 50 blues. At the start of the game each player takes the same number of chips (a *takeout*). A practical takeout might be 10 whites, 4 reds, and 2 blues, making 50 units in all.

The Riffle or Dovetail Shuffle

Divide the pack in two. Holding one half in one hand and the other half in the other hand, bend one corner of each half with each thumb. Then release them gradually so they interlock as they fall. Push the sections together and square the pack. Repeat twice.

The Overhand Shuffle

This shuffle, where one portion of the pack is pushed into the remaining portion, is not proper in most games since it doesn't redistribute the cards sufficiently.

chances of improving it are small. A player who folds is out of the game until a new hand is dealt, and loses any chips he may have already put into the pot. (Only the ante is lost if a player folds on the first round of betting.)

• *Call the bet,* by putting into the pot the same number of chips as the last bettor. A player calls when his hand is good, or has a good chance of improving. Essentially, he's sticking around to see what will happen.

• *Raise the bet,* by putting in more money than anyone else in that round so far. A player raises when he has a strong hand, and a good chance of winning the pot. (Of course, a player may also raise as part of a bluff—to make the other players think he has a better hand than he really does.) By raising, a player increases the bets yet–to–be–made (all bets subsequently made in that round must call that raise, or raise again) and, therefore, the size of the pot. A raise on the first, or early, round also eliminates those players with so–so hands by scaring them into folding early. This is part of the skillful player's plan, because weak hands can improve—even perhaps to the point of winning—if they remain in the game.

• *Check,* if no other bets have already been made during that round. If someone else bets later in that round, the chance to bet will return to a player who previously checked. (See sandbag, below.) If all players check, the round of betting is over.

• *Sandbag,* by checking during the first round and then raising later during that round. In essence, a player who sandbags is raising the stakes after having given the impression that he was ready to drop. Although this can liven the game considerably, such behavior is frowned upon in some games. (Often, the player who checks is only allowed to call the latest bet when the chance to bet returns to him in that same round.)

A player's decision to drop, call, raise, or check depends on the strength of his hand and how strong he thinks the other players' hands are. Since all players make this decision in turn, where you stand in the order of the bettors is a consideration. If your turn is after the first bettor, for example, you don't have any clues as to how the other players rate the strength of their hands and their chances of winning. If your turn to bet is near the end of the round, you know which players think they have strong hands because they have stayed in the game by calling or raising.

After the first round of betting, the players can be given the opportunity to improve their hands in some manner. (The specifics of how this is done depend on the type of poker being played.) Then, one or more rounds of betting generally follow. After the final round of betting comes the showdown, during which the active players (those who have not folded) expose their hands and the highest-ranking hand wins the pot. If only one active player remains after any betting round (that is, if a player makes a bet or a raise that no other player calls), no showdown is needed. That player wins the pot, and no one will ever know whether or not he was bluffing, because he doesn't have to show his hand. In poker, "You gotta pay to see."

The deal passes to the player on the previous dealer's left for the next game.

A Bold Bluff. (Reproduced by permission of and copyright by Brown & Bigelow, St. Paul, Minnesota.)

A Short History of Poker

Poker has no detailed, documented history. It probably began when card players mixed the Persian game *as nas* with its offspring, the French game *poque*. Then they threw in a little English *brag*, added a pinch each of *bouilotte* and *ambigu* (more French ingredients), stirred (or rather, shuffled) well . . . and out popped American poker. Ever since the game was introduced by way of New Orleans in the early 1800s, it has enjoyed a steady popularity, perhaps because it so well exemplifies our pioneer spirit. It's especially associated with the winning of the West, but still gives the bold and adventurous among us the perfect excuse to display our courage and wits.

The Thanatopsis Literary and Inside Straight Club

One of the more fabulous events of the 1930s was the formation of a poker club by the members of the Round Table, an illustrious literary luncheon group that met every day at the Algonquin Hotel in New York. Every Saturday, after dinner, five to twelve literati would sit down to a marathon game that lasted until Sunday afternoon.

At first, players were of a uniformly modest financial status: the game was for table stakes, but no one lost more than $100 a night. Eventually the group included better-heeled celebrities; among its members were Harpo Marx, Alexander Woollcott, Prince Antoine Bibesco, Jerome Kern, George S. Kaufman, Alfred Lunt and Lynn Fontanne, Ring Lardner, Robert Benchley, and Paul Robeson.

The stakes rose to $250, then $500. Reports of exaggerated winnings and losses inevitably began to circulate: Alexander Woollcott was said to have lost $4,000 in one evening. (His reply: "My doctor says it's bad for my nerves to lose so much.") Harpo, too, was the target of rumors: He was supposed to have won $30,000 in one game, but he denied this by saying, "The most I ever won in a session is a few thousand dollars."

BETTING LIMITS

Most social poker players agree that setting some betting limit is necessary. Whatever limits are decided upon will affect more than how much you can win or lose. Because the betting is so crucial in poker, the betting limits will affect the play itself. In a high stakes game you'll probably play more cautiously and so may your opponents. A bet made in relation to the limit set is also important. A 10-chip bet made in a 10-chip-limit game, for example, will mean something quite different than a 10-chip bet in a 25-chip-limit game. And if you're down to $10, you may not be as willing to risk a $10 bet as you would be if you had $40 left to bet with. This same reasoning also applies to your opponents. If an opponent low on betting money bets ten dollars, maybe he really *is* pretty sure of his hand. These considerations are easier to weigh when playing with your usual Friday night poker buddies, because you have some knowledge of their betting and playing habits; playing with strangers makes interpretation much more difficult.

The following are the most common betting limits:

● *Fixed Limit.* With a fixed limit, no player may bet or raise by more or less than a certain amount of money or number of chips. Usually two amounts are specified, fixing the high and low betting limits. In a 5–10 game, the least a player may bet is five chips (or pennies, or dollars, or whatever); the most he can raise is ten chips. The lower figure is usually also the ante. In a 5–25 game, a player may bet anything between 5 and 25, in units of five (5, 10, 15, 20, 25). In draw poker, the fixed limit may increase after the draw. In a 5–10 draw poker game, the betting limit may be 5 before the draw (first betting round) and 10 after the draw (second betting round). In a 5–10–25 draw poker fixed limit game, the limits are 5–10 before the draw and 10–25 after the draw.

• In *penny ante* poker, one cent is the basic limit, with pennies used exclusively. Everyone antes one penny, and the betting limits are 1–5, with bets allowed anywhere in between (1, 2, 3, 4, 5). Some penny ante games are actually high-powered, because pennies merely take the place of poker chips, each representing up to a dollar or more.

• *Pot limit.* In a pot limit game, any bet or raise is limited to the number of chips in the pot at the same time the bet or raise is made. A player who wishes to raise may count the number of chips needed to call as part of the pot. For example, if there are ten chips in the pot and the last bet made was four chips, the player may raise by fourteen chips (ten plus the four needed to call). When pot limit is played, there should still be some maximum limit set.

• *Table Stakes.* Table stakes is one of the most popular betting limits. The limit for each player is the number of chips he has in front of him. If he has only ten chips, he may bet no more than ten. A player may add to his stack, but only between the showdown and the beginning of the next deal. A player isn't allowed to withdraw any chips from the table, or return them to the banker, until he leaves the game.

• *Limits on Raises.* In addition to betting limits, you may want to limit the number of raises any one player may make to two or three in each betting interval; or to have no more than three raises—no matter by whom—in any interval.

Whangdoodles and Roodles

No, they're not new snack foods to munch on while playing poker—these are terms for a special pot with an increased ante or stakes in a fixed limit game. When a whangdoodle or a roodle is declared, either everyone antes double, or the betting limit is doubled for that round. For the next round, it's betting as usual.

Risk is rightly thrilling, fate is fascinating, and luck is luring . . . the timid man seldom forges ahead, and the one who fears to gamble will never have the thrill of a win. He may console himself that he will never lose either, but he probably has little to lose, and worry will kill what fun he gets from hoarding what he has.

(The Only Game in Town *by Hank Messick [T.Y. Crowell]. Reprinted by permission of Harper & Row, Publishers, Inc.)*

HOW TO PLAY DRAW POKER

A Mighty Mecca

There are over 400 licensed and legalized draw poker card clubs throughout California, but the biggest concentration of them is in Gardenia (about 20 miles south of Los Angeles). Only five-card draw poker is allowed, but high draw and low draw variations lend spice to the proceedings. Players need only pay an hourly rate to the house (rental for the use of gaming facilities); patrons play among themselves and the entire pot goes to the winner. The action is definitely cutthroat, and the unsuspecting rookie can be fleeced of his rent money in a few games by the pros. But that doesn't stop the four million poker addicts that show up every year.

Draw poker is played by the basic poker rules already described, except that each player is given the opportunity to improve his hand by discarding unwanted cards and being dealt replacement cards (the *draw*) after the first betting round. This feature also helps the player bluff his opponents. What better way to make them think you're holding four strong cards than by requesting only one replacement card?

Any number from three to seven can play draw poker, but six is best.

After each player antes up, the dealer gives each player five face-down cards, one at a time, in turn. The players look at their cards, and the first betting round begins. The first player on the dealer's left may open the pot or check. (Some rules don't allow checking.)

If all players check, the cards are collected and new ante is added to the ante already in the pot. The deal passes clockwise to the next player. New cards are dealt and a new betting round begins. Once the pot is opened, however, players may drop, call, raise, but not check. Most players will still be active at the end of the first betting round, waiting for the draw, which begins after the first betting round. Each player in turn may declare how many cards he is discarding and place them face down in front of him. The dealer replaces them in turn from the undealt portion of the deck.

Replacement cards are usually limited to three. But there are games where the dealer only can draw up to four, and in rare games five cards may be drawn. Of course, the player may also elect to *stand pat*, and stay with all five cards originally dealt to him.

When every player has either drawn or chosen to stand pat, the second round of betting begins.

Draw poker is usually played with a fixed limit, with both the low and high limits increased after the draw—on the second betting round. (See Betting Limits, pages 78–79.)

The player who opened the pot for the first betting round has the opportunity to make the first bet in this round as well. If he dropped on the first round, the next active player on his left makes the first bet. When everyone has bet, checked, raised, or dropped there is the usual showdown, where all active players show their hands and the highest ranking hand wins the pot. If only one player has bet and nobody calls, the lone bettor wins the pot without showing his hand.

How Many Cards Should You Draw?

In draw poker, you have a chance to draw additional cards, and so improve your hand. If you've got K, K, 8, 8, 5 you won't have to think too much about which one to discard. More often, however, some hard thinking is involved. Let's say, for example, you've been dealt Q(H), Q(D), J(H), 10(S), 9(C). Should you hold onto the pair and draw three cards in the hope of getting three of a kind? Or should you sacrifice the pair in hopes of a straight? Table position can help make up your mind. If you are the last to draw, you know how many cards everyone else has taken and have a clue to what they may be holding. (A player who draws three cards, for example, probably holds a pair.) Some knowledge of your chances of getting what you need is also important, and the table that follows shows the probability of improving various hands with various draws.

Draw	When you need . . .	Probability of improving hand
5 cards	A whole new hand—you have practically nothing in your hand. (Note: Draw poker rarely allows a player to replace his whole hand.)	Very slim, and whatever you get you're stuck with.
4 cards	To match a high card (you have only an A or K) for a pair.	1 out of 4 to match high card.
3 cards	To improve a pair.	1 out of 3½
2 cards	To improve three of a kind.	1 out of 10; if you do improve your hand, chances are 2 out of 3 that you'll get a full house rather than a four of a kind.
	To improve a pair and a *kicker* (a high card, such as an ace or a king).	1 out of 3. The 2-card draw also has bluff value, since the other players may think you have three of a kind.
	To improve an open-ended straight (Q, J, 10).	1 out of 12 to make a straight or a flush. There's a very slim chance of making a straight flush.
1 card	To improve two pair.	1 out of 12 to make a full house.
	To improve an open-ended straight (10, 9, 8, 7).	1 out of 6 chances of filling the straight.
	To improve an inside straight (Q, J, 10, 8).	1 out of 12 chances—it's rarely worth the try.

(continued)

The Trap: the Second-Best Hand

One of the main ideas in winning poker is to stay out of the big pots when you are not going to win. A hand which was hopeless all the way should never have gotten going. The place where the real money is lost is in the vain pursuit of a hand just a bit stronger than the one you hold. You must recognize that some hands, while they are possible winners, are just not worth following through. A common example is a small pair, particularly at draw. I know you hate to throw away a hand and then find that you could have held it and won this particular pot, but this sort of chasing the will–o'–the–wisp will cost dearly in the long run. It is far better to recognize that hands like this are best gotten rid of with a fond farewell.

(Go With the Odds *by Charles H. Goren. Copyright* © *1969 by Charles H. Goren. Macmillan Publishing Co., Inc.*)

Draw	When you need . . .	Probability of improving hand
1 card	To improve three of a kind.	1 out of 12 but opponents may think you have two pair or a possible straight or a flush.
	To fool opponents into thinking you are trying to improve your hand when you already have four of a kind.	
	To fill a four-card straight	1 out of 12 to fill a straight either in the middle or at one end; 1 out of 6 to fill a straight open at both ends.
	To fill a 4-card flush	1 out of 5.
No card (Standing Pat)	Nothing. You have a straight, flush, full house, or a straight flush.	No improvement possible.
	To bluff your opponents into thinking you have a strong hand. (You may consider the chances of getting a full house too slim to be worth a one-card draw.)	
	Anything! Use as a bluff to make your opponents think you have a great hand: flush, straight, straight flush, five of a kind, full house. Or as a double bluff to make your opponents *think* you're only bluffing—and don't really have a great hand.	? ? ? ? ? ? ? ? ? ? ? ? ? No improvement, but your chances of making a successful bluff depend upon how well you know your opponents—and how well they know you.

Cheating at Poker

There's relatively little cheating in poker games between friends, aside from giving in to the temptation to sneak peeks at a neighbor's card or the bottom of the deck. Few of your friends are likely to pull off card mechanics' tricks like stacking or marking the deck, or dealing seconds or bottoms. (See Confessions of a Card Mechanic on pages 96–99 for more about those tricks.)

One veteran player suggests, however, that you be on the lookout for two players who are in cahoots. Such partners can cheat by signaling each other to indicate the strength of their hands. The one with the weaker hand builds the pot by raising the bets a few times. He then drops out at the last moment, and his partner wins the pot (which they split later).

Jackpots, or Jacks or Better

In this popular form of draw poker, one of the players must have at least a pair of jacks, or a hand that would beat a pair of jacks in a showdown, in order to open the pot. Once the pot is opened, however, the other players don't have to have jacks or better to stay in the game; if they don't, however, they usually fold anyway, because they know they're beaten already.

When you play jackpots you increase the size of the pot with additional antes. Since a pair of jacks is a better–than–average hand, often all the players check (no one can open the pot). The ante remains in the pot and the deal passes to the next player, which means another ante is added to the pot and a new hand is dealt. If no one can open the pot on the second deal, a third is dealt, and everyone puts in another ante. This continues until a player is dealt two jacks or better and the pot can be opened. The game progresses as usual: each player calls, raises or folds; then comes the draw, and another betting interval. Lastly, the showdown.

In a variation called *progressive jackpots*, every time all the players check on a hand the opening requirement is raised. So, for the second hand you would need a pair of queens to open the pot, a pair of kings in the third, then a pair of aces. After aces, you can raise the opening requirement to two pair, but things seldom progress that far.

Should you open the pot in either jackpots or progressive jackpots, you may decide to split your openers, that is, discard one of your opening cards (such as a jack or king) from a pair, in order to go after a higher hand, such as a straight or a flush. The opening player should keep the discard handy so that at the showdown he can prove he was qualified to open the pot.

Poker headache #23: You've been dealt four spades on the third deal of jackpots. There are a lot of chips to be won and you are well on your way to a flush—but no one can open the pot.

Poker Ethics or "When in Rome . . ."

Since poker customs vary so much, and since card playing is most of all a social pastime, the only way to remain social is to follow whatever house rules are agreed upon by the folks you're playing with. A fine of a few chips might be imposed for an occasional broken rule but, if you break such rules often enough, you'll probably not be invited back to play.

It's in the nature of poker to allow—yes, even to encourage—a certain amount of hanky panky, as long as you don't cheat outright. In many games it's okay to sneak a look at your opponent's hand if he's dumb enough to let you. And speaking of roving eyes, in some circles the last card of the deck is never dealt, because it's assumed that any player worth his salt has taken a peek.

Another sensitive area is bluffing, and the boundaries of acceptable behavior vary a great deal. In some games, a player is expected to do anything to fool his opponents. Lies, misstatements, misleading facial expressions, etc., are just part of the skill of the game. Others frown upon such activity as announcing that you have improved your hand when you really haven't.

All this could be a rather touchy subject, especially since behavior of this type is never discussed out loud. So, pay attention to what everyone else is doing—you'll soon figure out what's tacitly sanctioned, and what isn't.

BLUFFING, MOXIE, AND PSYCHING OUT

In the original game of poker, each player was simply dealt five face-down cards and was forced to bluff his way through the game. Draw and stud poker players can actually improve their hands, but the principle of bluffing is still one of the most important—and certainly one of the most fascinating—components of the game. In fact, some say bluffing is the most important factor in a game of poker. This is especially so when you always play with the same people, and get to know their habits, their strengths, and their weaknesses.

A purse of the lips, a shift of the chair, a sigh, or the absence of any of these can be construed (or misconstrued) as signals of the inner workings of your fellow players. For some, the cards and money are simply tools that create situations enabling them to probe their opponents' psyches in a game of wits.

A player who bluffs is essentially a liar. He's trying to fool his opponent into thinking he has either a better or worse hand than he really does. The most common bluff is when a player stays in or bets aggressively when he knows his hand is probably not the best in the game. Another common ploy in draw poker is to stand pat on a "nothing" hand. Either tactic may scare your opponents (who may have better hands than you have) into dropping out, or not calling or raising your bet. You may then win the pot without even showing your hand. To do this takes guts or moxie, and the ability to follow through once you've decided to bluff. Another form of bluffing is to stay cool when you have just drawn a fifth card to an inside straight flush. Although you know you've got everyone beat, you must remain calm and not raise your bet too high or you will scare off your opponents and their bets. Unless, of course, you want to try a double bluff: get them to think you're only bluffing that you have a great hand.

Leave it to Nick the Greek to fit the state of affairs into a nutshell. He said poker can consist of "not what is going on, but what someone thinks is going on."

HOW TO PLAY STUD POKER

In stud poker each player is dealt face-down cards (*hole cards*) and face-up cards (*up cards*). The fact that players can see part of each others' hands can produce some intriguing situations. Because stud poker has more betting rounds than draw poker (where the betting limits before and after the draw often vary), players usually decide to keep the same betting limit throughout the game. Exceptions, if any, are usually made on the last betting round where the upper limit on bets is raised.

In both five-card and seven–card stud the basics of poker apply, along with the distinguishing characteristics that are described below.

Five-Card Stud Basics

Two to ten may play the game, but it is best with seven to nine players. Some players like to vary the action by stripping the standard 52-card deck of 2's and 3's.

Players ante up as usual, and the dealer gives each player in turn (starting at his left) one hole card, face down. Each player is then dealt, in turn, one up card. Each player looks at his hole card (he doesn't show it to the others until the showdown), and the player with the highest up card (the *high man*) begins the first round of betting. Of course, he may check instead, in which case the opportunity to open passes to the person on the left of the high man. (In some games the players don't ante up before the

cards are dealt. The first betting round becomes an ante of sorts, because the first bettor *must* open the pot and each player to bet after him, therefore, must at least match that bet.) If two or more players hold the same high card, the one who was dealt the card first starts the betting. The other players in turn then check, call, raise, or fold. With three more cards to be dealt, however, no one folds—it's too early in the game.

The dealer then gives each player a second up card. The high man (player with the highest ranking combination of up cards) begins the second betting round. If he bets, others may call, bet, raise, or fold in turn.

In stud poker, up cards and hole cards remain on the table. Players do not hold their cards in their hands.

The following table shows the hands on which you have an even chance of holding the highest hand originally dealt:

Hand Required	To Beat
Any pair	1 opponent
Pair of eights	2 opponents
Pair of jacks	3 opponents
Pair of kings	4 opponents
Pair of aces	5, 6, or 7 opponents

Values of Hands

A player must know what constitutes a good hand in the form of poker he is playing. Following are the average winning hands in various forms of poker, with seven players in the game:

Type of Poker	Winning Hand
Draw poker, nothing wild	Jacks up
Five-card stud	Aces or kings
Seven-card stud	Three 8's
Draw poker, joker wild	Three 8's
Draw poker, with the bug	Aces up
Draw poker, deuces wild	Three aces
Draw poker, high-low	Jacks up, high; 10 or 9, low

The dealer then gives each player still in the game a third up card. This is again followed by another round of betting started by the high man. Each player's last card—a fourth up card—is then dealt. Then, the high man starts a final round of betting. After all remaining players have called, thereby evening up all bets, they turn up their hole cards for the showdown.

When Should You Fold? / The rule of thumb is, fold unless your hand beats any exposed combination. If, however, your first two cards make a pair, stay in. If any player's up card is an ace, and you have anything less than another ace or a pair, consider getting out of the game. If a second player also shows an ace, however, then the chances of either of them holding (or being dealt) two aces are reduced and your pair may beat them.

As the game progresses, continue to pay careful attention to your opponents' up cards—they can be powerful clues as to what the hole cards may be.

Here's a handy tip from one expert: if a player's hole card is any good, he'll remember it the first time he takes a look at it. It's only the worthless cards that a player keeps peeking at. *But*—and this cannot be repeated too often—get to know your opponents before you apply such a rule. Some keep sneaking peeks at a queen in the hole to reassure themselves that she's still there.

Seven-Card Stud Basics

Seven-card stud (also known as *down the river*) and five–card stud follow the basic procedure of getting both face-up and face-down cards, but the similarity ends there. In seven-card stud each player gets to choose the five best from the seven cards he is dealt, so the ranks of hands are usually higher. Additionally, three of the cards are face down, four face up, so a great hand is often well concealed from the eyes of opponents. Still another difference is in the size of the pot, which is likely to be much bigger in seven-card stud, since there are five betting rounds (as opposed to four in five-card stud).

Two to seven players may participate, and the game begins with the ante and then with each player being dealt two hole cards and one up card, one at a time in turn. Then comes the first round of betting; initiated by the high man.

Each player still in the game is dealt three more up cards, one at a time, in turn. After each card is dealt there is a round of betting.

Finally, the dealer gives each remaining player his seventh card—the last hole card. Then there is the final round of betting, followed by the showdown, where players choose their five best cards to form their hands and discard the other two. A player cannot reclaim discards should he discover at the showdown that he could have made a better five-card hand.

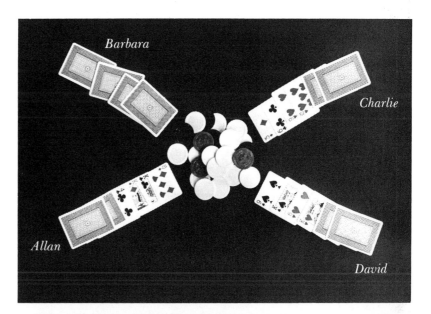

The aftermath of the third betting round in a seven-card stud game looks like this.

Allan and David, each with a pair of kings up, are still in the game and have each raised the bet a few times.

Barbara folded after the second up card was dealt.

Charlie seems to have little prospect of victory judging from his up cards but he has stayed in the game and called Allan's and David's raises. On second thought, Charlie could have the makings of a flush, a straight, or a straight flush.

In the last deal, Allan was dealt an ace (face down) Nice—but he doesn't think it's enough to beat David's pair of kings and whatever else is hiding in the hole. He folds. So, it's one-on-one between Charlie and David, who battle it out a while, raising the pot considerably in the process. Comes the showdown, Charlie (who had weak cards showing) ends up with a straight flush, beating David's straight, and he rakes in the pot.

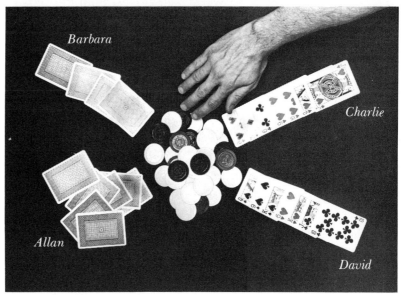

The game:

Players	Hole Cards (three)	Up Cards (four)	Final Hand (five out of seven)
Allan	8(S), 7(C), A(H)	4(C), K(D), K(C), 10(D)	(folded)
Barbara	9(D), A(S)	5(S), 7(H)	(folded)
Charlie	J(H), Q(H), 8(H)	10(H), 9(H), 6(C), 3(D)	Q(H), J(H), 10(H), 9(H), 8(H)—the winner.
David	10(C), J(C), Q(S)	9(S), K(S), 6(H), K(H)	K(H or S), Q(S), J(C), 10(C), 9(S)

Strip Poker

When it comes to strip poker, some loose players play a very tight game. *Playboy's Book of Games* (Edwin Silberstang, Playboy Press, 1972) devotes a whole chapter to the game. Here are some of the author's recommendations:

• Alternate sexes at the table.

• Play draw poker, not stud. Both five- and seven-card stud (where five and seven bets are made, respectively) would leave most of the players stark naked after a few hands. In draw, you stand to lose only three articles of clothing if you stay in a game.

• Only bona fide articles of clothing constitute bets. This includes shoes, but not band-aids, eyeglasses, jewelry, bobby pins, wigs, false teeth, hearing aids, false eyelashes, fake fingernails and false noses. Outer garments must be removed before undergarments. Once a garment has been removed, it may not be put on again. (It remains a part of the winner's stake.)

• No player may withdraw from the game unless agreeing to remove all of his or her clothing.

• The game ends when: all the players are naked; half the players are naked—this calls for a vote as to whether everyone should strip, and end the game; the game has gone on too long and the majority of players vote to strip, and end the game.

• What you play after the game ends is up to you.

When Should You Fold? When Should You Raise the Bet? / One of the reasons for the popularity of seven-card stud is the skill and strategy involved. You must be able to recall cards that have been folded, pay close attention to your opponent's up cards to figure out what's lurking in the hole, and be aware of the odds.

Some players, usually those who can be characterized as "tight" (or conservative), fold in seven-card stud unless, by the third card, they have a concealed pair, a split pair (one in the hole and one up card), or three cards of the same suit. Others will stay in at least until the second up card is dealt. They say it takes until then to know whether your hand is improving sufficiently.

It is rarely good strategy to raise on the first bet, no matter how good

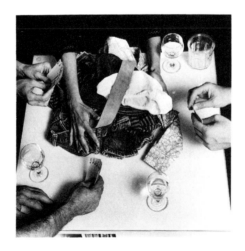

your hand is. Consider a raise this early in the game only if you are to the right of the high man and the last to bet. You then are in a position to judge how many other players have good hands and how heavy the betting action may get. Raising the bet after the second up card makes more sense, but once again, you should consider your position in relation to the rest of the players. The best time to begin to raise is after the third up card has been dealt. The betting limit is higher, and so is the pot. And the poor players who have stayed in will probably stay a while longer just to protect the money they have already invested. By the sixth and seventh rounds, you should raise freely, to build the biggest pot you possibly can—*if* you still think you have the winning hand.

TEN THINGS EVERY WINNING POKER PLAYER MUST KNOW

1. You figure to lose unless you have the best hand going in.

2. Treat every bet as though it were your first one—forget the money you put in the pot before.

3. Call only when your hand should be good enough to win, not merely because you suspect a bluff.

4. Don't try to bluff a poor player, a heavy winner, or a heavy loser.

5. Drop a doubtful hand if you may later be in the middle between two strong hands.

6. Most Stud players would win instead of lose if they never tried to draw out against an open pair.

7. Raise on an early round to avoid calling a big bet later.

8. A loser will drop a close hand if raised early, a winner will stay in.

9. When you're sure you'll win a Stud pot, wait till the last round to raise.

10. The more wild cards and crazy rules, the greater the expert's advantage.

(From How To Be a Consistent Winner in the Most Popular Card Games *by John R. Crawford. Copyright 1953 by John R. Crawford. Reprinted by permission of Doubleday & Company, Inc.)*

In gambling, ignorance is fatal.

(John Scarne)

How to Be a Good Loser

Nick the Greek once lost the biggest single pot in the history of poker: $605,000 to Arnold Rothstein. Actually he came out $70,000 ahead, since in the seven hours of play preceding Rothstein's coup, Nick had won a total of $675,000.

Rothstein presented Nick with a brand-new Rolls-Royce the next day. Nick returned the car with the comment, "Who needs a car in New York?"

TIGHT/LOOSE

The way you play a game should suit the occasion. Most low stakes poker games are played rather "loose"—people play to gamble and have fun, so everyone stays in on almost any hand, good or bad. The players are "chasers," who keep betting and trying to buy better cards. They tend to bet rather than raise, not wanting to scare off other players. In high stakes poker games, though, players are more serious, and play a "tight" game—they wouldn't dream of staying in a seven-card stud hand with anything less than a concealed pair, a split pair of 7's or better, or three cards of the same suit during the first round of betting. They like to have the goods at the beginning, and raise the bet whenever they have a strong hand.

If you play tight in a loose game, you won't lose much money, but you will lose your poker partners. (No one likes a consistent folder.) And if you play loose in a game where everyone else is playing tight, you're not only a fool, you're a loser. Generally, though, most social games rarely consist of all tight or all

A Low Blow

Brian Roberts won fame and fortune by winning the 1975 World Series of Poker. What's so great about that? Well, he did it with a pair of jacks, the lowest hand ever to win the series. The final pot was $115,500; Roberts' total winnings came to $210,000.

That's Dedication!

Two Austin, Texas, planters began playing poker in 1853. They continued playing all through the Civil War and Reconstruction, until 1873, when they died simultaneously.

loose players. You'll get to know how others play after a few sessions.

Let's see what happens when the same hands are played by two different poker players—one loose and one tight. The game is five-card draw; Donald is the loose player (playing for fun and low stakes), and Mark is the tight player (playing a more conservative game for higher stakes).

The deal:
A(S), 10(S), 6(C), 5(H), 3(S)

Donald will stay in the game, drawing two cards to try for a flush.
Mark will fold. Although there is a possibility of drawing two more spades, he won't take the chance on this poor hand.

The deal:
K(H), 10(H), 9(H), 8(H), 3(C)

Donald stays, drawing one card for a flush.
Mark decides to stay too, since the betting isn't very heavy. (If it had been heavy, he would have folded.)

The deal:
K(H), 10(D), 8(H), 8(C), 3(C)

Donald plays his pair of 8's, and draws three cards.
Mark folds. The pair's not high enough for him.

The deal:
K(C), Q(D), 9(D), 7(S), 5(H)

Donald keeps the king and queen and draws three, going for a pair or two pair.
Mark folds.

The deal:
K(C), 7(S), 7(C), 5(H), 3(D)

Donald keeps the pair of 7's and draws three cards.
Mark folds.

The deal:
6(D), 5(S), 5(C), 3(S), 3(C)

Donald draws one card, hoping to turn his two (low) pair into a full house.
Mark folds. The betting is too heavy to count on such low pairs. He'll save his money for a stronger hand on the next deal.

The deal:
A(C), A(H), J(S), J(D), 4(S)

Donald draws one card and feels (rightly) pretty excited, with two aces.
Mark draws one card too, but won't raise or call a raise.

The deal:
A(D), 8(S), 7(H), 6(S), 4(H)

Donald bets, drawing one card and looking for a 5 for a straight.
Mark folds.

The deal:
10(S), 9(H), 7(D), 4(H), 3(C)

Donald folds.
Mark folds.

The deal:
K(D), K(H), K(S), 7(D), 7(C)

Donald and Mark play this hand all the way, boldly raising and calling raises.

DEALER'S CHOICE

Once a poker player has mastered the basic forms of draw and stud, he is ready to go on to the game at its most sociable and enjoyable—dealer's choice games.

In dealer's choice, each dealer in turn has the right to name the form of poker to be played during his or her deal, or to announce a variation in a "standard" rule, like declaring there will be no ante.

The options that govern dealer's choice rules are at least as imaginative as their names. There are so many variations, in fact, that even old hands at poker are occasionally stumped by contrivances they've never heard of. What follows is a description of some of the basic rules that underlie these variations. Most can apply to either draw or stud poker. To whet your appetite, a few of the hundreds of games that are based on them are also described. Others can be found in the books on poker and card games listed at the end of this volume. However, the importance of being familiar with local or house rules, which take precedence over book rules or those based on past experience, cannot be overemphasized.

Wild Cards

The dealer can announce that any card (a joker, for example, as in *joker poker*), or rank of cards (all 2's, for example, as in *deuces wild*) is *wild*, which means it can represent any other card the player designates. This small change alters the entire structure of the game. It adds the rank of five-of-a-kind to the game; it allows double or triple ace-high flushes and straights; it makes three-of-a-kind hands more common than a pair. This, in turn, changes the odds, and the expert player will do better, because of his ability to figure odds quickly. The novice or average player who holds a wild card often loses sight of the fact that all the other players may also have improved their hand with a wild card. On the other hand, some say serious gamblers don't play wild-card games—the luck factor is too high.

• *Five and dime* is a form of seven-card stud where 5's and 10's are wild provided that the player holds both ranks. Even if you hold three 5's, nothing is wild without at least one 10. (You should fold if you don't have at least four of a kind.)

• *Low hole card wild* is another seven-card stud variation, where each player's lowest hole card is wild. For example, a player with a 3 in the hole would have two wild cards if an up card, or his last hole card, were also a 3. Unfortunately, he's out of luck if, for his last hole card, he is dealt a deuce.

The dealer could also announce that each player's first card, third card, or whatever, is wild. Wild card designations can, therefore, be different for each player in the game.

• In *Mexican stud* (also known as *flip* or *peep-and-turn*), two cards are dealt to each player face down. Players look at their cards and de-

Dealer's Choice—
A Sampling of Names

Anaconda with Pass Along
Around the World
Baseball
Bedsprings
Betty Hutton
Bimbo
Blind Tiger
Bobtail Stud
Butcher Boy
Cincinnati Liz
Crisscross
Doctor Pepper
Double-Barreled Shotgun
Down the River
Fiery Cross
Five and Dime
Football
Free Wheeling
Gruesome Twosome
Guts
Heinz
Hilo Picolo
Hokum
Hurricane
Lalapalooza
Lamebrain Pete
Misere
Mustached Jacks Wild
New York Stud
Omaha
Pass the Garbage
Pussy Cat
Queen City Poker
Rangdoodles
Rickey de Laet
Roodles
Screwy Louie
Shifting Sands
Shotgun
Shove Them Along
Slippery Elmer
Southern Cross
Spit in the Ocean
Sudden Death
Take It or Leave It
TNT
Twin Beds Wild
Whangdoodles
X Marks the Spot
Zombie

Watch out

Short thick eyebrows could mean an independent, aggressive player who accepts challenges readily. Since he can also be full of surprises, you'd better watch this potential bluffer carefully.

The proud possessor of thick, upturning eyebrows has a brave, generous, enterprising character. This "born to succeed" type is an especially challenging opponent when the texture of brows is rough, because this adds a cruel, relentless element to his personality.

The owner of eyebrows with a broken line is treacherous and deceitful—a good bluffer who may also be into cheating.

If the end of the eyebrow curves upward and is relatively thin, the person has enough courage to bluff and hold his own during aggressive betting.

Upward-slanting eyes indicate a courageous, opportunistic, and decisive personality. This person may even be reckless at times, and apt to bet and bluff wildly.

Diagonal eyebrows that do not touch in the middle indicate a poker player with imagination, foresight, and enough guts to take a risk.

THE POKER FACE

The Chinese have been reading faces for centuries and have, in fact, made a science of the art. It's called *physiognomy,* and it makes a person's character as plain as the nose on his face. Since bluffing, and the inscrutable poker face it requires, is a large factor in the game, you may want to try adapting this

The Chinese call cheek lines that extend all the way from nose to mouth snake mouth. *They say a person with this facial characteristic is untrustworthy, and so would certainly make a dangerously good bluffer, if not a cheat.*

A firm mouth that droops at the corners is called a fish mouth in Chinese physiognomy. It indicates a strong-willed character, a person who is resourceful, and not easily influenced by others. He may also be a loner—an I'll-do-it-myself type, and a good poker player.

A broad face with a broad jaw and chin indicates a strong personality. This person has lots of determination and the craftiness to see a bluff through.

When you see lips that are thin and don't close well, be very careful. He's a likely bluffer and a possible cheat.

Drawings by Amanda Wilson

ancient method for your own poker-playing purposes, by comparing the facial characteristics on these two pages with your poker opponents'. Of course, the method is not infallible—in fact we couldn't guarantee it any more than advice found in a fortune cookie—but neither are probabilities, nor the grace of Lady Luck.

Relax

Heavy eyebrows that meet in the middle belong to a rather straightforward person–he's unlikely to bluff.

A drooping eyebrow indicates a droopy personality–this person is shy and cowardly. If his coloring is pale and lifeless, you should really be wondering what this guy is doing in a poker game at all.

People with large irises are calm and gentle, and not apt to take risks. They tend to be unadventurous and conservative. If their eyes are very glittery, though, they may have a heartless, mean streak.

Eyes that slant downward often belong to a person who is shy and easily victimized. He has no self-confidence, is pessimistic, and wouldn't dream of bluffing in a game of poker.

A large, bulbous nose tip usually belongs to a kind, warm, self-sacrificing type. But take a look at the owner's eyes, too—uncontrolled glittery eyes can cancel out his good nature.

The relatively long nose usually belongs to a conservative personality. Although he's not likely to bluff, his intellectual capacity is impressive, so he might play a well-thought-out, intelligent, albeit "tight" game.

Anyone whose upper lip is long and broad, but whose lower lip is small or pointed, is gullible. These people are easily taken advantage of, so any bluff you might decide to make would probably succeed.

A wide mouth with thin lips is usually the sign of a cowardly nature, so this type would pose no threat to your poker-playing plans. If, however, these lips are surrounded by a heavy beard (or stubble), the person is as dangerous as someone who has the snake mouth.

A small mouth indicates a person with an exceptionally weak character, especially if the lips are thin. A player of this type is nothing to worry about.

Low-set ears (especially if the upper edge of the ear falls below the eye level) indicate mediocrity. If they are smaller than average, the owner may be slow-witted and easily influenced by others. If the ears, however, are pointed and small, the person is stubborn and cruel: a possible cagey player.

Who Plays Poker?

David M. Hayano of California State University came up with some interesting findings during an informal two-year study of poker games played in legal card houses. Some players are regular part-timers, but many are full-time addicts who scoff at the idea of holding down a nine-to-five-type job.

For them, poker is a more exciting way of life. They play every day, earning an average of $15,000 a year. They make detailed notes of games and opponents, and study gambling books and magazines, incessantly computing the odds. Some indulge in a bit of old-time hustling; compulsive gamblers and inept players (especially rich ones) are juicy targets.

In sort, they have made a full–time career of cards. But the fact that they have been unjustly relegated to the bottom of the social and moral heap has led them to go to some amusing lengths to conceal their real "job." They leave for "work" in the morning, perhaps with a briefcase, just like any other businessman, and return to their respectable homes at night.

cide which one is to be placed face up. Each player's face-down card becomes his wild card. (This card, and all other cards of the same rank, is wild only for the player who holds it face down.) After a round of betting, another card is dealt face down and each player again decides which of the two face-down cards to turn up, and which to keep for a wild card. Then, another round of betting. This continues until each player has four cards face up and one wild card (face down). At the showdown, each active player shows his face-down cards and announces the rank of his hand.

Ranks of Cards

It isn't always the highest-ranking poker hand that rakes in the pot at the showdown. Sometimes it's the lowest, as in these variations:

● In *lowball*, the lowest hand wins the pot, and the rank of poker hands is reversed. Aces rank below 2's so a pair of aces ranks lower than a pair of 2's. Before you begin, decide if flushes and straights count. If straights and flushes don't count, as they often don't in lowball, the perfect low hand—called a *wheel* or *bicycle*—is A, 2, 3, 4, 5 (two or more suits).

● Playing *high-low* adds spice to low stakes games but it's a very demanding addition to any game, since the amount of deception possible and the number of decisions required is greater. In high-low, both the lowest-ranking hand (as described in lowball, above) and the highest-ranking hand win the pot, and the

players who held each one divide the pot between them. The pot is almost always a good deal more than double that of a high-only game. High-low may be played in either stud or draw poker, but *high-low seven-card stud* is considered the quintessence of poker playing. A player can select any five of his seven cards to comprise his hand, and must declare whether he is going for high or low—usually before the final round of betting. A player can also declare he's going for high *and* low but, if he does, he must end up with both to win. Declarations can be made out loud, beginning with the last player who raised a bet. But simultaneous declaration is preferred: each player conceals a number of chips in his hand (one chip represents high, none represents low, and two represent both), and then all players open up simultaneously. Simultaneous declaration is used especially in high-low draw poker since it prevents the dealer (who always bets last) from declaring "low" because everyone else has declared "high." Generally, it is advised that you stay in a game of high-low only if your original hand is quite low or quite high to begin with.

Number and Order of Cards Dealt

Usually the best five-card hand wins, but the number of cards and/or the order in which they are dealt can be changed by the dealer.

● *Two-card poker* is the simplest variation in this category—though it can be embellished with wild cards or the high-low feature—and can accommodate up to 15 players. Players ante up and are dealt two face-down cards. After a round of betting, there is a showdown. The best hand is a pair of aces, and flushes and straights don't count.

• In *acey-deucey,* each player is dealt two cards, one face-down card and one up card. Players may stand with the cards originally dealt or may, in turn, discard one card at a time for new cards. (If a face-down card is discarded, the player is dealt a replacement face-down card. If an up card is discarded, the player is dealt a replacement up card.) Players can draw up to three replacement cards: for the first card drawn, a player puts one chip in the pot; for a second card, he pays two chips; for the third card, five chips. The betting doesn't begin until each player has stood with his hand or folded; the player with the high card bets first. Acey-deucey is usually played high-low, and only pairs and high cards count. So the highest hand is A, A and the lowest hand is A, 2. (A, A is never treated as a low pair.)

• *Five-card stud, last card down* is played as regular five-card stud except the last card is dealt as a hole card instead of an up card. A variation gives each player the option of having his last card dealt as a hole card or an up card. This is done by having the player turn up his first hole card before the last round is dealt and asking for his last card face down. Or, he may keep his original hole card, and then his last card is dealt as an up card.

• *Roll your own* takes more luck than skill to win, and the game is best with six or seven players. Each player is dealt seven cards, face down. The first bettor turns one card over and bets. The second player turns up his cards one at a time until he exposes a card that beats the first bettor's up card. Then, the second player bets. The play passes to the third bettor, who also turns up his cards one at a time until he gets a card (or combination of cards) that beats the highest card or combination showing (the last bettor's cards). The play continues, with players only allowed to bet when they show the best combination. When all cards are turned over, or all but one player has folded, the best five out of seven cards win.

Mutual Cards

Mutual card games, where players share one or more of the same cards, can be played high–low too.

• In *around the world,* each player gets four cards, followed by a round of betting. The dealer places a single card, face up, on the table. This is considered each player's fifth card. Then comes another round of betting. The dealer places three more mutual cards, face up, on the table—and each card is followed by a round of betting. A player wins with the best five cards out of a total of eight (four of his own and four mutual cards).

• To play *criss-cross,* each player is dealt four face-down cards. Five mutual cards are dealt in the shape of a cross face down in the center of the

Sino-sensation

Poker is thought of mostly as an American game, but it's actually popular all over the world. In fact, in 1907 the rules of poker were published in Chinese. The first edition of 100,000 sold out fast; sales had hit the million mark by 1937. At that time, it was the only book to receive such a wide distribution in that country.

The Kitty

By unanimous or majority agreement, card players may establish a special fund called a kitty. The kitty is usually built up by *cutting* (taking) one white chip from each pot in which there is more than one raise. The kitty belongs to all the players equally and is used to pay for new cards, refreshments, or a "free" night on the town—any night except the usual poker night, that is.

Now There's a Thought

Possibly the single most important thing to know about poker odds is this: keep friendly games to table stakes and you'll increase the odds in favor of their remaining friendly.

Professional poker player Allan Goldberg says, "Bluffing is both an art and a science. The art in bluffing is in the way the bluff is executed. The timing of a bluff, and against whom it is used, constitute most of the science."

In the West, cards were dealt to the left in a poker game so a man could reach for his pistol with his right hand if he suspected cheating.

table. After each betting interval, one mutual card is turned face up. Each exposure is followed by another round of betting. The center card is turned up last. (It may be declared to be wild, along with the other cards of that rank.) When all five cards have been exposed, the players choose the best five cards out of seven (the four hole cards, plus three vertical or horizontal cards from the mutual cross) to form their hands.

• To begin *pass the garbage*, each player is dealt a closed hand of seven cards. (If there are more than eight players, they get only six cards apiece.) After the first betting round, each player discards three of his cards and passes them to the player at his left. Then each player reduces his hand to five cards by discarding two, followed by a round of betting. When the dealer gives the signal, each player simultaneously exposes (*rolls*) one card on the table. The player with the highest card exposed begins the next betting round, which is followed by another roll. After the fourth round of betting, which is again begun by the holder of the highest card or combination of cards, the players each expose their last card for the showdown. Play is often complicated by the addition of one or more wild cards.

CONFESSIONS OF A CARD MECHANIC

One should always devise ways to achieve the ultimate goal: to win. And helping the hands of fate to deliver the best cards is one way to assure that goal.

I learned to mark cards when I was eighteen, from a lady gambler in Jersey City. Of course, there are professional card markers who specialize in rigging gambling equipment. But these are the makers, not the doers. I am a maker *and* a doer.

As I work, there is constant mental and physical pressure. My mind must respond twice as fast as my hands, because it has more to handle. As dealer, I must plan and remember in what order the *dead cards* (hands folded and exposed by players in the previous hand of play) are picked up. I must accurately read four or five cards down in the deck. At the same time, I've got to remember

what cards I'm holding in play. I must consider the bet and my own raise, whether I want a player to stay or fold, whether I'm going to skim a card off the top of the deck to place with the dead ones, or whether I am going to deal seconds.

My hands are my most valuable tool. They must not sweat and become slippery. Nor must they shake, because then there would be a herky-jerky motion, and precision is required at all times. Even though it's hard to be 100 percent correct, I still must be as smooth as possible. I always keep my hands clean and my fingers nimble, to manipulate the cards fluidly. My fingertips are sensitive; I let them roam all over the deck so the cards will become familiar to the touch.

I owe most of my success to the fact that no one is able to detect the slight defects that

"Keep an eye, too, on your friends and acquaintances"

Even this dignified 19th century gentleman was not above improving his luck at the expense of playing a fair game.

mark the cards. I try to keep each opponent's mind on his face-up cards and I praise his ability even if he should lose. He's a fish that I reel in slowly. Of course, the fact that he's losing continuously helps, because it increases his desire to try harder, and he won't be casually inspecting anything and everything around him. He'll be concentrating on his own cards, not mine or the other players'.

I never work with a partner, because I'm trying to take everyone to the cleaners. I keep the rounds of hands that I win close to 75 percent, or three out of four. Even if some slight mistake occurs, at the end I'll still be 50 percent richer.

A little help here and there builds my confidence to play in any game, anywhere, anytime. I incorporate many tricks as different situations arise.

As a conscientious professional, I always carry two *guns* (marked decks). One is red, for extremely bright electric light or sunlight. The other is blue, for gloomy areas. And if anyone at the table smokes, it's an additional

advantage—smoke camouflages the cards.

If the game begins with someone else's deck, I make a big show out of requesting a change of decks after a reasonable amount of time. To facilitate the switch, I may bend a couple of the cards. Then I'll open one of my guns. I never ever let another player keep the cards after the game is over. Idle inspection can result in discovery, and place me in a precarious position. I also always carry a regular, unmarked deck and switch to it if anyone gets suspicious. The loser always has the right to ask to change the cards for another deck. This works in my favor because I can always ask for the same courtesy if luck's against me. Then, my second gun is ready.

My first task when marking any deck of cards is to get them out of the box in such a way that the other players won't notice the box has been opened. To do this, I carefully cut the celophane wrapper along the bottom of the box with a razor blade, and then slide the box out, leaving the rest of the wrapper intact. There's a seal on the top of the box that must be lifted without any sign of ever having been broken. For this delicate operation I first steam the seal to soften the glue, then use a very small needle to pick up the seal. Steady hands and a lot of concentration are required to avoid tearing the seal. I keep my hands extremely dry at all times, because one smudge and the complete procedure is aborted. Next, I slide the cards out of the box by holding the sides between forefinger and thumb. After marking the cards I put them back in the box, use a smear of clear glue on the seal, place the box in the cellophane and glue the bottom. Once the method is completed the deck is known as a gun, for it's surely loaded.

My favorite method of marking cards is called *guider.* The cards best suited for this method are the Bumblebee brand, because the design on the back of the cards—rows of tiny red diamonds—lends itself easily to marking. To mark the cards I carefully nip one of the four tips of one diamond with a razor blade. This diamond signifies ace, king, queen, or jack, depending upon which tip is marked. I do the same thing to a second diamond, directly underneath the first, to tell me if it's a 10, 9, 8, or 7. The third diamond down in the same column shows 6, 5, 4, or 3. This is done to the upper left and bottom right of each card, so the markings are visible no matter which way the cards are held. I leave the four deuces unmarked and I don't bother marking suits as in most games it's the count that's important.

The *liner* method of marking cards is easy, and not too obvious. Sometimes I think that since I can see it so easily, so must the other players. But they are not looking for signs of marked cards, especially after I've flashed a large bankroll. If there were no greed, there would be no suckers. The liner is best done on decks of cards with diamonds on the back design. Of the sixteen lines surrounding each diamond, I use only twelve for marking purposes—the eight on the upper portion and the four on the left of one diamond. Starting with the ace and ending with the 3, I remove a line to signify each unit. For this I use a razor blade, and again mark both the upper left and

the lower right of each card. The four deuces remain unmarked.

When an opponent supplies the cards, you can be sure I give the first hand a very close inspection. In a poker game with heavy stakes, sometimes all the players are marking cards. When an unmarked deck is in play. I have to come up with a new system. To improvise in this situation is not easy, but all playing cards can be rigged if you study them intensely. I might decide to mark the aces with ear wax; or I might erase some of the ink off the backs of the kings with a moistened fingertip. Or, slowly and methodically, I might start leaving slight nail imprints along the edges of important cards. This I will accomplish while continuously shuffling the cards dealt to me. The poor suckers think I'm nervous. So I encourage this impression by picking my fingernails, hoping that will attest to my fidgetiness. When I'm done, aces, kings, queens and jacks will be marked along the top and bottom edges; 10's, 9's, 8's, and 7's will have marks on the side edges.

When I'm not using a marked deck in a game and I'm dealer, I'll usually *stack* it. The other players will probably be discussing the previous hand, not paying attention to what I'm doing. (No opportunity to enhance a chance of winning should be passed up.) Stacking a deck is done with mathematics and plenty of concentration. Holding the deck in my hands sideways, I place the four aces (or any other cards I want) on the bottom as I pick up the dead cards. If there are four players in the game, I pull one ace off the bottom, then count four cards off the top and place the ace there as I shuffle. The second ace is placed eight cards from the top; the next twelve; the last one, sixteen. Thus I am assured of being dealt four aces. All of this must be done rapidly and exactly while I pick up and shuffle to ensure receipt of the cards I want. If there are more than four players, I just add another card as a place holder for each extra player.

Are you wondering how the shuffled cards stay where I want them if the deck is subsequently cut? Well, I just mark the deck where I want it cut by *crimping.* I hold the

Be on the lookout for any dealer using the mechanic's grip (right). Card cheats use it to enable them to deal the exact cards they want, as well as to take peeks at the top card of the deck. A card mechanic will often crimp the deck (left) so that the cards are cut exactly where he wants them to be cut and his carefully stacked deck stays intact. A professional's crimp is much more difficult to detect than the one shown above.

bottom half of the deck on the sides between thumb and forefinger, and make a crimp by bending up the sides slightly. This will leave a small break in the deck and if the player who cuts isn't looking carefully at the cards—or doesn't make some extraordinary type of cut—he'll lift the cards exactly where I want him to. Most players will cut the cards and leave two stacks for the dealer to pick up. I love this type of player because I can place the top cards I've stacked back on top without his noticing.

To manipulate the cards easily and without detection, I always use the *mechanic's grip*. If you see anyone holding the cards this way, you'd better leave the game. I hold the deck in my left hand with the palm slightly cupped. Three fingers rest lightly along the outside of the deck. I keep my forefinger in front of the deck to securely hold the cards and place and hide as best I can the last card's number and suit. My thumb slides the cards off the top of

the deck into my right hand to deal. This way of holding the cards is also good for taking peeks. When I'm not dealing, my right hand rests lightly on top of the deck. This shields it so I can slide the top card forward with my thumb toward my index finger. The card buckles and I can take a quick peek. Or, my thumb slides the top card back, so by bending my wrist quickly, I can see the next card.

These tricks are helpful to know, but the true keys to success are *dealing* or *pulling seconds* (dealing myself the second, third, or fourth card from the top instead of the first one) and *drawing the bottom card* (dealing a player the bottom card from the deck instead of the top card). Sometimes, you see, the cards stick when I stack the deck, or a player cuts the cards slightly off my marked target. If I know what the top few cards are, I can pull the one I want as the need occurs. In a fast deal, these moves are undetectable.

To deal seconds, I hold the deck in an extremely tight mechanic's grip. With my thumb, I slide back as many top cards cards as I need. Then with my right thumb and forefinger, I grip the tip of the second, third, or fourth card down, and pull swiftly. The player gets this card in place of the top one he's supposed to receive. Before deciding to deal seconds, I wait until everyone has bet or folded, and then adjust the cards as the need requires.

To draw the bottom card, I put my right thumb on the bottom and stretch the four fingers out straight over the top of the deck. I wet the tops of my thumb and forefinger, pull backwards, freeing the bottom card from the deck, and deal it to the player.

Even all these tricks and more, however, are not always the signs of a professional card mechanic like me. Many sociable card players will cheat if they think they can get away with it. Take it from me—leave the game if you suspect any cheat, professional or amateur.

BLACKJACK OR BUST

Blackjack is a relative newcomer to the United States, although some forms of it have been played in Europe since the 15th and 16th centuries. The game only became popular here after thousands of servicemen stationed in Europe during World War II brought it back with them.

"Hit me!" cries the blackjack player whose card total is a mediocre 15. The dealer gives him another card, and his total is now 20. "I stand," this lucky player replies with a smile. "Stand," echoes another, whose cards total 17. "Hit me. . . . Hit me again," says a third player—then "Dammit!" as he goes bust with a total of 23. The dealer decides to give himself another card; it brings his card total of 15 up to 22. He goes bust too, and the first two players gleefully collect their winnings from him.

People tend to think of blackjack as primarily a casino game. Though this is justifiable—it *is* the most popular casino card game—its simple rules and fast pace make it equally enjoyable as a private game. The object of both private and casino–style blackjack is to get a higher card total than the dealer without going over 21. Both are stimulating games that test a player's luck, skill and fast judgment. But the rules described here for private blackjack make this sociable game a better gambling game, and a more exciting one.

BLACKJACK BASICS

Blackjack is usually played as described below, with a *changing bank*, where the deal passes from player to player. It can also be played with a *permanent bank* (which resembles casino blackjack), where the same player always deals. The same basic rules apply.

Any number from two to fourteen may play blackjack, but the game is best with from five to nine players. Within this range there will be plenty of betting action and enough cards exposed for players to figure the odds.

One standard deck of 52 cards is used. The dealer (who is playing against all the other players) gives one face-down card to each player, including himself. Bets are made, then everyone is dealt a second card. The second card is dealt face up to all the players, including the dealer. Players can, if they wish, be *hit* (dealt additional cards), or *stand* with the original two cards. The dealer can also stand or hit. The ace counts as 1 or 11 (whichever the cardholder prefers), picture cards count as 10, and all the other cards are counted at their face value. Any player who has a higher card total than the dealer, without going over 21, wins.

In one standard deck of 52 cards there are 171,060 possible combinations of cards that total 21.

HOW TO PLAY

To begin the game, any player picks up the deck and shuffles. He deals one face–up card to each player in turn, beginning at his left, until a jack of spades or clubs shows up. The player who was dealt the black jack is the first dealer.

The dealer reshuffles the deck and the player to his right cuts the cards. The dealer then shows the top card to all players and places it, face up, at the bottom of the deck to mark the end of the shuffled cards. This is called *burning a card* and whenever that card is reached in play, the deck is shuffled before the deal is resumed. If the card to be burned comes up an ace, the cards are immediately reshuffled. Some use a joker to mark the end of the deck instead of burning a card.

For the first round, the dealer gives one card face down (the *hole card*) to each player in turn, including himself, beginning at his left. Each player looks at his hole card, and everyone except the dealer makes a bet, placing it in front of his cards. (Some play that all bets must be made prior to the first deal.) Bets must stay within the limits established by the dealer. A common range is a 25¢ minimum and a $2 maximum. The dealer usually lowers the limit while on a losing streak, and raises it when he is winning.

Madame Vestal

Belle Siddons was born of good stock, well educated—and a confederate spy who traded physical pleasures for military secrets. She was caught, imprisoned, and eventually released. Realizing a change in career was in order, she learned how to deal blackjack and became so adept that she changed her name to Madame Vestal and opened her own gambling tent in Denver. Her staff of shills lured the suckers into the tent, where, in her honey–coated Southern accent she would croon, "Cards, gentlemen?" And play they would, recklessly asking to be hit again and again simply because watching her flip the cards was, as one of them put it, "better than Lillian Russell with all her clothes off."

The death of her lover is blamed for her decline, which took the form of an endless spiral of liquor, opium, and destitution. Madame Vestal, with the enigmatic Mona Lisa smile, and the dark hair and eyes that set her apart from all other professional gamblers, ended up in a hospital in San Francisco. Near death, she made a full confession of her life story to a chaplain, who passed it on to all the newspapers as a lesson in the wages of sin.

After all the players other than the dealer have bet, the dealer has the option of requiring that all bets be doubled. Doubling gives the dealer a chance to win a great deal, and is usually done when the odds against him are low. After the dealer doubles, a player may redouble his bet. For example, if you make a two-dollar bet and the dealer doubles, you and every other player must put up another two dollars. If you then were to redouble, you would have to put up another four dollars (for your total bet of eight dollars).

When all bets are on the table, the dealer gives each player in turn, including himself, another card, face up.

If a dealer's first two cards total exactly 21 (an ace plus a picture card or a 10), he holds a *natural,* and he wins the game. He immediately shows his hole card, and all players pay him double the amount of their bets, including any previous doubles made. If another player holds a natural too, he loses only the amount of his bet (but including previous doubles). If a player holds a natural and the dealer doesn't, the dealer pays that player double the amount of his bet and the game continues with the remaining players.

Each player in turn must decide whether to stand or be hit. If a player decides to stand because he is satisfied with his card total, he says, "I stand," or "stick," and places his bet on top of his cards. If he wants to try to improve his card total, he asks for additional cards one at a time by saying, "Hit me." This continues until

he decides it's best to stand, or until he goes over 21 (*goes bust*). A player who goes bust must turn over his hole card and fork over his bet to the dealer immediately.

When all players have stood or gone bust, the dealer turns up his hole card and may draw cards until he wishes to stand. If he goes bust, he pays even money to all the standing players. If he stands on a total of 21 or less, he pays all players who stood with a higher total, and collects from all players who stood with the same total or lower.

As each player's bet is settled, the dealer gathers that player's cards and adds them, face up, to the bottom of the deck. He continues to deal from the deck until he comes to the burned card, which marks the end of the shuffled deck. At this point he interrupts the deal, shuffles all cards not in play, has them cut, burns a new card, and continues the deal. If the dealer doesn't think there are enough cards to go around, he may reshuffle the cards before beginning a deal.

When another player is dealt a natural without the dealer matching it, the player holding the natural becomes the next dealer after all bets in the current deal have been settled. If two or more players have naturals and the dealer does not, the one nearest the dealer's left becomes the next dealer.

Should You Stand or Hit?

A smart player is able to figure out the chances of getting the cards he needs. These expectations change constantly during a game and are based on counting, or keeping track, of the values of the cards that have been exposed since the last shuffle. By counting cards, you can figure out how many cards of the value you need are left in the deck, then use that information to calculate your odds of getting them. Say, for example, that 21 cards have already been played since the last shuffle in this and previous games. In this game your cards total 13 and you need to be hit with an 8 to get 21. By paying close attention throughout previous deals, you have seen that three 8's have already been dealt. This means that there is only one 8 left, and your chances of getting it are 1 in 31. Of course, an added complication to remember is that a player may be holding that 8 as his hole card.

The other players' face-up cards are important to you for card counting, but you need not be concerned with their card totals. However, you must give thought to the dealer's card total and his chances of winning, since he's the one you want to beat. In the above situation, for example, your chances of getting 21 with an 8 were 1 in 31—not very good. You would stand if you suspect that the dealer's total would be 21. If, however, you felt you could beat the dealer with a 19 or 20 card total, then, by this same card-counting method, you could figure out what your increased chances were of getting a 6, 7, or 8. Special note, therefore, should be taken of the

Hit or stand?

dealer's face-up card, since it is an important clue to his card total. If his chances of going bust are greater than yours, then stand. If the dealer's chances of getting 21 are greater than yours, run the risk of going bust and take another card. You can't figure out his exact expectations because you don't know his hole card; you only suspect what it might be, based on your memory of the cards that have already been exposed.

The experts' advice on specific moves varies, including whether an ace is counted as 1 or 11. In general, however, ask to be hit if your total is 11 or less; stand if your total is 13 or more and the dealer's up card is 8 or less; stand if your total is

Madame Moustache (Eleanor Dumont)

Called "perhaps the greatest of all professional women gamblers," Eleanor Dumont opened her own gambling house in Nevada City during the 1870s. She was so skillful at dealing blackjack that card players of some repute made special trips just to watch her at work. But eventually her luck soured. Times grew bad, she lost her good looks and even the down on her upper lip lost its charm. She ended up committing suicide, apparently after losing her bankroll to a band of professional gamblers.

Bonus Payments

If you should be lucky enough to form any one of the following combinations during the course of a game, you would collect from the dealer immediately. And you get to keep the money, even if the dealer eventually gets a higher total.

• If you have five cards and your total is still under 21, you collect double your bet; this coup is called a "Five-card Charlie" in some circles. If you have six cards totaling under 21, you get four times your bet; and so on, doubling the amount for each additional card you hold.

• If you make 21 with three 7's, you collect triple the amount of your bet.

15 or more and the dealer's up card is 9 or more.

When you are dealer, card counting is more complex, since you have the face-up cards and the card totals of all the standing players to consider. In general, however, hit when your total is 16 or less.

Whether you are dealer or player, a knowledge of your opponents' playing habits can help you make the stand–or–hit decision. Some conservative players, for example, consistently stand on fairly low totals.

Two-card total	Number of combinations	Probability of two-card total occurring
20	136	1 in 9.75000
12	118	1 in 11.2372
13	112	1 in 11.8392
14	102	1 in 13
17	96	1 in 13.8125
15	96	1 in 13.8125
18	86	1 in 15.4186
16	86	1 in 15.4186
19	80	1 in 16.5750
21	64	1 in 20.7187
11	64	1 in 20.7187
10	54	1 in 24.555
9	48	1 in 27.6250
8	38	1 in 34.8947
6	38	1 in 34.8947
7	32	1 in 41.4375
5	32	1 in 41.4375
4	22	1 in 60.2727
3	16	1 in 82.8750
2	6	1 in 221

The probabilities of all card totals for the first two cards dealt are shown in descending order. These probabilities change with each additional card dealt.

The Dealer's Advantage

The dealer always plays last. He sees every player's face-up card and the hole cards of busted players before he makes his stand-or-hit decision. The dealer also sets the betting limits for individual games, so he has the power to lower them when he's on a losing streak or raise them when he's been winning.

The dealer immediately collects a bet placed by a player who goes bust, and keeps it—even if he ultimately goes bust himself.

The dealer can lose big, since he must pay off every standing player when he goes bust. But he can win big, too. Ties, including a tie of a natural, favor the dealer. And he has the option of doubling all bets on any game he wishes.

The Player's Advantage

Any player matches his skill and luck against only one person—the dealer. Stand–or–hit decisions are made solely for the purpose of beating the dealer and decisions are made without the added burden of dealing cards.

A player can give himself more of a chance to win in a single deal by *splitting pairs*. If the first two cards dealt to him are a pair, such as two 2's, a player can elect to split them into two hands by turning up his hole card and announcing that he is splitting pairs. His original bet remains on one card, and he matches that bet on the other card. The dealer then gives him one face-down card for each hand. The hands are played separately, and the dealer settles each bet independently. A player need not split a pair if he wants to play them together, and not all pairs should be split. A pair of aces should always be split, because it gives you two chances of making a natural. Splitting a pair of 10-count cards requires some consideration. On one hand, a two-card total of 20 is very good, so why split them? On the other hand, splitting a 10-count pair gives you a good start toward two total counts in the 17 to 21 range. The experts don't always agree on which pairs to split.

Players also have the option to *double down*. If the first two cards total exactly 11 (9-2, 8-3, 7-4, 6-5) a player may double his bet, and is dealt only one more card. The player must stand on these three cards. (A two–card total of 10 may also be doubled down if all agree to this prior to the game.) A player indicates he is doubling down by turning his hole card face up and asking to be hit with one more card. Since the odds of making 21 with three cards when the first two total 11 (or 10) can be as favorable as 1 to 2, this is an excellent opportunity to bet above the set limit and increase your winnings. Doubling down, however, isn't always the best move. Don't double down on a total of 11 (or 10) if this total is achieved by counting an ace as 1. An ace (counted as 11)

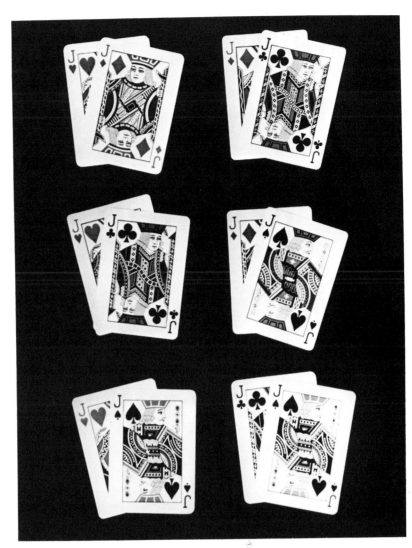

Six ways a pair may be dealt.

plus a 10 gives you a natural, and an automatic win. (A 20—ace-9—is a good total, and shouldn't be tampered with.)

Players are also eligible to collect bonus payments (see page 104), which the dealer can't collect.

Getting Pairs

Each card in a suit can be paired with a similar card from another suit in one of six ways, as shown with jacks. The probability of getting a specific pair with the first two cards dealt is 1 in 221. The probability of getting any pair with the first two cards dealt is 1 in 17.

Blackjack Misdeals / With all those cards flying through the dealer's hands, blackjack's fast pace can result in a few accidents. Follow these rules in event of a misdeal or other error:

1. If the dealer forgets to burn a card, he shuffles the remainder of the deck and burns a card before continuing.

2. If the dealer skips over you during the first round of dealing, he deals you a card from the top of the deck as soon as possible. If no one notices the error until the second round of dealing, stay out for that deal.

3. If you get your first card face up, you should still make your bet, but you get your next card face down. If your next card is dealt to you face up, drop out and withdraw your bet.

4. If you stand, turn up your hole card as soon as the dealer has stood or gone bust. If you get caught with a total of more than 21, you must pay the dealer *twice* your bet, even if he has gone bust.

5. If you are dealt two cards during the first round of dealing, take a look at both cards; then keep one card and discard the other. Or keep both cards, play two hands, and place a bet on each. (You never play both cards as belonging to the same hand.) If you get two cards during the second round of dealing, keep one and discard the other.

6. If the next card you would be dealt is found face up in the deck, you may either accept it or refuse it. If you refuse it, discard it and place it face up at the bottom of the deck.

7. If the dealer hits you and you did not ask to be hit, keep the card if you wish, or refuse it and discard it. (The next player may not claim it.)

Golf

Golf fans like to wager on the pros—at many invitational tourneys spectators can buy pari-mutuel tickets right on the course—but a lot of betting action goes on among weekend foursomes too. The most popular wager is the *Nassau,* where three individual points are competed for: the lowest score on the front nine holes, the lowest score on the back nine, and the lowest score on the total 18 holes. A player with a ten dollar Nassau actually has three individual bets with his fellow golfers.

In *skins,* the players determine how much a skin is worth before teeing off. A skin is awarded to the winner of each hole—ties don't count. The solution for two players who deplore the thought of competing against each other in a foursome is *team skins.* Before teeing off, teams are decided on along with the value of a skin. At the end of 18 holes the two teams settle up, with each player winning skins for his team, not for himself.

Another type of bet is the *greenie,* where players bet on who will wind up closest to the cup on a par three hole.

Then there's *bingle–bangle–bungle*—definitely not for the weak of heart. Three points are awarded at each hole, players decide how much they're worth beforehand. One point goes to the player who gets to the green first, one to the player nearest the cup after all have made it to the green, and one for the player who holes out first. After the 18th hole, the points are counted, and the bets settled.

Golf Hustlers

Whether you play the public links or the country clubs, stay away from the guy who comes on like the biggest sucker you've ever seen. He could be a hustler. If he says he can out–putt you blindfolded, or drive faster than you with one hand tied behind his back, then he is a hustler—and you can be sure he can perform all those feats. Most golfers fall for his bait because they think they play better than they really do.

The hustler might try the "give the sucker an edge" come-on, especially if the golfer he approaches is a lot older. He lets the golfer play the best of three balls on every hole but he'll play only one ball. This might sound like a smart bet if you were Jack Nicklaus; it means that by the end of the 18th hole you'll have actually played 54 holes. But *your* game is sure to fall apart by the time you're halfway through even if you are in condition.

The hustler may try to fleece you with the "loudmouth drunk routine," practically forcing you to take his money because he's so damned obnoxious or he's so drunk it looks easy. He'll be real sober by the time he's ready to count your money on the 18th hole.

It's wiser never to bet with strangers—especially strangers with deep tans. Hustlers spend countless hours in the sun. Pigeons who work for a living only get to play on weekends.

Types of Bridge

Auction bridge was the first
form of bridge, developed from
a game called Whist. Next came
contract bridge, a refinement of
auction bridge devised by
Harold S. Vanderbilt in the
1920s. This is the type most
often played today. A variation
called duplicate bridge, devised
in attempt to exclude the
elements of luck from the game
by giving opposing players
identical hands to play, is played
in virtually all tournaments—
except for those taking place in
Las Vegas, where rubber bridge
is played. Other variations include:
four–deal or Chicago bridge,
pivot bridge, progressive bridge,
honeymoon bridge, cutthroat
bridge or towie, blackout or
pshaw, and goulash.

A WORD ABOUT BRIDGE

If you don't play bridge, the rules and procedures may seem so
complex, and the terminology so strange, that you find yourself
either completely intimidated or simply unconvinced that all that
intricacy of play is worth the effort. (If takes longer to master than
any other popular card game—usually three months to learn to
play even tolerably well.) Tens of millions of aficionados will firmly
attest, however, that it is worth it. In fact, they'll tell you it can be
positively addictive.

Its very complexity is what makes bridge so challenging, and is
responsible for its reputation as a highly stimulating and
intellectual form of entertainment. Dealing with cards always
involves some luck, but a good player can turn a lousy hand into a
good one. As bridge expert, Alfred Sheinwold says, "The effect of
the cards is almost zero. . . . You control your own fate by how
well you play."

Bridge can be played on a more casual level and also, since two
teams of two players are needed, it's the perfect game for
entertaining guests in this couple-oriented society.

The best way to learn is to have another person teach you, and
then to play as often as you can. Enlist the aid of a friend, or better
yet, take a course at your local Y, bridge club or adult recreation
center. Most have classes on both the beginner and advanced

*Each hand in bridge offers the challenge of a new problem to be solved. The game appeals to the
intellectual, the adventurous, the courageous, and to those who enjoy mental stimulation.*

levels. Once you become familiar with the game, pick up one of the many books on the subject (the best-known author is probably Charles Goren) or start following the bridge columns that appear in many newspapers. Try one of the "Auto-Bridge" sets that are sold in adult games departments. Using these kits, you "play" with experts who analyze your bids, responses and plays.

Once you've learned the game, play often. Try forming a group of "regulars," and you might find yourself winning more consistently because a knowledge of your partner's and opponents' tendencies is important. Improve your game by visiting a local bridge tournament. Almost every town has its bridge club and its attendant tourneys. Find out who the best players are, then watch. Most players will not only let you observe a game, but will be more than happy to share their knowledge with you after the game.

Gambling at Bridge

Bridge tends to be downplayed as a gambling game. Some don't like the emotional effect playing for high stakes can have on players. (Bridge players, unlike poker players who use the amount of the pot as a part of their strategy, are supposed to play the cards, not the players.) Others feel that having money at stake tightens up the play by preventing wild bidding. Purists insist that the game should be played only for the sheer enjoyment of exercising and improving one's skill. Others point out that the high scores and large point differences that exist in bridge lend themselves perfectly to gambling, and that the money is simply a barometer of a player's skill. The fact is that bridge club and home games are usually played for a certain amount of money per point.

When gambling at bridge, the winners with the highest score collect the money equivalent of the difference in points from the losers. Since scores and point differences can go so high, most social players limit their betting to a tenth, a twentieth, or even a fiftieth of a cent per point. The stakes at bridge clubs can range from a quarter of a cent per point to a half a cent per point. (Occasionally you'll find a club where the stakes are exceedingly high—one cent to ten cents per point.) In a ten-cents-a-point game, one bad hand can mean a loss of up to $200—even in a penny-a-point game that would mean $20. Never play in a game where you cannot afford the stakes. Besides the risk of losing money you do not have, opponents can usually sense your concern and use it as a psychological weapon.

Popular Bridge is a bi-monthly magazine directed toward the average player. Articles are often written by leading experts in the field, and range from the humorous to the technical. It's sold on newsstands, but if you can't find it, write to Popular Bridge, 16001 Ventura Blvd., Encino, CA 91436.

Watching bridge is like watching two people making love—you want to get into the act.

(*Anonymous tournament player and cheat*)

When you're playing bridge for money, know your partner like a book.

(*Bob Martin, odds-maker*)

A TOAST TO GIN

History of Gin

Gin is a popular two–handed game that belongs to the extremely large family of rummy games. Rummy's history is somewhat vague, but its best–known and sure–fire ancestor is the Spanish game of Conquian, a name which was Americanized into Coon-can when introduced here. The game soon acquired a slew of elaborations and variations, along with the catch–all name, rummy. In South America, rummy gave birth to canasta, samba, and others.

Gin rummy is rumored to have emerged from the brain of Elwood T. Baker of New York's Knickerbocker Whist Club. At that time (1909) it was dubbed gin poker. The game received an enormous boost when the "beautiful people" in Hollywood took it up, and it has grown in popularity ever since.

An early form of gin rummy was popular with American blacks.

Gin rummy—or gin, as it's known to its more intimate fans—is one of the easiest games to learn. It's rife with variations, but the classic game described here is a two-handed contest. If you have more than two players, switch to another type of rummy.

Novices and old hands alike find that playing for money adds spice—whether playing for "peanuts" (four points for a penny), a penny a point (the usual), or up to a dollar a point (the big time).

HOW TO PLAY

Gin is essentially a race to see which player can empty his hand first (get rid of his cards, or *go out*) by forming certain combinations with the cards. At the end of each hand, the scores are computed according to the cards left out of the combinations, and entered on a score sheet. When a player has scored a predetermined number of points (or at the end of each hand in some circles), the winner collects the money equivalent of his point total from the loser.

The standard 52-card deck is used, with the king ranking highest. Then queen, jack, 10, 9, 8, 7, 6, 5, 4, 3, 2, ace. When scoring, each picture card will count ten points; an ace counts one point, and the rest count their face values. To keep the game moving along, most players use two decks, so that while one player deals one deck, the other can be shuffling the second to ready it for the next deal.

After the deck has been shuffled, each player draws one card, and the holder of the highest card becomes the dealer. The dealer shuffles the cards once more, the nondealer cuts them, and the deal begins.

The dealer alternately gives one face-down card at a time to his opponent and to himself, beginning with his opponent. When each has a total of ten face-down cards, the deal is complete. The dealer places the remaining cards face down in the center of the table, to form the *stock*. He puts the top card of the stock face up next to it, to begin the *discard pile*.

For the first round, the nondealer has the option of taking the up card from the discard pile, adding it to his hand, and discarding another card, face up, in its place. If the other player doesn't want the first up card, the dealer may take it, replacing it with a discard from his hand. If the dealer refuses it too, the action passes back to the nondealer, who takes the top card from the stock. He may decide to keep that card to add to his hand, and discard another card he is holding, by placing it face up in the discard pile; or he may decide he doesn't want the stock card and discard it by placing it face up in the discard pile. In either case, a new face-up card ends up on top of the discard pile. (Some people play with the nondealer being dealt 11 cards, the dealer 10. The first round begins with the nondealer discarding. The dealer then takes his turn, and subsequent rounds follow as usual.)

The rounds continue from this point on with the players given alternate chances to replace cards in their hands (and thus improve them) by adding and discarding one card at a time. The replacement card is either the top card of the discard pile or the top card of the stock. Discards are always placed face up on top of the discard pile.

Tournaments

In the numerous card clubs around the country, the weekly or monthly gin rummy tournament is an accepted ritual. As players get better, they move upward and onward in the ranks, progressing from club championships to interclub championships, area championships, and on up to the Gin Rummy Tournament of Champions where the total prize money may reach $35,000. High–ranking tournaments are played in resort hotels. If you want to enter (or simply rubberneck) during your next vacation, you can obtain information about upcoming tourneys by writing to: Chet Wander, Box 803, Woodland Hills, CA 91365. Tournament maven Chet Wander shares this tip: "The losers are the wild, reckless, devil–may–care players; the winners are the calm, cautious, percentage players."

Three gin rummy hands, showing various melds. A winning hand can be formed by: matching cards of face value (top), forming a sequence of cards from the same suit (middle), or any combination of the two (bottom).

The aim of each player, as he adds and discards, is to go out, and the first to do so wins the hand. A player goes out by forming *melds* with the cards in his hand. A meld is a matched set of three or four cards of the same rank, such as 9(C), 9(D), 9(S); or a meld may be a sequence of three or more cards of the same suit, such as J(D), 10(D), 9(D).

If, during a turn, a player picks up a card and finds he can arrange ten cards into melds, he has gin and declares it as he discards one card face down onto the discard pile. His hand, arranged into melds, is then exposed. His opponent's hand is also arranged into melds and exposed. The winner's score is the point total of his opponent's unmatched cards (*deadwood*). The more unmatched cards you can catch your opponent holding—and the higher the value of those cards—the higher your score.

A hand can also be won by *knocking*, instead of going gin. A player would knock if, during one of his turns, he picks up a card and finds he can meld enough cards so that the value of his deadwood totals ten points or less. He indicates he is knocking by declaring it as he places a card face down onto the discard pile. He then exposes his hand, arranged into melds and deadwood. His opponent's hand, similarly arranged, is also exposed. The winner's score is the total point value of his opponent's deadwood minus the point value of his own deadwood. His opponent can try to lower the point value of his deadwood (and, therefore lower the knocker's score)

The player on the left has ended this hand by knocking with a deadwood total of five. (He could have continued to add and discard cards until he had gin—either a queen, an 8, or the 3(D) or 7(D) would have done it. But he decided to knock and catch his opponent with, hopefully, a lot of deadwood.) The player on the right is caught with two melds, and four cards as deadwood that total 23 points. He can, however, lower this score by laying off his 8 (C) onto the knocker's meld of 8's. His 2(D) and 3(D) can also be laid off onto the knocker's 4-5-6 sequence. By doing so, he lowers his deadwood score to 10 and the knocker only scores five points (10 minus 5).

by *laying off*. He can lay off by adding his deadwood to the knocker's melds where he can. For example, if you, as knocker, have a 3-4-5 of diamonds, he can lay off the 6 of diamonds onto your meld, reducing your score by six points.

The winner of each hand deals the next, until the game is over.

Scoring

Scores are tallied at the end of each hand, after one player has gone out by going gin or knocking. The first player to reach 100 points (or any other total mutually agreed upon prior to play) wins the game and merits a game bonus of 100 points.

The player who goes gin earns points for the total of his opponent's deadwood. Cards may not be laid off onto a gin hand. In addition, going gin merits a bonus of 25 points.

The player who knocks adds up the total point value of his opponent's deadwood—after his oppo-

	Betsy	*Phyllis*	
FIRST HAND	10	7	**THIRD HAND**
SECOND HAND	18	14	**FIFTH HAND**
FOURTH HAND	36	28	**EIGHTH HAND**
SIXTH HAND	54	+75	**BONUS FOR HANDS WON**
SEVENTH HAND	73	103	
NINTH HAND	104		
BONUS FOR WINNING GAME	+100		
	204		
BONUS FOR HANDS WON	+150		
	354		

In this example of a typical gin rummy score sheet, you can see that a running total of each player's score is kept. Betsy won the first hand by 10 points and the second hand by 8 points, so a total of 18 appears under her name after the second hand. Betsy was the first player to reach 100 points so she gets a bonus of 100 points plus another 150 (25 x 6) for the six hands she won. Her total game score is 354 points. Phyllis' total score is 103 points, including her bonus points for hands won. Betsy wins by 251 points, or $2.51 in a penny-a-point game.

nent has laid off—and subtracts from that the total value of his own deadwood. Even without laying off, an opponent's deadwood point value can turn out to be the same or less than that of the knocker. When this happens, he has *undercut* the knocker, and is considered the winner of that hand. The player who undercuts a knocker scores the difference in points between the deadwood totals, and in addition is awarded a *box* (a bonus of 25 points). In effect, he scores as if he were the knocker plus an extra 25 points. He also gets to be the next dealer. Some players also add a bonus for each knock.

A game during which one player doesn't score at all is called a *blitz* or a *schneider,* and the winner's score is either doubled, or fattened by a bonus of 100 points.

When a player has reached 100 points, he wins the game and gets a game bonus of 100 points. The difference between the winner's and loser's score is used to determine cash winnings. For example, a 53-point difference between players in a penny-a-point game means the loser pays the winner 53¢.

Knock or Go Gin?

This is the agonizing question every gin player must face. The first rule to remember is this: When opportunity knocks, KNOCK! A variation of the old "a bird in the hand . . ." school of philosophy, it sums up the mundane fact of life that most hands should not be played for gin. So try to knock as soon as you can, and don't give in to the temptation to hold out just a little longer in the hope of going gin and being awarded bonus points. When you try to go gin instead of being satisfied with knocking, you run the risk of getting caught with deadwood if your opponent goes out first. And the additional turns that going for gin requires give your opponent the opportunity to improve his hand as well.

When to knock is another matter that takes some thought. Naturally, the faster you can lay down your cards, the more points you are likely to end up with, since your opponent will have had less chance to pick up cards to improve his hand. In general, follow this rule of thumb: it's safe to knock after your sixth turn if you have ten points or slightly less. Experience has shown, however, that the more turns played in a hand, the lower the deadwood point count you need to safely go out—without being undercut. By the ninth or tenth turn, don't knock unless you have six points or less in deadwood. Otherwise, the odds are simply too great that your opponent will undercut you.

If the hand is a long one, however, and you're still playing when the stock is down to a dozen cards or so, it's best to go for gin. The reasoning is that the difference in points between your deadwood total and your opponent's is probably dangerously low by this time, and you could easily be undercut if you knock.

Which Card Should You Discard?

In general, discard an unmatched high-point card rather than a low one. This reduces your deadwood total should your opponent knock before you do. Of course, there's more to discarding than that. You also want to avoid discarding a card that your opponent can use to form a meld. A good gin player, therefore, tries to remember every card his opponent has picked up from the discard pile, and those which were passed over in favor of replacement cards from the stock. These give you clues as to which cards your opponent needs, and which are safe to discard. When you have a 10 and a 2 you don't need, you would normally get rid of the high card. However, if you remember that your opponent picked up a 10 on a pre-

vious turn, then he may be trying for a meld of matched 10's—so you should discard your 2, and risk getting caught with the higher card as deadwood. Taking this strategy a step further, both the value and the *suit* of your opponent's picked-up, discarded, and passed-over cards should be considered clues as to what he needs. If you remember that both the 9 and 10 of hearts were picked up by your opponent in previous turns, then you can be pretty sure he's trying to form a sequence meld and can take the chance of discarding a 10 of another suit.

Another factor to help you decide which cards to discard is the likelihood of melding your remaining cards. If you are faced with the possibility of holding onto a pair (which could lead to three matched cards) or splitting the pair to go for a sequence, it's usually advisable to play for the sequence (depending, of course, on your opponent's previous discards). You can always add to a sequence at both ends, but a three-of-a-kind meld can only be improved by getting the fourth card of that rank.

Paying close attention to the contents of the discard pile can help your play in still another way. Abandon all hope, for instance, of improving your pair of kings if the other two lie buried among the discards.

Another point to ponder is this: the 7 is the most valuable card in gin, because it can be used to form more melds than any other card. The 9, 8, 6 and 5 come next; then 10 and 4; then jack or 3; then queen or

The Odds

It's twice as hard to improve a three-card sequence of the same rank (e.g., three 7's) as it is to extend a three-card sequence in the same suit. The former can only be improved with one card—the fourth card of the same rank; the latter can be improved with two cards—extending the sequence at both its low and high ends. In addition, the four-card sequence in the same suit can be extended to five cards—even six or more. The same-rank sequence has no such possibilities.

The chances of a dealer having a meld in the first ten cards are 2 out of 5. The chances of a non–dealer having a meld in his first 11 cards are 1 out of 2. So, if you're a smart dealer, you'll deal ten cards to yourself and ten to your opponent; the smart opponent will request the variation which allows him to be dealt 11 initial cards.

In such an 11-card hand, the odds that the dealer will be able to use his opponent's first discard to form a meld are:

Odds of Dealer Forming a Meld are:	When the Discarded Card is:
1 out of 6	king or ace
1 out of 5	queen or deuce
1 out of 4.7	any other card

Gin on Broadway

Depending upon the relationship and personalities of the players, gin rummy can be an amusing, friendly card game, or an extremely competitive, even cutthroat battle. Or, if you're a playwright, it can be the basis for a successful two-character play, as was the case with D. L. Coburn, author of the Pulitzer Prize winner, "The Gin Game." During the play, the two characters, who meet and get to know each other over a game of gin, actually get to play fourteen hands on stage. The game, according to Coburn, "becomes the binding agent that at once brings them together, and serves as a catalyst for conflict that repeatedly tears them apart."

The play, which opened on Broadway with Hume Cronyn and Jessica Tandy as the original cast, was performed using a stacked deck, loaded with a proportionately high number of face cards. The actors had to change their lines to go along with the play of the cards. Even so, Mr. Cronyn admitted that he occasionally got over–involved in the game to the point where he'd want to pick up a particular card to improve his hand–but the script wouldn't let him.

Miss Tandy and Mr. Cronyn, who are married in real life, never play cards together off stage.

(Zoe Dominic/Franz Furst.)

deuce—with the king or ace being the least useful for melding purposes. This is something you should remember when deciding what to discard, especially early in the hand when you have few clues to your opponent's needs. On the other hand, melding isn't everything. Don't be too eager to get rid of an ace, deuce, or 3, since their low count is valuable when knocking.

Psychological Warfare

Poker by no means holds the monopoly on bluffing. In gin you can bluff by using the tactic known as *advertising*. A player who advertises discards a relatively useful card in order to encourage his opponent to discard a similar card (one of the same rank or suit) that would be even more useful. For instance, if you discard the 10 of diamonds, it would appear you haven't the slightest interest in 10's. Your opponent thinks it's safe to discard his 10 of spades. But you promptly pick it up

to add to your spade sequence— K, Q, J.

Another useful ploy in this game of wits is that of card sorting. Observe the way your opponent picks up and holds his cards, and how he arranges his matched sets: watch where he inserts the cards he picks up, and where his discards come from. If you get to know his habits, after a few turns you may be able to deduce what percentage of his hand is deadwood.

By the same token, your opponent can pick up valuable clues about your hand. When you pick up your hand, it's a natural instinct to group together your melds, your possible melds, and your unmatched cards. But once you have the groups memorized, intersperse your groups, and mix them up during the play. Throw off your opponent by first intermingling a card you've drawn with the other cards in your hand, even if you don't need it. Then pull it out from your hand and discard it.

HOW TO PLAY HOLLYWOOD GIN

The distinguishing feature of this variation is the scorekeeping: hands are scored as if they were being played in three games simultaneously. This means lots more action, and the interesting possibility of winning three times as much money in about the same time it would ordinarily take to win one game. Others like it because a player who has lost games one and two could still win game three.

To play Hollywood gin, follow the rules for gin rummy, but set up the score sheet with three columns, as shown. The point total of the first hand won by each player is scored once, in game one. The point total of the second hand won by each player is scored twice, in games one and two. The point total of the third hand won by each player is scored to his credit in all three games. Once a player has won three hands, results of subsequent winning hands are scored to his credit in all three

A TYPICAL HOLLYWOOD GIN SCORE SHEET

	Game one		Game two		Game three	
	Shelley	Steve	Shelley	Steve	Shelley	Steve
hand #1 (Shelley wins by 12)	12	—	—	—	—	—
hand #2 (Shelley wins by 25)	37	—	25	—	—	—
hand #3 (Steve wins by 21)	—	21	—	—	—	—
hand #4 (Shelley wins by 10)	47	—	35	—	10	—
hand #5 (Steve wins by 25)	—	46	—	25	—	—
hand #6 (Steve wins by 7)	—	53	—	32	—	7
hand #7 (Shelley wins by 28)	75	—	63	—	38	—
hand #8 (Shelley wins by 30)	105	—	93	—	68	—
game one is over						
hand #9 (Shelley wins by 24)			117	—	92	—
game two is over						
Game Total	105	53	117	32		
Bonus for hands won	125	75	125	50		
Bonus for winning game	100	—	100	—		
Game Total	330	128	342	82		
Minus losers total	−128		−82			
Shelley's final score for game	202		260			

202 *Shelley's* final score for GAME ONE
260 *Shelley's* final score for GAME TWO
462

This shows the procedure for scoring three games of gin simultaneously. Shelley won Game One, and has a total score for this game of 202 points, including bonuses. She also won Game Two, so Steve's losing score is subtracted from her score for that game. The difference, 260 points, is added to her final score from Game One. If she wins Game Three, which at this point is more than likely, Steve's losing score would be subtracted from her winning one, and the difference added to her running total of 462 points. At a penny a point, Shelley would win at least six dollars from her opponent.

Card-Playing Etiquette

The ability to play card games is a social asset that you can make the most of by observing the common sense rules, set forth by the U.S. Playing Card Company:

1. Sit up straight at the card table, and avoid unnecessary and distracting noise.

2. Learn how to shuffle, cut, and deal neatly and gracefully.

3. Try to conceal any nervousness, and don't take forever to make a decision on your next play. Nothing is more infuriating to other players than hearing someone moan, "Oh, I just don't know *what* to do." An incorrect bid or play is preferable to imposing long periods of waiting on your fellow players.

4. Don't pick up your hand until the deal has been completed.

5. Don't express sympathy for the loser—especially yourself. When you play, you should realize that losing is part of the game.

6. Don't gloat when you've won.

7. Unless they ask for advice, don't point out your opponent's or partner's mistakes.

8. If you are just watching a game, confine your observations to one player's hand per deal. Shifting from one player to another is very bad form, since it could imply the previous hand was uninteresting or not very good. Observers should be seen and not heard: make no comments and ask no questions.

games until one player reaches 100 points in any game, thus ending that game. The other games continue until 100 points is reached in each. Bonuses for winning hands and winning the game are credited. Although the three games are played simultaneously, their totals differ, because each starts later than the last. (Scores are not credited in game two until a player has won two hands; scores are not credited in game three until a player has won three hands.) The games run out as each is won, until only game three is scored.

Hollywood gin can also be played with more than three games, using the same scoring patterns.

HOW TO PLAY OKLAHOMA GIN

Oklahoma gin is played like regular gin, with one rule change: the rank of the first up card from the stock determines the maximum number of points with which a player may knock in that hand. For example, if the first up card is a 5, a player must have five points or less of deadwood (instead of the usual ten) in order to knock. The knocking point for picture cards is ten or less; all other cards have knocking points equiva- lent to their face values. In some games, an ace means you must play for gin—no knocking allowed.

A variation of Oklahoma gin calls for doubling the scores, including bonuses, from any hand where the up card is a spade. However, since doubling means higher scores for individual hands, these games are usually played for 150 or 200 points instead of the usual 100.

HOW TO PLAY PARTNERSHIP GIN RUMMY

Any even number of players may participate, with each half forming one partnership. All partners sit on the same side of the table: each plays a regular two-handed game against the player facing him. The results of each individual hand are combined to determine the team scores. The margin of win for winning scores is added up; the margin of loss for losing scores is deducted. For example, if one member of a two member team wins a hand by twelve points, and the other member loses by ten points, that team still wins the hand by two points. The total for each hand determines the winning side for the next deal.

When one player knocks, players in other hands may stop their play until they learn the result. A player whose hand is finished may advise any of his teammates, but only if he has not seen any opposing hands.

Bonus points are awarded as usual. For a two-team game with four players, the game ends when one team reaches 125 points; with six or eight players the game ends when one team reaches 150 points; 175 points if there are ten players; 200 points if there are twelve players.

GIN RUMMY FOR THREE PLAYERS

The most popular three-player method begins with each player cutting the cards. The person with the lowest-ranking card stays out during the first hand, and the person with the next-lowest card is the dealer. At the end of each hand, the loser goes out and the third player takes his place. Each plays for himself and maintains his own individual score. The game ends when a player reaches 100 points or more, and after game and box bonuses have been added in, each player pays the difference between the scores to each higher-scoring player. If one player is shut out, an additional 100 points is awarded to the winner.

Another method for three players is called "chouette." The principle is described on page 65—just substitute cutting cards for throwing dice to determine the *man in the box*. Keep one score for the man in the box, another score for the partnership. If the man in the box wins, he collects in full from each opponent; if the partnership wins, each partner collects in full from the man in the box.

AROUND THE CORNER

The special feature of this variation is that aces are either high or low. So a player could form a sequence such as 4, 3, 2, ace (as usual), but he could also meld 2, ace, king, queen. The hitch is that if you're caught with an unmatched ace at the end of a hand, it's worth fifteen points, not the usual one.

MAH-JONGG

Essentially a kind of rummy played with tiles instead of cards, mah-jongg is a manufacturer's name for the ancient Chinese game of ma-tsiang (sparrows). Long popular as a gambling game in the Orient, it became all the rage here during the 1920's, a decade that saw more than its share of crazes.

Mah-jongg sets come with a set of complex rules and procedures which, like those for rummy, consist basically of forming combinations by picking up and discarding tiles. There the similarity rapidly breaks down. There are 144 beautifully colored tiles, of three suits (bamboo, circles, and characters); honors (the four winds, and red, green, and white dragons); and four seasons or flowers.

During the course of the game, players *break the wall, create a garden,* and form *chows, pungs, kongs,* and *pillows.* A player who is lucky may even get the opportunity to *rob the kong.* Instead of knocking or going for gin, players *go woo,* after which a complex system of scoring is used to compute each player's points. Astronomical scores are common, because doubling is a part of the system.

Supposedly, once you have mastered the terminology, it's just like playing gin. But there have been complaints from some players that an hour after finishing one game, they feel like playing another.

B*I*N*G*O

There isn't much risk involved when gambling on bingo. The only money a bingo player puts up is his admission fee (usually one dollar) and a minimal stake, which is the total price of the cards used to play the game (usually a quarter a card). Prizes, depending on state regulations, may be cash—which can reach thousands of dollars—or merchandise, from kitchenware to new cars.

Bingo can be a purely sociable pastime, played among friends at home, or it can be played for fun and big prizes in bingo parlors. These public games are sometimes sponsored by professional bingo operators who run them strictly for profit. More often, however, they are sponsored by churches, or fraternal or charitable organizations, who use bingo to raise money for worthy causes.

Bingo's enormous attraction as a fund raiser has stirred heated controversy. Advocates argue that the benefits—money for schools, hospitals, the needy, and so on—are reason enough to support its legalization. Opponents say that bingo is gambling, and charitable groups should not be allowed to earn money by methods denied to the general public. As of now, bingo is legal in only half of our fifty states, but it is often played just as ardently in the others. Police tend to ignore fund-raising games, especially when they take place in churches. Organizations also wriggle around the game's illegal status by featuring it as a nameless activity that is part of "entertainment"—a brief period of recorded music, for instance, may be played before the game begins. In states where bingo has been legalized, it often suffers beneath the yoke of crippling rules. New Jersey fans who campaigned vigorously for legal bingo felt cheated when legalization killed the game by reducing jackpots, prohibiting refreshments, and imposing other nuisance regulations that made it much less enjoyable.

In truth, however, the devoted bingo player is probably not primarily attracted to the game because of its charitable applications. It's the opportunity to risk a little money for a prize—in a game that requires no mathematical talent, and no skill other than the ability to pay attention—that makes bingo so popular.

Playing bingo can't be described as exciting, but many players are attracted to it for the companionship it offers. For this reason bingo has a strong appeal to the elderly.

Set Up Your Own Bingo Night

If an organization you know needs to raise money, try having a bingo night. First you'll need to check local bingo laws and regulations. This can be done by consulting the state law in your local library. Check the index under "B," which will direct you to the appropriate volumes. Laws on bingo are often long and involved, but your local municipal offices will be able to explain them to you. The place where you rent the equipment will also be able to help you, since they must comply with state laws too. Some states, like New York, require a license to operate a bingo night. Failure to comply with the law is a misdemeanor in some states. In New Jersey and Nevada, however, it's a felony.

You'll need to rent admission cards, bingo cards, lap boards (or heavy pieces of cardboard), markers (buttons, bottle caps, dried beans, or even small squares of heavy paper can be used), bingo balls, and a bingo cage or blower. (Unlike a bingo cage, which is cranked by hand, a blower or automatic hopper mixes up the balls and shoots them out with air under pressure.) You'll also need a microphone for the caller to announce the letters and numbers. If a large turnout is expected, consider an electric flashboard, where the numbers and letters light up (like a scoreboard at a baseball game).

BINGO BASICS

The bingo player purchases one or more bingo cards for about 25¢ each. Each card is divided into 25 small squares: 24 bear numbers between 1 and 75, in five columns of five numbers each; the central square is unnumbered, or "free." Each column is headed by a letter: B–I–N–G–O. An announcer, or "*caller*," randomly draws a small ball, bearing a number and a letter, from a bowl or wire–mesh cage, and announces its number and letter to the players. If a player finds the same combination of letter and number on his card, he covers that square with a plastic marker. (Some bingo cards have shades that slide down to cover the called number.) If the announcer calls "N32," for example, and the player finds the number 32 in the N column on his card, he covers it. The unnumbered or free square counts as a covered number.

Each player's card, of course, is printed with different numbers. When a player covers five numbers in a straight vertical, horizontal or diagonal line, he shouts "Bingo!" A *floor man* then reads the covered numbers on the player's card aloud,

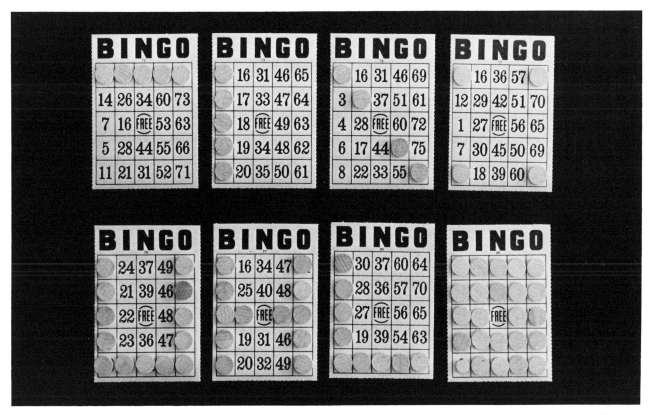

The many ways to win at bingo include the usual horizontal, vertical, or diagonal line, as well as variations such as the four corner squares, letter formations such as U, H, or L, and the cover-all.

and the announcer verifies that they have been drawn. The player is then declared the winner of the game, and the whole process starts over again. If two or more players win at the same time, the prize is divided between them.

Some bingo parlors add new wrinkles to the game by featuring a two- or four-way play, in which there is more than one winning pattern. For example, in addition to the regulation ways to win, a player who covers the four corner numbers, or the eight numbers surrounding the free center square may also be de-clared a winner. Sometimes the winning pattern will be the form of the letter X, U, L, H, or T. A bigger prize, or *jackpot*, may go to the first player who covers the entire board, for a *cover-all* or *blackout*. Or, a player may win a jackpot by winning within the first 50 numbers drawn. Sometimes a *wild ball*, which bears no number, may be added to the hopper. When drawn, it can be used by players to cover any vacant number on the card. If no one wins the jackpot, the cash may be added to the next session's jackpot prize.

HOW TO PLAY BINGO

LEGALIZE BINGO- Keep Grandma off the streets

(Photo from the Joel Rudinger collection.)

The "World's Biggest Money Bingo Game"

A prize of $60,000 was at stake in the "World's Biggest Money Bingo Game," held in Las Vegas in 1977. The manager of the game, who only deals with big money games, said he felt the little-old-lady image of the avid bingo player no longer holds true. The fans that attend his games belong to "a chic group that includes all ages and both sexes."

As with other games of pure chance, there's not much strategy involved that can increase your odds of winning. Some players decrease the odds against them by purchasing two, three, four or more cards. There are bingo fanatics who play with as many as 20 or 25 cards in a single game, checking all cards simultaneously for the called number. As simple a game as bingo is, this kind of playing is not easy.

3rd	31	32	33	34	35	36	37	38	39	40	41	42	43	44	45	3rd
4th	46	47	48	49	50	51	52	53	54	55	56	57	58	59	60	4th
Last	61	62	63	64	65	66	67	68	69	70	71	72	73	74	75	Last
1st	1	2	3	4	5	6	7	8	9	10	11	12	13	14	15	1st
2nd	16	17	18	19	20	21	22	23	24	25	26	27	28	29	30	2nd
3rd	45	44	43	42	41	40	39	38	37	36	35	34	33	32	31	3rd
4th	60	59	58	57	56	55	54	53	52	51	50	49	48	47	46	4th
Last	69	70	71	72	73	74	75	68	67	66	65	64	63	62	61	Last
1st	8	7	6	5	4	3	2	1	15	14	13	12	11	10	9	1st
2nd	23	22	21	20	19	18	17	16	30	29	28	27	26	25	24	2nd
4th	53	52	51	50	49	48	47	46	60	59	58	57	56	55	54	4th
Last	75	74	73	72	71	70	69	61	62	63	64	65	66	67	68	Last
3rd	38	37	36	35	34	33	32	31	45	44	43	42	41	40	39	3rd
1st	9	10	11	12	13	14	15	1	2	3	4	5	6	7	8	1st
2nd	24	25	26	27	28	29	30	16	17	18	19	20	21	22	23	2nd

Numbered dart target used to select numbers in old-time bingo. (Photo from the Joel Rudinger collection.)

Bingo Cheats

The popularity of bingo draws millions of players to individual games. Admission fees and card purchases, in combination with large prizes and jackpots, can also draw the bingo cheat.

Games organized by legitimate charitable organizations are safe, as are games run by honest bingo operators. It is the unscrupulous bingo operators who have developed ingenious ways of rigging the game in their favor.

Sometimes a *house player,* usually a woman, is planted among the other players. She is paid to win the jackpot, and returns it later. The announcer may record the numbers of the house player's card, and miscall the numbers he does draw. Sometimes the house player sits near the announcer and communicates the number she needs with prearranged gestures or silent lip messages.

Bingo fans can protect themselves against cheats by selecting a player to sit near the announcer and verify that the numbers called are the same as those on the balls he draws. If an operator approves of this plan, he's probably honest.

Players, too, have been known to cheat—by using plastic markers that have numbers pasted to the underside which are transferred to the bingo card. Most bingo cards now bear an individual serial number in each square which makes this cover-up trick virtually impossible to use.

BRIGHT LIGHTS AND BOOBY PRIZES

The midway of every neighborhood fair, carnival, boardwalk, penny arcade or amusement park is lined with games designed to tempt the gambling streak in any red-blooded member of the human race. It only takes 25¢ to play the wheel, toss the hoop, or throw the ball and win yourself a giant pink stuffed elephant, a fancy radio, or—if it's a *money store* game—even cash. The thrill of the midway's noise, crowds, and colored lights, and the chance to win a prize, even cheap merchandise (known as *slum*), often conquer one's common sense, making one forget that it's not all in fun—there is money involved.

Though there are innumerable carnival games, most of them fall into two basic categories: games of skill, in which you throw a ball, ring, hoop, dart, or coin toward a specific goal; and games of chance, in which you wager on the outcome of a spin of the wheel, a roll of the dice, or which slot a ball will land in when tossed. Some games require that a player score a specified number of points to win. All of these games can be operated fairly, or gaffed so that the player always loses—a *flat* game. Even when the games are fair, the odds always greatly favor the *carny*, or man who runs the game. Carnies and their shills will do everything in

their power to arouse the player's gambling spirit and entice him to bet big money—especially if they spot a sucker, or a *live one*, a sucker with money.

The following are the most popular carnival games, and the ways they can be rigged.

The Wheel of Fortune

The wheel of fortune is divided into sections, each of which bear a number, a color, or both. The player lays his money on a square on the playing board that corresponds in number and/or color to a section of the wheel. The wheel is spun on its axis, and when it stops, a pointer indicates one of the sections on the wheel—the winner. If a player bet

on that winning number (and/or color) he takes home the prize.

Some operators rig their wheels with hidden brakes that are controlled by pressure. The carny gives the brake a belly push, by leaning against the counter where the brake is concealed, and stops the wheel where he wants it to stop. According to John Scarne, renowned gambling authority, honest wheels tend to have a sturdy indicator at the top of the wheel which makes a loud tapping noise as the wheel is spun and hits the posts dividing the numbered sections on the wheel. Gaffed wheels have softer, more flexible indicators that bend easily, making the wheel easier to control. *Horizontal wheels*, or those that remain stationary while a pointer or arrow is spun, are very often gaffed. Wheels are often forbidden in states where only games of skill are permitted in carnivals.

The Mouse Game

In this amusing version of the wheel of fortune, a live mouse is placed in the middle of a circular cage mounted horizontally, which is covered while spun. When the wheel-like cage stops, the dizzy mouse is forced to choose one of many holes around the wheel for a hiding place. Players bet before the spin on which hole the mouse will choose.

The operator may rig this game by installing a device that enables him to close off any hole he wishes, or by simply scaring the mouse into a losing hole by shouting when the mouse gets close to it.

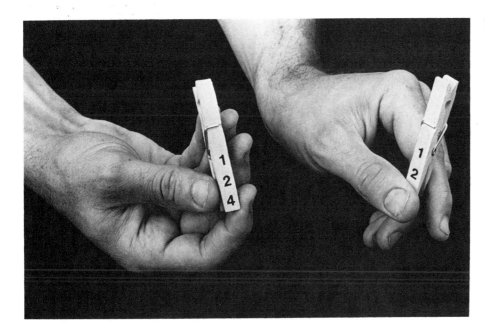

The clothespin gaff.

The One-Ball Game

The one-ball player throws a rubber ball against a backboard. As the ball rebounds, it falls into one of many numbered containers, each of which is worth a specific number of points or pays off at different odds. Players bet any amount on any number.

The one-ball game is not often rigged, but the odds of winning greatly favor the carny.

The Clothespin Game

In the clothespin game, also known as "Aunt Mary's Clothesline" among other names, the operator clips clothespins to a wire line and the player attempts to ring the pins with wooden hoops or ordinary jar lids. Each pin has a number on the back, invisible to the player, and, if hooped, the prize claimed depends on the number. The values of the prizes vary.

This game is rigged by sleight of hand. The operator either covers one of the numbers with his thumb when he shows the pin to the player (so 42, for example, appears to be 2 or 4), or turns the clothespin upside down, so that 61 appears to be 19, and so on. Thus, the pins that award the big prizes are never seen to be the ones the player rings. The fish pond game, where players try to hook a numbered "fish," is often gaffed in the same manner.

Hoop-Tossing Games

Hoop-tossing games—called hoopla, watch-la, ring-toss, and ring-it, among others—require the player to throw a wooden ring over a square stand to which a prize is fastened. A watch, ring, lighter, or pen are the usual prizes.

Chuck-a-Luck

Chuck-a-luck is played with three dice in a metal cage. The players can bet on the numbers 1 through 6. The dice are shaken by rotating the cage. If your number appears on one of the dice you win even money; on two of the dice, you win 2 to 1; on all three, you win 3 to 1. The house enjoys an edge of almost 8 percent in this game.

The urge to gamble is so universal and its practice is so pleasurable that I assume it must be evil.

(*Heywood Broun*)

There is a wide gambling streak in nearly every American man and woman, a fat streak, fat as a prize hog's bacon.

(*Will Rogers*)

The operator gaffs this game by constructing the stands at an acute angle, so the hoop can only pass over a prize if it approaches from the rear. The operator behind the counter can demonstrate how easily the hoop slips over the stand, but in reality it is impossible for the player to win. Sometimes the stand is composed of several smaller wooden blocks covered by a piece of velvet. The operator demonstrates how easy it is to win, then moves one of the blocks so the stand is no longer squared off, and the hoop cannot settle over it.

Cat Game

In this game, the player throws three baseballs—three for 25¢ usually—at stuffed cats on a shelf. If he knocks three cats off the rack with three balls he wins a prize.

In a fair game, the cat must be hit squarely in the center before it will fall—which is difficult enough to do. Some carnies will weight the cat at the bottom so it may topple, but will not fall off the shelf.

The Penny Fall Game

This is the latest addition to the dishonest carny's roster of rip-offs. For some reason it's called the Penny Fall—although players lose quarters, not pennies. Depending upon the individual game, one to twenty people can play. Each puts his quarter in a slot, which opens out into a slide or chute. This in turn feeds the quarter onto the game's playing surface inside the machine, where it joins a spread of already captive quarters. The playing surface, visible under glass, is constantly swept over by a wood bar, which first pushes against the player's quarter, which in turn moves the others. The player then has the privilege of watching the mass of quarters *almost* go over the edge of the playing surface—and thus *almost* into his lap.

He should be so lucky. Of course, the quarters seldom go over the front edge, because it has a slight lip that creates just enough resistance to divert the quarters out to the sides, and then back into the mainstream. Often, in the center of the playing area (covered by quarters) are one or more round-headed screws which also tend to cause the sliding quarters to pile up on each other, rather than to force other quarters into the payout chute.

Carnival games, whether games of chance or games of skill, rarely offer you a fair opportunity to win. The only control you have over the amount of money you lose is your ability to walk away from the game.

PORTRAIT OF A CARNY

No operator in the gambling world is more gifted at squeezing the greenbacks out of your jeans than the professional carny. As you stroll down the midway, he uses hypnotic powers to convince you he's dying to give you a thick bankroll or a color TV. With a dazzling pitch, he invites you to try his game. "Just tip 'em over, you win," he sings. "One little quarter for a brand new watch." And before your very eyes a man on crutches knocks the cats off the shelf and takes home the prize. He is however, probably a *stick*, or shill, who's hired, along with little old ladies and beautiful girls, to win the sympathy of the crowd and draw you into the game.

The carny demonstrates that any fool could hook a fish from his pond and win a ham, or toss a ring around the digital watch on the velvet stand. When he pays winners of the fortune wheel he makes the coins ring like bells (he sweeps the money he takes off the counter into his cashbox as silently as possible). Yet when you try to hook the fish, ring the watch, or beat the wheel you · inevitably fail, and he will use every gimmick he knows to keep you trying, and losing.

If you suspect the game is gaffed and start to complain, he'll have a plausible-sounding alibi to explain your loss. He also uses subtle psychological ploys to kid you, embarrass you in front of your companion, or in other ways cool you out. If you summon the police he has gimmicks to fool them, too, or has paid them off. If his game is fair and you demonstrate the winning skill, he'll go out to lunch—for the rest of the day. He'll never let you win if he can help it.

The carny often uses a language of his own. One type is a sort of pig latin, called cazarny tazalk. *The smooth-talking carny who handles payoffs and settles any customer disputes is called a* patch-man.

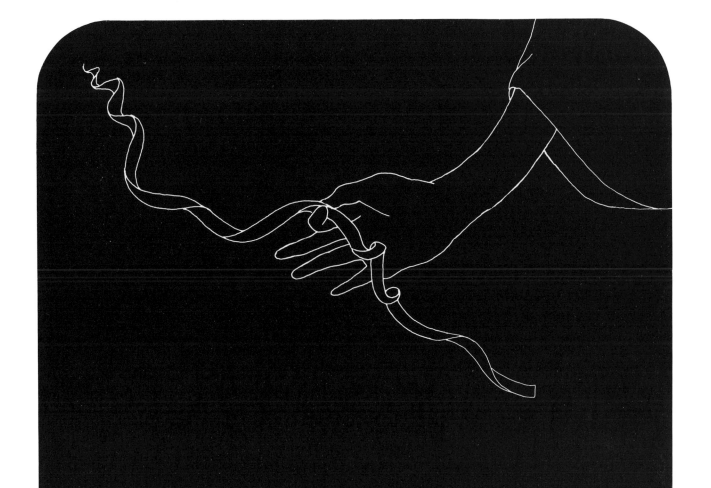

THE
PAPER
PLAYERS

GREAT EXPECTATIONS

Paper gamblers are those who play lotteries, sweepstakes, numbers, the stock market, and the like. They all create a mountain of papers: tickets, entry forms, leaflets, punchboards, chain letters, betting slips, receipts, prospectuses, ticker tape, etc., are but a portion of the resulting volume. But that is not their only common element. They are all risky gambles.

Aside from the "winner" in the stock market—whose skill probably overrode luck—winners of paper gambles succeed against heavy odds. But losing is at least done in privacy, since these are the most solitary forms of wagering.

Large amounts of money are to be won if the risks pay off. If not, well . . . it's only paper money after all.

THE STATE OF THE LOTTERY

Lottery fever, a strange malady spread by mass communication and word of mouth, has been around for centuries. But the current form—state lotteries—is particularly virulent and can strike anyone.

Victims buy chances to win prizes that range from a free ticket (and so another chance to win) to $2 million (in New York's 1979 Olympic Lottery). Most instant lotteries pay a top prize of $5,000 and weeklies tend to give away $100,000. That's not all: when enough tickets have been sold, both instants and weeklies spice up the game with "jackpot" draws for $500,000 to $1 million. Some lotteries give away merchandise too, as Illinois did in its successful Car-A-Day-Give-Away game. The most valuable prizes, though, are the chance in a lifetime giveaways of up to $1,000 a month for life. Sociologists suggest that state lottery fever is caused by a desire to escape social woes and the economic uncertainties of modern living. In other words, the dream of becoming rich overnight, combined with the unbeatable attraction of a chance to win something for (almost) nothing.

If you suspect you might have been infected, ask yourself these questions. If you answer yes to one or more, you've definitely been smitten.

• Are you obsessed with numbers?

• Does your weekly budget include an allowance for the purchase of lottery tickets?

• Do you hang around newsstands waiting for the latest edition?

• Do you find yourself turning on the TV evening news just to get the lottery results?

• Are you subject to blackouts after which you are mysteriously covered with tell-tale bits of instant-lottery ticket coating?

The disease has no known cure, although a select few do find dramatic (though temporary) relief by purchasing a winning ticket. The multitude of lottery fever victims need not worry, however. It's seldom fatal and the symptoms can be contained by periodic purchase of additional state lottery tickets.

In lottery states, it's almost impossible to turn on a TV set without seeing a commercial for the newest, most exciting game in town. Close to $10 million a year is spent by state lotteries on television advertising alone.

Drawing winners at a Baltimore Lottery.

There Ain't no Justice!

Poor Barry Brunelle is crying, but not all the way to the bank. Although he won the Connecticut lottery, the state refused to give him his prize because he was only sixteen years old at the time, two years below the legal age of eighteen. The Commission did, however, refund the dollar he paid for his winning ticket.

Professional Players

Have you ever thought that the only way to win a million would be to make a full–time job of it?

Tom and Philomena Drake of McMurray, Pennsylvania decided to do just that. They took their life savings— $15,000—and invested in Pennsylvania's Instant Bingo game, which ran from May to September, 1976.

They didn't achieve their goal of becoming millionaires. Their $15,000 investment won them just over $17,000—a profit of only $2,000. But they did come out way ahead, thanks to the fringe benefits they received from selling their story to magazine and book publishers and even a movie producer.

HOW STATE LOTTERIES WORK

The basic principle of every state lottery is the same: to distribute prizes by selling chances in the form of numbered tickets. The winning numbers on tickets are drawn randomly either by computer or by referring to a pre-selected, randomly changing figure (such as closing stock market volume or the daily U.S. Treasury balance). Prizes are then paid out of the pool of money created by ticket sales—minus commission fees, operating expenses and profits. This shrunken pool is commonly called the payout, and there is a set of rules in every lottery that sets the size and number of prizes, the number of drawings and the percentage of the payout. Lotteries are successful when they offer a number of big prizes, frequent drawings, a generous payout and an imaginative yet simple game to play. A popular lottery also has to make it easy for people to buy tickets and find out results. And, of course, the ticket price has to be right. In the United States today there are three common types of lottery games operated by state lottery commissions, and it is the states that decide upon the size of the prizes and the frequency of the lottery.

The Draw

Despite its many ingenious disguises, this is the most common lottery around, and the simplest one to play. Ticket buyers hope to match all or some of the digits on their ticket with a drawn winning number. Sometimes the number of winning tickets drawn depends on total sales. Matching can involve any number of digital variations or bingo–like combinations and patterns. The drawings for prizes of fixed amounts are usually held weekly. And since it is the bettor who must find out if his numbers match the winning numbers drawn, the drawings are often hyped–up televised affairs. These lotteries pay the really big prizes.

The draw, where winning lottery numbers are drawn by random selection and holders of tickets that match those numbers win.

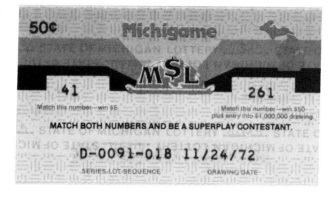

Most weekly draw tickets cost 50¢. New York set the record for the highest ticket price when it charged $10 a ticket in its Olympic lottery. But the prize was worth it—$2 million, estimated to be $1 million after taxes, the largest guaranteed prize ever offered in a U.S. lottery.

Instants

An instant lottery game is usually designed to last four to twelve weeks before it's replaced by a new, bigger, better, simpler, or kookier instant game. Instant games are the most popular lotteries in operation today. They work on the principle that people would rather win something small than nothing at all—and find out immediately if they're a winner. Instants give you more chances of winning, but the prizes are considerably smaller. Tickets usually cost one dollar; you find out if you are a winner and what you have won simply by rubbing off the coating to reveal a number or symbol beneath. If the symbol(s) you reveal match the one(s) printed on the ticket, you're a winner. Sometimes top-prize instant lottery winners become eligible for larger prizes in a random drawing.

Numbers

Legal "numbers" lotteries are almost exact duplicates of the illegal numbers racket.

These lotteries are designed for people who like to control the "action" by choosing their own numbers, and by betting as much as they want on various combinations of the three or four digits they choose. To win, players must match their numbers—in the correct sequence—to randomly drawn winning numbers. Bets range from 50¢ on up to $10. Most games have a fixed pay-out of 50 percent of the odds. For example, if the odds against a bet are 999 to 1, the winning payout is $500 for every dollar bet.

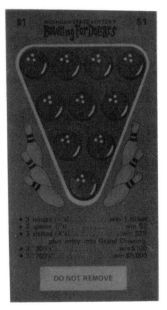

In a numbers lottery the bettor picks the numbers and must match the randomly drawn numbers to win.

Buyers of instant lottery tickets find out if they have won, and how much, by rubbing off special coating.

A HISTORY OF LOTTERIES

When the word "lottery" is heard today, we think of people selected by chance to win big money prizes. But the idea of random selection goes as far back as biblical times and, in its early usage, was not always a source of entertainment.

In classical mythology, Greek youths and maidens drew lots for the dubious prize of being served up as a snack to the monstrous Minotaur. Roman emperors entertained their dinner guests with door prize drawings for such lavish gifts as villas and slaves, inter-mixed with booby prizes such as a live ostrich and six dead flies.

The first recorded money lottery, *La Lotto di Firenze*, began in 1530 to raise money for the Italian government. It started a chain reaction that spread rapidly throughout Italy, then Europe, then crossed the Channel to England. In 1566, Queen Elizabeth sponsored the first British lottery to raise money for the defense of the channel ports. The prize was £5,000 in gold and goods, and ticket buyers were also given a seven-day guarantee against arrest for minor crimes. By the time James I succeeded to the throne, lotteries were financing everything in London from public works to private corporations and ladies' dowries.

It was only natural that the Virginia Colonization Company should seize on the ideal of a lottery to raise money for its expeditions. Virginia's success was quickly

"It says 'Rub all six spots. If same amount appears. . . .'"

copied by other colonizing enterprises, and the American colonies themselves held lotteries too. These lotteries were popular and eminently respectable. The result was that the Thirteen Colonies were virtually floated on lotteries. Ben Franklin sponsored a lottery to raise money to buy new cannons for the defense of Philadelphia. George Washington sponsored (unsuccessfully) a lottery to build a road over the Cumberland Mountains.

Thomas Jefferson summed up the American attitude toward lotteries when he endorsed them as "a salutary instrument wherein the tax is laid on the willing only." After the American Revolution, money was raised for the continuation of military defense as well as for public improvements, and institutions that benefited include Harvard, Yale, Princeton, Columbia, and hundreds of now–historical churches, schools, town halls, and hospitals. Despite their noble ends, these lotteries were still considered entertainment, and inspired other gambling games—such as the Wheel of Fortune, which was popular in marketplaces and town squares.

In 1831, in eight states alone there were 420 lotteries with estimated sales of more than $66 million (about five times the cost of running the federal government in those days). An anonymous poet described the lottery craze in these two lines:
"The name of Lott'ry the Nature bewitches And City and Country run Mad after Riches."
But as the number of lotteries grew, so did lottery swindles.

The most famous lottery scandal of the nineteenth century was the "Washington Swindle," in 1823. In that year Congress had approved a lottery to raise money to beautify the capital city, but when the winning ticket was drawn, it was discovered that the promoters had absconded with the money. To curtail such swindles, most states had banned lotteries by 1840, and in 1895 Congress passed a law forbidding the transportation of lottery tickets across state borders.

With the demise of legal lotteries, illegal and foreign lotteries boomed in the early twentieth century. Sports lotteries and numbers games flourished, and for years lotteries were burdened with an unsavory reputation. Of the hundreds of crooked lotteries that sprung up in the U.S. in the 1920s and 1930s, most were fly–by–night affairs operated by small–time con men. But one man thought big and made millions on the phoniest lottery in history—the Tijuana Lottery.

The American public was led to believe that the Tijuana Lottery was operated by wealthy Mexican horse owners. But "Doc" Peters was the one brain behind it. He operated the game from a dingy second–floor office in the Mexican town of Tijuana, conveniently close to the U.S. border. All he actually did was print fancy—but phony—tickets. His success lay in his marketing system: a network of American agents sold one-dollar tickets across the country, and Doc provided them with phony lists of "winners." There were no winners, however, because the drawings never took place. It was reported that Doc took in $240,000 a month at his peak, and made a 700 percent profit.

Scandals like the Tijuana Lottery managed to keep legal lotteries out of the United States for years. And our Puritan heritage, mixed with a little Protestant work ethic, made many Americans frown on the idea of trying to get something for nothing. But eventually the American dream of instant riches won out and resistance began to break down in 1964, when the modern strain of lottery fever was injected into the American way of life. That was the year that New Hampshire introduced its sweepstakes game, giving away almost $2

England's State Lottery, 1763. (Reproduced by Courtesy of the Trustees of the British Museum.)

million to winners in four draws.

In the years that followed, 14 more states authorized lotteries—New York, New Jersey, Maine, Massachusetts, Rhode Island, Connecticut, Delaware, Maryland, Pennsylvania, Ohio, Illinois, Michigan, Vermont, and Colorado—and ticket sales have climbed to epidemic proportions. In 1977 a delirious public spent more than $1.5 billion on lotteries—23.6 percent more than ticket sales in 1976. And the fever shows no signs of abating.

WHAT ARE YOUR CHANCES OF WINNING?

First, the good news: your chances of winning a lottery with a single ticket are as good as those of anyone else who holds a single ticket. And now, the bad news: everyone's chances are pretty slim.

Payouts and odds for lottery winnings vary greatly but, in general, buying a lottery ticket is actually one of the worst gambles around. Though the odds in favor of winning small prizes may be worth the gamble, the chances decrease dramatically as the amount of prize money increases. The fact that a lottery is extremely popular works against you, since a ticket holder's chances of winning a big prize usually vary according to the number of tickets sold. The more buyers there are, the poorer your chances of winning. (For example, if one million people buy lottery tickets the same week you do, your chance of winning is one in a million.) The odds remain constant for smaller prizes, since there is a fixed number of these prizes added for every 1,000 or 1,000,000 tickets sold depending on the lottery.

The only sure winner is the state itself. While total takes at race tracks are reduced usually less than 20 percent, the state takes anywhere from 50 to 60 percent off the top of lottery sales. (The state keeps an average of at least 45 percent of all ticket money. Operating costs generally take up another 15 percent. The prize money is the 40 percent that's left.) The exact financial breakdown is available from the individual state lottery commissions. Some games use the pari–mutuel pay-out system, where all the bettors holding winning numbers share in a fixed percentage of the total money bet. If a lot of people bet on a winning number, the payoff will be proportionately smaller than if only a few people bet on it.

It's impossible to list all the current lotteries operating in the United States, since new games and new gimmicks to attract players are constantly cropping up. The chart on the next page lists games offered by most of the states operating lotteries (Colorado is not included), along with the all–important information on your chances of winning. These figures are useful basically for general comparison: note how the odds vary dizzyingly from state to state, and even from game to game. For the odds of winning the newer lotteries that are sure to appear, check the back of your ticket—the odds are often listed there. Or, contact the state lottery commission.

As you can see, the odds of winning big in any lottery are so astronomical that it's difficult to influence them appreciably. As the tired lottery joke goes, you increase your chances only slightly by buying a ticket.

The Big Winners

The biggest winner in any lottery is, unquestionably, the state government. Some states simply deposit their lottery profits in that state's general operating fund. But the more politically astute state governments earmark the funds for highly–publicized, vote–catching projects. Kids and senior citizens are usually the biggest beneficiaries of these projects, since lottery revenue is often spent on education, health and community services.

In Maryland, property owners were the winners recently when lottery funds were used to ease a rise in property tax assessments.

In Massachusetts, the state government pays more than lip service to local governments—it also allocates a yearly share of lottery funds to every town or municipality in the state.

In New York, the lottery promoters borrowed a gimmick used in Canadian lotteries that not only provided money for a popular cause, but also promoted ticket sales—the Olympic Lottery. Profits from this lottery go directly into building permanent facilities for use in the 1980 Winter Olympics and for the support of education and training programs for U.S. athletes.

STATE LOTTERIES: THE WEEKLY DRAW GAMES—BASIC ODDS

State	Name of game	Ticket cost	Average weekly sales	Chances of winning per SINGLE ticket (one-in-...)					
				$1 million or more	$100,000 or more	$10,000 or more	$1,000 or more	$100 or more	Any cash
Connecticut	The Money Tree	50¢	750,000	none	3,750,000	384,600	48,500	48,500	90.9
Delaware	Double Diamond[a]	50¢	25,000	none	(1,900,000)	487,200	79,200	9,740	91.0
Illinois	Big Payday	50¢	800,000	none	6,000,000	750,000	54,500	8,450	90.1
	Goldstrike[b]	$1.	300,000	none	none	none	42,400	42,400	21.4
Maine	The 50¢ Ticket	50¢	120,000	none	none	600,000	85,700	27,300	90.8
Maryland	Super 50¢	50¢	550,000	(20,000,000)	10,000,000	1,044,100	136,100	4,400	89.1
	17-For-$1	$1.	230,000	none	(1,030,600)	134,700	16,800	2,180	74.3
Massachusetts	New Big Money Game	50¢	1,100,000	(11,000,000)	11,000,000	647,100	35,500	7,860	83.9
Michigan	Michigame	50¢	1,250,000	(30,000,000)	30,000,000	194,800	96,800	96,800	90.8
New Hampshire	50/50 Sweeps	50¢	160,000	none	(1,000,000)	1,000,000	55,600	5,050	212.0
New Jersey	The New Weekly	50¢	1,000,000	(20,000,000)	20,000,000	666,700	95,200	9,050	99.9
New York	Playoffs	$1.	1,000,000	(11,000,000)	11,000,000	500,000	66,700	66,700	113.5
	Olympic Lottery[c]	$10.	630,000	630,000	157,500	63,000	22,500	250	25.0
			1,800,000	1,800,000	257,100	69,200	12,900	143	14.3
Ohio	Weekly 50¢ Game	50¢	965,000	(50,000,000)	25,000,000	119,300	49,600	8,390	90.9
	Lucky Buck II	$1.	375,000	none	1,000,000	250,000	71,400	71,400	99.9
Pennsylvania	Big 50	50¢	1,400,000	(20,000,000)	20,000,000	190,500	70,200	8,830	91.0
	Baker's Dozen	$1.	333,000	none	1,000,000	200,000	22,200	22,200	247.0
	Multi-Million				2,500,000				
	Sweepstakes[d]	$5.	250,000	(1,250,000)	(1,250,000)	100,000	990	990	9.9
Rhode Island	Grand Lot	50¢	86,000	none	4,000,000	266,700	125,000	20,800	225.0
Vermont	Green Mountain	50¢	200,000	(1,000,000)	(1,000,000)	1,000,000	28,300	23,080	75.1

[a] Game has been discontinued.

[b] Combination draw and instant game; odds are for draw game only.

[c] Draws held at 2–3 month intervals. Prize structure and odds vary with ticket sales; odds shown for two sales levels.

[d] Ten weekly draws held once annually.

FOOTNOTES

1. All data and calculations are based on information provided by the lottery agencies up to time of printing.
2. All prizes paid by installment have been valued at their estimated cash cost to the lottery (using an annuity discount rate of 7½%) for purposes of categorizing "chances of winning." "Chances of winning" shown in brackets refer to nominal rather than actual present cash value (cost to the lottery) of installment prizes.
3. Prizes have been categorized by their before-tax value.

(Copyright 1978. Whole World Lottery Guide, Toronto, Canada, and Bryan Elwood. Not to be reproduced without permission.)

The $100,000 grand prize winners of New Hampshire's Bingo Instant Sweepstakes Game.

However, any advantage you can gain may make a difference. So here are a few tips, courtesy of the Whole World Lottery Guide (P.O. Box 6576, Postal Station A, Toronto, Ont., Canada M5WIX4):

• Ticket sales usually follow seasonal slumps and peaks. July and August sales tend to go down, when a lot of people are on vacation and away from their usual ticket source. But December sales usually soar as people buy tickets as gifts, or hope for a big Christmas win to help pay the bills. Since the fewer tickets sold the better your chances are of winning, check with your local lottery commission to find out when they anticipate slump periods, and make sure you get in on those draws.

• Enter those lotteries that give you the best chances of winning. You can get an idea of what the odds will be by dividing the number of tickets sold by the number of big prizes offered, or by reading the fine print on the back of the ticket, or contacting the state lottery commission.

• The lottery that takes the least amount of each ticket dollar and gives out the best–value prizes is a better gamble. Figure out each lottery's payout by dividing the total value of cash prizes offered by the number of tickets sold. Compare each lottery on the basis of the payout per dollar spent to find your best buy.

• Multiply your chances of winning, although you may win a smaller amount, by multiplying your bets. If you have $5 to play with, it's better to buy ten 50¢ chances than five $1 chances.

Winning Woes

There are some lottery winners who have found that money does indeed buy happiness. But others undergo such traumas that their dream of winning turns into a nightmare.

Winners find themselves besieged by the media looking for a classic rags–to–riches story, and it's not uncommon for winners to have their stories (filled with extraneous and often incorrect information) exposed to millions—complete with their addresses, phone numbers, and employers' and relatives' names.

Charities, investment brokers, and individuals track them down for a parcel of the prize money. Friends, relatives and co–workers often start showing jealousy, and resent it when the winners are not as generous as they swear *they* would be in the same situation. The instant notoriety brings fears of kidnapping for ransoms winners couldn't possibly afford to pay with their prize installments. Many are forced to quit their jobs to avoid even higher taxes than those they must pay on their winnings. Many move to new neighborhoods with unlisted phone numbers— becoming virtual recluses.

The most disheartening stories involve the winners who are simply not prepared to handle a lot of money and end up deeply—and very quickly—in debt.

In countries such as Greece, lotteries are an integral part of the inhabitants' lives and cultures, and lottery ticket vendors are a common sight. (Photo by Michos Tzovaras.)

The Tax Bite

After the euphoria of winning most big winners are usually brought crashing down to earth when their first prize check arrives. It's known as the million-dollar misunderstanding, for the million dollar prize printed on your ticket is not what you'll get.

A million dollar prize is parceled out in $50,000 installments over 20 years. (Prizes of $100,000 are usually paid out over 10 years.) This procedure enables you to reduce the $700,000 in taxes you would have to pay on a lump sum of $1 million and

More than 50 governments around the world have established national lotteries. The U.S. Government does not encourage its citizens to enter, and various laws make it difficult to find out who has won (you can't be notified by mail) and to collect. Our government considers such winnings taxable income.

Picking the winning numbers in the Swiss National Lottery.

provides a steady guaranteed income. That's not too hard to take. But there's more. Unlike the rest of the world, where lottery windfalls are tax-free, in the United States the government withholds 20 percent of any lottery winnings of $5,000 or more. (This is only the withholding percentage. The total Federal tax may ultimately be higher, depending on one's tax bracket.) If you live in a state that also levies income tax, chop off some more. And the local government may get a share too. Most million-dollar winners end up, on an average, with a yearly check of $30,000. The cost of losing tickets can be tax deductible, but only if you have won on another ticket that year. So far, Vermont is the only state that has exempted lottery winnings from state tax.

If you continue to earn a salary, your winnings will catapult you into a much higher tax bracket, and you'll end up paying higher taxes on both your winnings and your earned income.

Winners of lesser prizes may receive the amount in one lump sum. These winnings are also taxable and must be declared as income.

THE LOTTERY DEBATE

Although public opinion is increasingly swinging in favor of state lotteries, some people still think governments shouldn't be in the gambling business. Critics point out that compared to regular forms of taxation, lotteries are an inefficient way to raise revenue, voluntary though the contribution may be.

The loudest criticism against lotteries has come from church leaders and morality–conscious politicians. But there are exceptions, such as the Million-Dollar Adventure sponsored by 71 Roman Catholic parishes in Eastern Pennsylvania, and the congressman who suggested that each Congressional District run a numbers lottery in conjunction with elections to encourage voters to come out to the polls.

On the pro side is the fact that feared government corruption and scandals have not materialized for the most part. Computers are the main bulwarks against fixes. Accountants keep a close watch on computer clerks, and the accountants, in turn, are monitored by spot auditors. The few scandals that have arisen have usually involved, rather than a crime, what the experts call a "design deficiency"—which either allows too many tickets to be sold or inadvertently duplicates numbers.

The U.S. Government is considering legislation to ease the mailing restriction on lotteries and allow them to sell tickets nationwide and worldwide. If that comes about, it won't be long before private enterprise, with its hungry eye on the potential profits, starts lobbying to take over the business. Private competition would probably mean bigger payouts—and more prizes to win!

And The Winner Is. . . .

How do you know you're a winner? It's pretty hard to miss the news, since winning numbers are announced in local newspapers, and on local TV and radio stations. Notices are also posted wherever tickets are sold. Some states even have a recorded message you can reach by telephone. Many states also televise the actual drawings, from the grand prize lotteries right down to the daily numbers drawing. In Michigan and Massachusetts, the lottery is run like a prime–time TV game show with contestants chosen from qualifying ticketholders.

Despite the wide publicity given to winning tickets, millions of dollars in prize money goes unclaimed each year. In Illinois alone, the lottery commission listed almost $4 million in unclaimed prizes among its assets in 1976–1977. Some states hold bonus drawings just to use up these lucrative leftovers.

Most players, though, know when they're winners and don't waste any time collecting. Instant lottery winners of up to $25 are usually paid on the spot by the ticket agent. Larger wins usually require the ticket–holder to mail in a claim form or, for the really big prizes, pay a visit to the nearest lottery office.

The Smugglers' Sweeps

Since both the sale of Irish Sweepstakes tickets and the use of the mails for sweepstakes transactions are illegal in the United States, a colossal smuggling operation has resulted, earning the game the alias of the "Smugglers' Sweeps."

Not only do tickets have to be smuggled in, but stubs and money have to be smuggled out. Then, counterfoils (official receipts) have to be smuggled back in. And, tickets and counterfoils have to be distributed within the United States. The smuggling operation is equal to rum–running in the days of Prohibition.

Over the years, the smuggling has taken many ingenious forms. U.S.–bound tickets have been hidden in hollowed–out religious books mailed to "devout" Irish—Americans; in the bottoms of false—bottomed bird cages; in one famous instance, in packages of Irish cereal; in the holds of ocean liners, tramp steamers, pleasure boats, and even in the de–icing tanks of airplanes.

Ireland–bound ticket stubs and money are usually mailed in opaque or lined envelopes to constantly changing Sweeps depots in Ireland, or indirectly via Canada or Britain.

THE IRISH SWEEPSTAKES

The Irish Hospitals' Sweepstakes, commonly known as the Irish Sweepstakes, began in 1930 as a pure-bred sweepstakes with prizes determined by the total ticket pool. Then, to attract more ticket buyers, the promoters provided more prizes by dividing the total pool into as many units of £120,000 as the ticket sales allowed. Each £120,000 unit was then divided into fixed value prizes. But the number of £120,000 units still depended on the total pool amassed.

The Irish Sweepstakes is popular worldwide, especially in the United States, and employs more than 1,500 people—making it one of Ireland's major industries. Although the government authorizes the enterprise, it is run by a private company—Hospitals Trust Ltd.—thus protecting the Irish government from any embarrassment stemming from violations of other countries' laws. It is illegal in the United States, but that doesn't stop thousands of U.S. citizens from entering.

When the Sweepstakes began, Irish immigrants provided ready–made ticket sellers. Today's sellers are not exclusively Irish, but don't expect to find any ticket for sale unless the seller knows you well. (Since women are the Sweeps' best customers, beauty parlor operators are likely ticket sellers.) Aside from its illegal status, U.S. ticket buyers should also be wary of counterfeit tickets, which float around by the thousands.

There are three drawings a year, coinciding with the running of three famous horse races: the Grand National, the Epsom Downs

Derby, and the Cambridgeshire Stakes. About ten days before each race, ticket holders' stubs are automatically shuffled in huge bins for three days. The tickets are drawn by Irish nurses at a colorful public ceremony, and matched simultaneously with the randomly drawn names of the horses scheduled to run the race. The matching is repeated once for each prize unit of £120,000. Holders of drawn tickets are notified by cable, but then must wait until the race is run to find out what the prize will be.

The horse that comes in first wins £50,000 (about $100,000) for the ticket holder whose stub matched that horse; the second horse over the finish line wins £20,000 for the ticket holder; and a third place showing wins £10,000 for the ticket holder. Another £30,000 in prizes is shared by the holders of the tickets matched to the remaining horses' names, and there are also residual prizes of £100 each. If there are twenty £120,000 units in the total pool, each prize is awarded twenty times. And there's a grand prize of £200,000 for the very first ticket drawn. If a player has the extreme good luck to hold both the first ticket drawn and the winning horse ticket, he could win £250,000 (about $500,000). The odds of winning this top prize have been estimated to be about 1 in 305,000—something the operators don't advertise.

United States winners have to contend with currency fluctuations that can drastically affect the value of a large prize. And, of course, there's the IRS, which holds that such winnings are subject to taxes once they enter the United States. The tax bite can be eased by sharing the ticket ownership among family members and then filing separate returns. (This is only legal if the partnership is made in good faith and not simply to avoid taxes, but how the IRS goes about making such a distinction is a mystery.)

Since 15 states now have their own legal lotteries, many ticket buyers and sellers have switched from the Irish Sweepstakes to one of them. Nevertheless, Americans still buy over half of the Irish Sweepstakes tickets sold. Although United States law forbids advertising of any foreign lottery, including the Irish Sweepstakes, news stories of winners are perfectly legal and these, along with word of mouth, fuel the Sweeps' popularity.

Sweeps to the Sweet

In 1931, Americans read about Emilio Scala, an Italian candystore owner in London who sweetened his life with an Irish Sweepstakes win of $1,773,660 and became the biggest money winner in the Sweeps' history. Shortly afterward, an American factory worker, Joe Hadley, shared a win of $860,000 with his brother and brother-in-law. The news of these wins created an insatiable demand for these tickets in the United States that persists to this day.

Something's Fishy

Because the Irish Sweepstakes is illegal in the United States, promoters in the early days went to great lengths to find ways to publicize it here. One method used was the dumping of thousands of fish-shaped bottles into the Atlantic Ocean. Each bottle contained a voucher for a free drink at the bar of the bearer's choice. The only proviso was that the drinker toast to good luck in the Irish Sweepstakes.

Of course the publicity that surrounded such a gimmick was worth its weight in gold in ticket sales. What the public didn't know was that the bottles had not floated all the way over from Ireland—they had actually been surreptitiously dumped in the ocean quite close to shore.

SWEEPSTAKES— THE CROWD PLEASERS

Taxes on Sweepstakes Prizes

Winners of cash prizes in sweepstakes must declare the prize: it is considered taxable income. Winners can claim as deductions any expenses incurred, such as postage, and money spent for supplies (envelopes, 3 x 5 cards used for proof of purchase facsimiles, etc.).

Winners of merchandise prizes can also deduct expenses but are required to pay income tax based on the value of the item they have won. The IRS will be aware of the retail price of the item won, so the declared value will be questioned unless it is fairly close to the retail value. It seems as though you can't win even when you win.

How often have you gone to your mailbox and found a bulky envelope bursting with the good news that you are just a postage stamp away from winning the house of your dreams or a truckload of cash—and along with it a wad of discount coupons and advertising hype to buy, buy, buy, or subscribe, subscribe, subscribe? How many magazine or newspaper ads have you seen asking you to simply send in the entry blank along with a proof of purchase or, if you prefer, the name of the product written on a separate sheet of paper, for a chance to be selected as a winner in a huge cash or merchandise give–away?

Each year, hundreds of these commercial sweepstakes sweep across the country, leaving behind cash and prizes of an estimated total value of more than $82 million. That's nothing to sneeze at. And commercial sweepstakes are big business. They support an industry that includes scores of judging firms, direct mail companies, and sweepstakes consultants and wholesalers.

The most active sweepstakers are the same people who bring you soap and soap operas—Proctor and Gamble. Hot on their heels are the magazine subscription sellers who work through wholesale distributors (such as the mammoth Publishers' Clearing House), or through independent promotions (such as Reader's Digest does with it's own patented sweepstakes).

There's no limit to the number and variety of products promoted by sweepstakes through the mails, on TV, radio and in newspapers and magazines. Companies use sweepstakes as an advertising tool—to induce a maximum number of the right people to read promotional literature, and to do it with a minimum number of mailings or advertising spots. And the chances are good that you are the right person if you know about the sweepstakes. That is, you are a person who is likely to use the product (or subscribe to the magazine, or buy the record, or the like), or you would not have come across the advertisement or been on the mailing list in the first place.

HOW SWEEPSTAKES WORK

As Long as You Asked . . .

Most people don't know the difference between a lottery and a sweepstakes. The line that separates the two has been crossed so often that it has all but disappeared. In fact, some so-called lotteries are really sweepstakes, while most so-called sweepstakes are really lotteries.

The crucial difference is that, theoretically, a sweepstakes ticket buyer doesn't know what the top prize will be. It depends on how many ticket buyers contribute money to the pool by buying tickets. Sweepstakes are also traditionally based on the outcome of a race, and one winner "sweeps" all.

Chance is the pseudonym of God when He did not want to sign.

(Anatole France)

All sweepstakes work in the same manner. You mail in your entry with no strings attached—you are not required to send in money, or a proof of purchase or an order. In some cases you need not even invest in the postage, as your entry may arrive with a postage prepaid return envelope. Each entry has as good a chance as any to be selected as a winner in a random drawing.

Once all entries are received, winners are picked at random in a drawing. Because hundreds of thousands, even millions of entries are expected in national sweepstakes, the judges usually hold a series of random drawings. The winners of these become candidates in the final random drawing for the winners of the sweepstakes.

Winners are usually notified by mail, or by phone.

WHAT ARE THE CHANCES OF WINNING?

Skeptics may scoff at the chance-in-a-lifetime hoopla, and even doubt the validity of these sweeps. Although you may enter them all and never win, it isn't because these offerings are crooked. All commercial sweepstakes have to register with the state government, and comply with strict state and federal regulations that require—for example —that all prizes be awarded, that lists of winners be made available upon request, that judges may have to be blindfolded when drawing winners. Most commercial sweepstakes are not run by the sponsoring company, but by an independent judging firm whose business depends upon compliance with the law. However, be wary of a sweepstakes that requires you to buy anything to be eligible, especially if it never mentions who the sponsoring company is (or mentions the company in vague terms only). Sometimes crooked sweepstakes will ask for money in the same letter that tells you you're a winner. (All you have to do to claim this valuable prize is to send in a minimal amount of money, which will be returned to you later.)

Your chances of winning any sweepstakes depend on how many others take the time to enter too. The hitch is, your entry could be one in several million. Some entry blanks include in fine print how many entry blanks have been mailed out, or the estimated number of entries they expect to receive. Though each entry has as good a chance to be drawn as any other, there are some how-to's that can increase your chances of winning:

• Fill in your entry form correctly. It sounds obvious, but as many as 40 percent of sweepstakes entrants don't, and automatically disqualify themselves as winners even if their entry is drawn.

• Follow instructions to the letter. Don't type, for example, if the instructions say "print."

• If you do print, print legibly.

• Double check all the rules and requirements carefully. Some sweepstakes are not legal in all states. Employees or relatives of employees of the sponsoring company, their advertising company, or the judging firm are usually not eligible to enter. Some sweepstakes have minimum age requirements. All winners will be checked and double-checked for eligibility, so make sure you are eligible to win.

• Address the entry exactly as instructed.

• Sweepstakes can't require that you send in money, or buy anything, in order to enter, but a facsimile of a label is often required. Your chances of winning are not greater if you send in a label instead of the facsimile, but you must send in whatever facsimile is required.

• Stamp your entry if it isn't pre-posted.

• Don't forget to mail it by the entry closing date.

The $100,000 Thaw

Does the thought of winning $100,000 in cold, hard cash send shivers of pleasure up and down your spine? If so, put on your long johns and trek on up to Nenana, Alaska this April. That's when thousands of gamblers from all over North America meet on the banks of the Tanana River, waiting for the ice to thaw. Each contributes a dollar to a pool, along with his guess as to the exact day, hour, and minute the ice will begin to break up. When it finally does—sometimes not until mid–May—a siren wails and the closest guesser walks away with as much as a cool $100,000.

No one ever became a millionaire without taking a chance.

(*J. P. Morgan*)

If you're having trouble finding enough commercial sweepstakes and contests to enter, consider subscribing to Contest Hotline, a newsletter you can obtain by writing to Box 88, Yorba Linda, CA 92686. It costs one dollar per issue or nine dollars for a yearly subscription, and runs between 25 and 30 sweepstakes and contests every month.

Back in the contest–crazy days of the 1930s and 1960s, contest clubs abounded and library shelves overflowed with how–to–win guides. Thousands of contest hobbyists spent hours composing poems, slogans and eulogies—in 25 words or less—about different brands of margarine and soap.

With the coming of sweepstakes—and randomly-selected winners—contest skills and rhyming dictionaries faded faster than the laundry of those unlucky housewives who used the wrong detergent.

A little common sense can save you the postage too. For example, don't enter any sweepstake if the prize doesn't interest you. If you had all the camping you ever want to experience in the army, and the prize offered is a fully-equipped camper, why bother? Substitution of prizes—cash for merchandise for example—is sometimes allowed, but read the rules carefully.

Also, since the chances of winning depend on the number of entries received, you do increase your chances by entering often. In fact, there are some people who have made entering sweepstakes a life-time hobby. They spend hundreds of dollars a year on stamps, labels and envelopes, along with the hours of time needed to fill in all those entries. What these people usually do is concentrate on the particular sweepstakes they want to win. This technique can pay off better in a local sweepstakes, however. Multiple entries have a greater impact there because the total number of entries is much smaller than in national ones. If you are conserving postage and energy, concentrate on local sweepstakes; entry blanks are often found in supermarkets.

THE NUMBERS RACKET

In most cities across the nation, millions of people wager their spare change in an illegal daily or weekly lottery called the *numbers*. The numbers game is also called *negro numbers* (because it is popular in black communities), *policy* (by law enforcement officials and journalists), *bolita* (a version played in Latin–American communities), *bug* (in the South), *wheel* (a special type played in some cities), or *Puerto Rican* (if based on the Puerto Rican National Lottery). Whatever the name, however, it is often followed by the term "racket," because the game supports a huge network of illegal operators who do not pay taxes on the bets they accept or on the profits made (this can be the most powerful weapon used against these illegal operators), and may resort to violence if the game (or their control of the game) is jeopardized. Adam Clayton Powell once estimated that bets in New York's Harlem alone totaled $50 million per year. A more recent—and probably conservative—estimate is that 15 million people play the numbers every day (except Sunday), wagering $6 billion a year.

What makes these numbers so staggering is that most players wager small amounts—dimes and quarters at a time. Of course, there are some players who are numbers addicts—those who not only wager daily, but have graduated from quarters to dollars.

The odds against the bettor winning the numbers are always large, and the payoffs are based on less than correct odds. Winning a three-digit numbers bet, for example, may pay off $500 for a $1 bet; but the odds against winning are 999 to 1. Nevertheless, players often prefer the numbers to some legal lotteries because they can choose the exact number their superstition tells them will *hit* (end up the winning number) and superstitions abound in numbers players.

Their resources include numerology, astrology, dream books, and plain old intuition.

PICKING NUMBERS

With odds of 999 to 1 against picking the winning number in a three-digit system, numbers devotees need all the help they can get to choose the lucky digital combination. Popular among numbers fans are dream books which give a numerical interpretation of one's dream. If, for example, a player dreams of a fish, the dream book may tell him that the number associated with fish is 213. The player assumes some mystical source is advising him to bet on 213—and he does.

Dream books are also used by the bank to anticipate heavily–bet numbers in light of some newsworthy event which the bank knows will influence its clientele. Lower than payoff odds are then offered on those numbers.

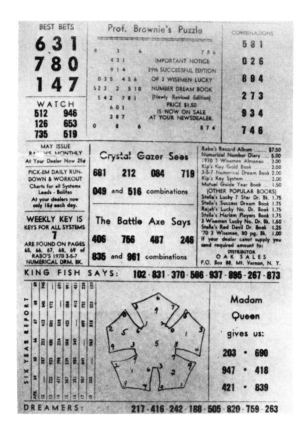

A typical numerology pamphlet and dream book used by players to pick winning numbers.

THE NUMBERS NETWORK

The numbers game is so large a network that it works like a private enterprise, with employees reporting to others higher up on the organizational chart. At the bottom of the chart would be the local numbers salesmen, called *agents, collectors, writers,* or *runners.* An agent is a small–time bookie who takes bets directly from the players.

Agents are ubiquitous in urban areas, frequenting newsstands, factories, office buildings, etc.; and they are usually people who have contact with the public, such as waiters, elevator operators, bartenders, vendors, etc. Some, called *route collectors,* will solicit bets at the players' homes. Agents are generally paid a percentage of the bets they collect,

The better the gambler, the worse the man.

(*Publilius Syrus*)

Aside from dream books and other numerology pamphlets which are sold at newsstands, players rely on intuition, hunches and fate to point out the lucky number—the license plate of a passing car, a significant street number, or any number which attracts their attention is the one to wager on that day. Palmists, astrologists, numerologists and psychic madames all do a healthy business imparting lucky numbers to gullible players—for a fee, of course.

In New York, some numbers fans consult Ching Chow, a one–panel comic strip in a local newspaper, for a tip to the winning number. They claim the comics' poses and actions are clues to the winning digit, which the fortunate eye—with a little help from a decoder pamphlet—may discern. The current artist/writer of Ching Chow had this to say in a newspaper article: "I do all the panels for a given week in one or two days. I don't consciously do anything connected with games of chance, yet I'm the source. It seems to me I ought to be getting a percentage."

and often they are given tips from bettors whose numbers have hit.

The agents bring the day's receipts to the organization's central office, called a *bank, clearinghouse,* or *countinghouse.* (In large operations, local agents bring receipts to—and report to—a *field man* or *controller,* who, in turn, brings the receipts to the bank.)

The bank is the heart of the operation, where all financial transactions are made.

Above the bank is the top management, the financial *backers* of the whole operation (frequently organized crime) who may or may not be involved in the day–to–day workings of the operation.

All gamblers [are] akin to thieves and robbers.

(*Aristotle*)

How the Bank Operates

Each bank employs hundreds of people and has access to a large amount of ready cash—as much as $500,000—to pay winners. It is run by a board of syndicate operators who seldom become involved in the complex, low-level machinations of the numbers game, and who often use their illegal profits to invest in legitimate businesses. Betting slips and cash reach the bank through a series of agents, who deliver the goods in secret containers such as baby carriages, hollowed-out auto steering wheels, even brassieres—in order to avoid police detection. The slips and cash are routed through *drops* (temporary receiving stations for money) to the office of a controller. The controller is a trusted employee who gets a commission or salary for collating agents' betting slips and delivering them and the cash, through other drops, to the bank itself—usually a heavily guarded private apartment. The controller also distributes winners' cash prizes to the agents when the number is announced. Drops, delivery methods and routes are changed regularly to circumvent police, who may also be on the bank's payroll for protection purposes. The banker's net profit is between 5 and 15 percent of the millions of dollars the numbers game pulls in every year. Anyone who poses a threat to the bank's security may be "eliminated" by racket hit men.

TYPICAL AVERAGE PROFIT

ASSUME $10,000 IN BETS DAILY AND AVERAGE PAYOFF AT 420-1. BASED ON CUT CARD.

GROSS WAGERING	$10,000
LESS AVERAGE PAYOFF	4,200
GROSS WAGERING PROFIT	$5,800
LESS 30% WRITERS' COMMISSIONS	3,000
* DAILY PROFIT	$2,800
DAYS IN WAGERING WEEK	X6
WEEKLY GROSS PROFIT	$16,800
LESS ESTIMATED FIXED EXPENSES (INCLUDING SALARIES, SUPPLIES, RENT TELEPHONE, PAYOFFS)	2,750
NET WEEKLY PROFIT	$14,050
DIVIDED BY GROSS WEEKLY WAGERING	$60,000

* PERCENTAGE OF PROFIT = 23.4%
* ANNUAL WAGERING = $3,120,000
* ANNUAL NET PROFIT = $730,000

723 NUMBERS CUT TO 399-1
112 NUMBERS CUT TO 299-1
165 NUMBERS REMAIN AT 599-1

AVERAGE LONG RUN PAYOFF AT 420-1
(NOT 600-1)

Some numbers operations may be so large that they have multiple banks. One New York City operation had, by conservative estimate, at least 10,000 employees on its payroll. Shown here is a numbers bank's typical daily and weekly average profit.

HOW NUMBERS ARE PLAYED

Players first select a number they want to bet on, then locate their local agent. A written record of the number and the bet is made (no names, please) and the bet collected.

Players usually bet on a three-digit number from 000 to 999. Players are betting that their numbers, in sequence, will match the winning number exactly. A bet on a single-digit number (called *single-action*), or a two-digit number (called a *bleeder*) may be allowed, but the payoffs are lower than payoffs on three-digit numbers.

Bets on all six possible combinations of a three-digit number, called *combination* or *boxed* bets, can be made, and those who do so are betting on six numbers instead of one. Any number that contains two digits that are the same is a *three-way combination* bet, because only three combinations can be made with it. Popular numbers, such as *777*, are not any more likely to win than others, but because they are played more frequently, they mean large losses to the bank if they hit. These numbers, called *cut numbers*, pay smaller payoffs, or the bank may even close the betting on them.

Numbers bets range anywhere from 1¢ to $10. Very small bets are discouraged (though many banks accept dime bets), and very large bets are uncommon. Players often bet on several different numbers at once, but the average player's daily bet usually remains under one dollar.

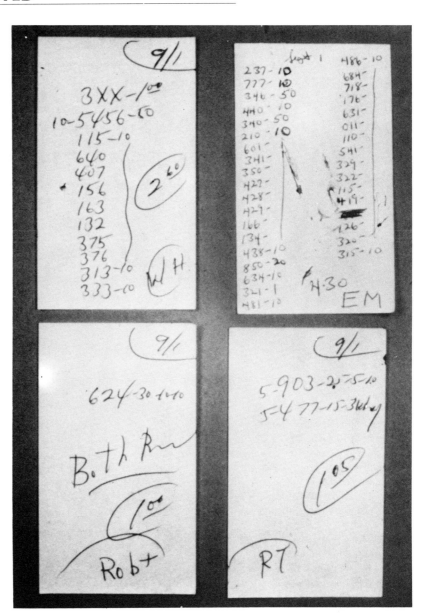

Typical betting slips, which the agents WH, EM, Robt, and RT delivered to the bank. There are several ways a bet can be written. Straight bets—which most of these are— include the number bet on and, to its right, the amount of the bet. Combination bets are written with the amount bet in a box, or with a small "c" next to the amount. Some agents record the amount of each permutation instead of the total wager. The longer line of figures on the above betting slips indicate various ways to record straight bets with a combination bet. The top bet on WH's slip is a single action bet on the number 3. It's a front action *bet because the bet is on the first digit, which is 3.*

CUT NUMBERS - 400 to 1
STARTING IMMEDIATELY

100	101	111	123	205	214	222
304	310	382	418	500	616	617	618
625	642	719	721	765	769	898

C - 125   C - 325   C - 974
No Claims After 72 Hours

Numbers play produces an unruly volume of paper that the bank holds onto for as long as a week in order to settle any claims made by bettors. Shown here is a part of that volume—a cut card which lists the cut numbers and odds (which have been lowered) for their payoff. An average numbers operation may cut as many as a third of the 1000 numbers to a half payoff, which can effectively increase the operation's gross profit margin 10 percent. The "C" means a combination bet on the numbers that follow.

Bolita

In bolita, winning numbers are drawn in what can seem to be a near-religious ritual. A group of men and women form a circle and pass around a sack or box of numbered balls. Each participates in the ritual by shaking the sack and one person is designated to choose the winning ball. Typically there are several witnesses to attest to the legitimacy of the drawing, but when the bank wants to make sure the winning number is a *cold* one (one on which few bets were placed) various methods may be used to that end. In Miami, for example, they reportedly use the *frozen ball trick:* a hollow ball is filled with water and then frozen. The person drawing the ball, who is in on the scheme, easily picks out a really cold number. Other organizations simply don't put any hot numbers into the sack to begin with.

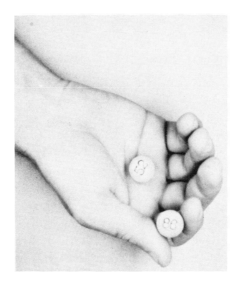

Bolita means "little ball," and that's exactly what's used in some forms of the racket to pick the winning numbers. Other versions of bolita are based on track results. Most bolita is a two-digit system, and its mispronunciation led to the term bleeder, *which is a two-digit numbers bet.*

Winning numbers are determined in different ways in different cities. Usually, an independent and well–publicized random number determines the winner. These come from the financial pages of the newspaper (a portion of the U.S. Treasury Balance for that day, or New York stocks and bonds sales for that day), or from the track (a portion of the *handle*—or total money bet—at a specific track for that day, or a digit from each of the total payoffs from certain predetermined races, such as the third, fifth, and seventh races at a specific track for that day). Sometimes a drawing is used, as in bolita, or a portion of a winning number in a legal lottery is used. In some cases, the bank itself proclaims the winning number—after making sure it won't lose too much on it.

In any event, the source for the winning number and the winning number spread through the city mainly by word of mouth. Payoffs vary, but are about 500 to 1 for a three-digit hit. Thus, if you wager a quarter on a three-digit number and it hits, you'll receive about $125, less the agent's bonus or tip. Single action bets pay-off about 7 or 8 to 1; two-digit hits pay off about 50 or 60 to 1.

Though the numbers racket is extremely profitable for the bank, it is not what you'd call a high-class way to wager, as the manner in which these winning New York-Brooklyn numbers are posted suggests.

SMALL–TIME SWINDLES

Chain letters and punchboards are the flimsiest of paper gambles. They've both been around for some time and, like numbers, are illegal. Most are small-time operations but some are large-scale hoaxes.

Chain Letters

Chain letters originated in medieval times when people formed good luck chains to ward off evil spirits. Modern recipients of chain letters are still almost always promised good luck—in the form of money—if they continue the chain, and threatened with bad luck if the chain is broken. People who don't even consider themselves superstitious may feel compelled to follow the instructions. It is doubtful, however, that it is fear of the bad luck as much as greed for the good luck that makes them responsive. But that is exactly what the originators of the chain count on.

In spite of the chain letter's illegality, almost everyone has gotten one at one time or another. Included along with the threatened curse and promised good fortune is a list of five names and addresses, and instructions on how to continue the chain. The

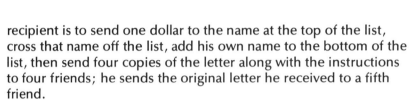

recipient is to send one dollar to the name at the top of the list, cross that name off the list, add his own name to the bottom of the list, then send four copies of the letter along with the instructions to four friends; he sends the original letter he received to a fifth friend.

Theoretically, each person on the list would eventually receive 3,125 letters, each with a dollar enclosed. But it never works that way because it is a fraud and a misrepresentation, and someone is pocketing that money. (Chances are that those first five names are all aliases of that same "someone.")

Some chain letters start out or are continued as a joke, or in the naive belief that everyone will profit from them. (Some don't involve money at all. But even when there is no fraud intended, it can still be misrepresentation and is still illegal. Most do, however, involve money and are started up by swindlers.)

If you ever receive a chain letter, do not pass it on. Send it to the Postal Inspector in charge of your area. (Look him up in the Yellow Pages, under U.S. Government listings.) If you add your name to the list and send it on, and another recipient reports the letter, you will probably receive a warning from the Postal Inspector as to its illegality. If fraud and misrepresentation are proven, it could mean a maximum fine of $1000 or five years imprisonment, or both.

Punchboards

The punchboard, or push card as it is often called, is simply two pieces of printed cardboard sandwiching a piece of paper with printed numbers (or sometimes names or symbols). Players pay to push out a perforated cardboard circle (or square), which then exposes the number beneath. After all the perforations have been pushed out—and paid for—the operator breaks the seal covering the winning number, and the player who punched out the matching number is the winner. Prizes can be money or merchandise.

The original punchboards were wooden, and made their debut in taverns back in the 1790s. Winning players were entitled to a free drink or a cash prize. Crooked operators put an end to their usage, but around 1870 they made their comeback in the present cardboard form. In 1910, with the first mass printing of the boards, punchboards began flooding the country. They reached their peak in 1939, when 50 million of them were in circulation—with an estimated potential revenue of $700 million. Their popularity declined again, due to the ease with which they could be fixed, and by the 1950s most states began enforcing the laws outlawing them.

On an honest board, no player's chances of winning on a single punch were better than anyone else's chances on a single punch. The payout was usually 40 percent. So if a board had 1000 punches costing one dollar each, for example, the total handle would be $1,000. Prizes would usually amount to no more than $400, and the operator got to pocket the remaining $600. However, nothing is easier to fix than a cardboard punchboard, which is one reason for its demise. Crooked operators knew the winning number and its location on the board. (Manufacturers even published catalogues of punchboards sold complete with the winning key.) The operator either punched out the winning number beforehand—creating a "bare" board where, the players had no chance of winning—or, a confederate punched out the winning number for him.

The ease with which the punchboards could be fixed also encouraged their control by small–time mobs. These racketeers wished to assure the punchboards' usage in certain establishments, collect the proceeds, and make sure there were no competing boards around. Their employees "enforced" these wishes.

Today the pickings are far too small to interest many criminal elements. You'll still see a punchboard occasionally behind the counter in some candy store, bar, or restaurant, but the merchandise prizes usually range from a roll of mints to a camera. Those who still play them do so for amusement only. The most valuable punchboards are the artistically printed ones found in antique shops.

Arthur Flegenheimer (a.k.a. Dutch Schultz) became the leader of the numbers racket in Harlem during the 1930s. A beer baron by trade, Dutch became restless and searched for bigger and better things. He soon muscled his way into the numbers racket, and was responsible for introducing a new twist: using the pari–mutuel handle at a racetrack to determine the winning number. (Up to that time, the daily U.S. Treasury balance provided the winning numbers.) What numbers players didn't realize was that Schultz owned the racetrack in question, and so had the power to manipulate the winning numbers.

Madame Queen

Always accompanied by her faithful bodyguards, Stephanie St. Claire (known as Madame Queen) was a well–protected numbers racket figure in Harlem. She alone was able to resist Dutch Schultz when he took over the Italian segment of the numbers racket. She had such a strong system of employees under her that she was never in any real danger of arrest. Only the guys at the bottom—the agents—weren't safe.

This typical 25¢ punchboard takes in $75 and pays out $60, for a profit of $15 to the operator.

PLAYING THE STOCK MARKET

The investor's nest egg.

People invest in stocks, real estate, collectables (such as stamps, art, etc.), gold, commodities, cattle ranches, broadway shows, and the like for the same purpose: they are hoping that the value of what they bought (as measured by its initial cost)—their investment—will increase. The stock market will be described in this chapter to illustrate how investments work in general. This is not meant to make you an authority. Stocks, like all investments, involve risks and are complicated. If you decide this is the kind of gamble you like, arm yourself with in-depth information. Know what you are buying, your reasons for doing so, and understand fully what the investment will mean for you—before you hand over your money.

HOW THE STOCK MARKET WORKS

Playing the stock market is not a game but, nonetheless, "players" (or investors) risk money in order to make money by increasing the value of their initial investment. The stock market's primary function is to raise capital for corporations, not to help investors get rich. And investors risk their money. However, with a lot of skill and luck, investors can come out ahead. The skill is in deciding which corporations to put your money into. Since the price of stock is based on a corporation's earnings, and especially its potential for future earnings, the element of luck enters the picture.

There are many different kinds of stock that investors can buy, and the risks vary too. But the basic idea is explained as follows.

Businesses often need more capital than they have available to establish themselves, or to expand. One way to get this capital is to sell a share of the business to people who are willing to buy it. People who buy shares of stock buy a part of the business, and the business gets to use the buyers' money. The price of the stock is an investment, because buyers are hoping that the future earnings of the business will increase, that the business will be worth more and, therefore, the value of their stocks will increase. But, there are no guarantees.

If a corporation's earnings do increase, the profits may be put back into the corporation for improvements, or expansion. Or, the corporation may share its increased earnings with its stockholders by giving them cash dividends.

When an investor wants to buy a share of stock, there must be someone willing to sell that share. When someone wants to sell a share of stock, there must be someone willing to buy it. Thus the buying and selling prices fluctuate, and are governed by the law of supply and demand. The buying and selling of stock is not done directly through the corporation, but through security or stock *brokers* (who work for brokerage firms) who negotiate an acceptable price between the buyer and seller, and receive a commission for this service. The collective average price of stocks is referred to as "the market," as in, "How's the market doing?" And there are several different kinds of averages, the Dow Jones average being the best-known.

Buying shares in a well-established corportion that has substantial assets (known as *blue chip* stock), means that one is almost always assured of a seller when one is ready to buy—or a buyer when one is ready to sell. It also means that you are assured of getting dividends, and that there is a greater chance for an increase in the price per share. Though the initial invest-

ment—the buying price per share—is high, there is less risk for the investor who buys this stock. People who buy blue chip stocks are playing it safe.

Investors who like to play more dangerously invest their money in new and innovative businesses—those whose financial growth is less certain. The initial investment per share is lower, but the risks are greater. Even the careful investors will now and then, however, risk some money in one of these more speculative stocks.

More than 26 million people play the stock market by buying and selling shares of stock. But add another 75 million to that figure for those who invest in the stock market without ever personally buying or selling a share, or even realizing their money is doing so. Savings banks and pension funds, for example, use their investors' money to, in turn, invest in the stock market.

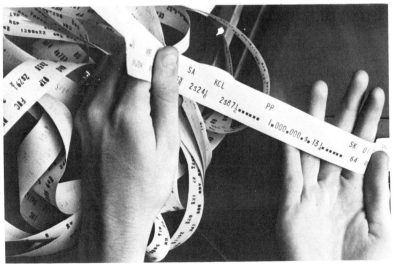

(UPI.)

Market Mystics

Are annual reports, stock–price charts, and sophisticated investment analyses a mystery to you? Well, you ain't seen nothin' yet. Here are some *real* stock market mysteries:

• Now a spry octogenarian, one ESP-guided investor began his career in the 1950s by investing $3,000. His first purchase/sale doubled his money; the second sextupled it. This type of lucky nonsense went on and on: he's now worth about $900,000. He attributes his success to the way his mind acts as a receiving station for all the thoughts floating around the stock market. This way, he claims, he can "see" the market's short-term future.

• A fifty–ish New Jerseyite has "visions" that tell her whether a stock's price is going to rise or fall. She has made accurate predictions about United Fruit, Telex (which went from $130 a share in 1968 to around $6 in 1973), Cox Cable Communications, and A & P, among others. Says one successful stock trader who follows such occult advice: "It sounds strange, but what else can I tell you?"

• One astrologer periodically makes market forecasts in her syndicated newspaper column—and is still in business. What's more, she takes her own advice when investing. Her most spectacular prediction was of the second worst crash in the history of Wall Street (when the Dow plummeted 300 points between 1969 and 1970); there have been other, lesser forecasts that add up to thousands and thousands of dollars.

A HISTORY OF THE U.S. STOCK MARKET

Today's stock market investor has a wide variety of stocks, and kinds of stocks, to buy. That's a far cry from the choice that the first U.S. Stock Exchange offered in Philadelphia in 1790. Then, investors had the exciting choice of buying either the first issue of U.S. Government bonds, or a few newly-issued U.S. bank securities. But it wasn't long before there were enough securities around to stir up competitive trading.

In 1792, 24 New York stock brokers met under a tree in Wall Street to set down some rules. They promised, for instance to charge no less than ¼ percent commission on all transactions. Thus was born the New York Stock Exchange—and brokers' fixed commissions. Some of the new stocks traded on the fledgling exchange were issued by companies that had formerly relied on lotteries for their financing. And many former lottery ticket agents switched from selling lottery chances to buying and selling shares of stock.

The risks of playing the stock market increased dramatically throughout the nineteenth century. Gold rushes, Confederate bonds, the industrial boom, and the race to build railroads created a turbulent and even violent market for stocks, as well as creating legends out of the men who won and lost huge fortunes.

After World War I, the little guy decided it was his turn to share in the spoils of capitalism. Millions of small investors entered the market, buying stocks on *margin* (credit). Banks and brokers were happy to overextend credit, and stock manipulators—from board directors to small-time swindlers—were delighted with the easy pickings.

PSST MISTER, WANNA BUY AN OIL WELL? AND OTHER SWINDLES

Despite the ever–watchful Securities and Exchange Commission, stock swindlers are still with us. And, it seems, the crazier the bait the more suckers there are who will bite. In 1957, a California promoter bamboozled $200,000 out of investors who bought his idea of a wingless airplane capable of carrying 4,000 people nonstop for 25,000 miles. The all–time favorite stock fraud, though, is the legendary oil well, located anywhere from Texas to a mythical Greek island. For a while after the ballyhoo over nuclear energy, phony uranium claims out-

The Crash of 1929 cast a gloom over the joys of playing the market from which the stock market has never completely recovered. And no wonder. The Crash ruined one out of every 20 families who had invested their life savings in the stock market.

Confidence in the market had largely been restored by the 1960s, chiefly through the efforts of the watchdog Securities Exchange Commission which, since 1934, has kept a tight leash on any wayward stock deals. The business boom of the 1960s also attracted millions of new small investors. Between 1970 and 1975, however, five million skittish investors opted out of the market.

Today's market is still a risky game, even for the cautious investor. But risk is the name of the game for those who like to play.

Witch Stock?

It seems there's a witches' coven on Manhattan's Upper East Side that operates an occult investment club. The high priestess, a mild–mannered bank employee by day, says they actually use their powers to influence the stock market. They buy stock with pooled money, and then "concentrate very hard," on forcing others to buy the stock, which in turn raises the price. Lest you rupture yourself laughing too hard, get a load of their record: two successes out of every three attempts.

"If you bet on a horse, that's gambling. If you bet you can make three spades, that's entertainment. If you bet cotton will go up three points, that's business. Get the difference?"

(*Blackie Sherwood, journalist*)

I never was much of a gambler, except in the stock market, where I get wiped out regularly.

(*Groucho Marx*)

numbered phony oil wells. But with the worldwide oil shortage, oil swindles have come back into their own.

One U.S. promoter successfully marketed shares in a "magnetic logger"—a device which he claimed could not only locate oil fields, but could also tell the precise depth of the oil and the exact number of bar-rels the well would yield.

Two Texas promoters gave the oil well swindle a religious rebirth by sending out a prospectus with an evangelical appeal, thanking Divine Guidance for leading them to the joyful oil flowing from the earth's bounty. Their collection plate brought in $1 million.

TICKER TIPS

There's no doubt that playing the stock market is risky and unpredictable. The only tip any investor, large or small, can trust is: deal with a reputable broker whom you trust. Bear in mind, however, that brokers can only recommend stocks and make buying and selling suggestions. The ultimate decision is up to the investor. And an investor should not let a broker make decisions for him. As we said initially, know what you are investing in, why you are doing it, and what the investment will mean for you. Using a broker to advise you is, however, wise, as following and interpreting business and stock market trends is his business. (Some brokers advise and buy and sell. Others only buy and sell, and their services cost less.)

Along with the advice of a broker, there are also hundreds of how-to-invest books, as well as financial newsletters and magazines. Some of the basic do's and don'ts these experts advise include the following (they adapt themselves well to any kind of investment):

• Do place a dollar limit on your investments and have patience. Some investments are only profitable long-term, and you must be able to afford to live without that money for the long term.

• Don't overextend yourself by buying too much stock on *margin* (credit).

• Do be leery of hot tips. You'll probably get burned.

• Do play it safe. Buy blue chip stocks to start, then use your dividends to buy riskier stocks.

• Do buy different stocks covering different areas of investment. If industrials sink, you'll still have your mines and oils to buoy you up.

The end of a day of heavy trading on the New York Stock Exchange. (UPI.)

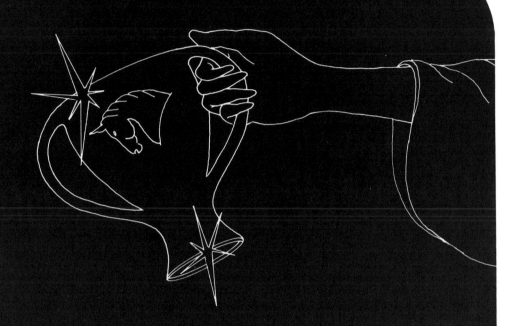

HORSE RACING— A RUN FOR YOUR MONEY

NOT FOR KINGS ONLY

Why do people bet the horse races? Why do people risk their hard–earned money in the pursuit of an improbable dream? How can the most rational creature on earth expect to analyze successfully the hundreds of factors that determine the winner, especially when the most important factor—the attitude of the horse—is unavailable? Computers have tried and failed. Yet people continue to try in ever–increasing numbers, risking ever–increasing amounts of money.

Horse racing and gambling have always been inseparable. No fan ever rooted for a horse simply because of team spirit. It is the wager in horse racing that is the adrenalin for the sporting heart. A racetrack is not a baseball stadium: at the track it's every man for himself, and greed is the prime mover.

Then there's the excitement—from start to finish, one horse race provides enough emotional stimulation in two minutes to last all day . . . or at least until the next race. First, you feel the anxiety of anticipation before the start. This is followed by the heart–stopping moment when you wait to learn if your choice dashed away from the starting gate without stumbling. Then, there may be the joy of watching a brilliant performance or the agonizing disappointment of witnessing a poor one. There is the

My First Bet

In a few moments the horses went to the post and were off! They all looked alike to me, colors, jockeys, and horses. I saw one mass of horseflesh over on the back stretch. In a moment or two they were at the quarter–stretch pole, and then, in a few seconds, they were rounding into the stretch. I still couldn't distinguish my horse from any of the rest, but about the time they reached the paddock gate I noticed the colors of the horse that I had bet on and saw that it was in front by about a length.

From the time I distinguished my horse until the finish I was like a crazy man. I stood on my chair and shouted, "Come on, come on!" I snapped my fingers, when the finish came I would have sworn my horse won by six or eight lengths, when as a matter of fact he only won by a nose.

(From Easy Money *by Harry Browlaski, Searchlight Press, 1911)*

(Courtesy of Sportsman's Park.)

Portraits at the horse race.

self–satisfaction derived from pre-dicting a profitable outcome, or self–flagellation at having lost, per-haps because an important indicator was overlooked.

All of these feelings are accom-panied by a quickening pulse, and a final explosion of relief and satisfac-tion as your choice crosses the finish line first; or dejection if your selec-tion finishes out of the money. In short, horse racing makes the juices flow.

To be a successful horse race bet-tor you must be knowledgeable. So before you rush off to the track, re-member the words of a man who had owned, raced, and bet horses his entire life: ". . . placing a bet requires a keen eye, an unfailing memory, an analytical mind, a steady nerve, a big ego, a little luck, and two dollars." You must supply the nerve, the ego, and the two dol-lars. What follows will help you de-velop the rest.

THOROUGHBRED, HARNESS, AND QUARTER HORSE RACING

A Short History of Thoroughbred Racing

Horse racing has been around a long, long time: Roman sportsmen stood in the Coliseum and cheered as Ben Hur whipped home a winner. But it was not until much later that Henry VIII put down his chicken leg and took time out from getting married in order to build a racetrack. It was not a Coliseum-like stadium that Henry built at Doncaster in 1595, but a simple track where members of the royal court raced their horses by jumping over hedges and streams, making sharp turns and stops, and doing all those things intended to separate rider from horse. This was steeplechasing. It is doubtful that Henry himself rode, so nothing changed until Charles II came to the throne. Charles did ride, and perhaps in regard to his royal personage he did not jump over anything and stuck to "flat" racing. It wasn't until late in the 1700s, during the reign of George I, that a public record of horses' births was kept. This record became known as the stud book, and with it came the recognition of the thoroughbred as a breed.

Most of the early races were simple one-against-one matches . . . "My horse can beat your horse . . ." The owners put up the stakes and the winner took all. There are five classic thoroughbred races run in England today (see boxed material) but the Derby at Epsom Downs is still universally regarded as the greatest horse race of all.

There are three basic forms of horse racing. In thoroughbred racing, a rider sits on a horse and races around a closed track. In harness racing, the rider sits on a cart and is pulled around a closed track. In quarter horse racing, the rider sits on the horse and runs in a short, straight line.

All three styles are popular, and each has its own following. Geographically, we find thoroughbred tracks across the country, harness tracks mostly in the Northeast, and quarter horse tracks in the West and Southwest. Horse racing in general is a daytime sport, but in recent years nighttime racing, especially at harness tracks, has become quite popular. Harness and quarter horse racing is also part of the scene at hundreds of rural fairgrounds.

Horse racing is no longer a seasonal sport, and many cities now have one or more tracks open year-round, so the racing fans have a choice of where to go. The reasons for choosing one type of track over another are diverse: "I can only go at night"; or, "I can't handicap the flats"; or, "I like to see the thoroughbred champs in action—they're poetry in motion"; or, "My brother-in-law knows a quarter horse owner, and I get great inside tips."

What style of race is the most stimulating, or the most rewarding, to watch or to bet is a personal decision. Try them all, to find out which is your favorite.

Thoroughbred racing takes place on a flat, closed track over distances that vary from three-eighths of a mile to two-and-one-quarter miles. Unlike their English cousins, the steeplechasers, the United States thoroughbreds do not jump over hurdles. Therefore, American thoroughbred racing is often referred to as the "flats."

The term "thoroughbred" refers to a breed of horse that is raised for beauty and speed over long distances in a gallop. In order to register a thoroughbred horse in the stud book, which is a "who's who" of thoroughbreds, the owner must

THE FIVE CLASSIC ENGLISH THOROUGHBRED RACES

The race and its origin	The horse
St. Leger	3-year-old males
Began in 1776 at Doncaster	
Oaks	Fillies
Began in 1779 at Epsom Downs	
Derby	3-year-old males
Began in 1780 at Epsom Downs	
Gold Cup	Any age males
Began in 1807 at Ascot	
Guineas	3-year-old males
Began in 1809 at Newmarket	

Nighttime harness racing. (Courtesy of Sportsman's Park.)

This triple dead heat is indicative of the speed of the quarter horse race. (American Quarter Horse Association.)

know the lineage of the animal. Every thoroughbred in this country can trace its ancestry to one of three Arabian stallions listed in the 1793 stud book.

Harness racing takes place on a flat, closed track, with the most common distance being one mile. The horses bred specifically for this kind of running share a common ancestry with the thoroughbred, but are of a distinct breed called *standardbred*.

These horses will pull a two-wheeled vehicle not unlike a rickshaw, called a *sulky* or *bike*. The standardbred harness racehorse is trained to move his legs in two distinctly different ways. These two gaits are called *pacing* and *trotting*, and, although they are almost indistinguishable to the average bettor, they each require considerable training. A harness race is run for either trotters or pacers only.

Quarter horse racing is a style of racing that may be likened to the sprint events in track and field. The quarter horse is bred to run fast over short distances (usually a quarter of a mile) in a straight line. The sport originated in the South, but has flourished in the Southwest as well, and is a part of many county fairs. Its popularity continues to grow throughout the United States.

Thoroughbred Racing in the U.S.

It was Charles II of England who was responsible for building the first racetrack in the colonies. Following his orders, the English forces that liberated New Netherlands from the Dutch in 1664 established a racecourse on Long Island called Newmarket. Here, the English liberators and the liberated Dutch could watch the match races with a florin or sovereign occasionally changing hands. As the English army moved about and new settlers arrived, other racecourses were built in New Jersey, Pennsylvania, Virginia and the Carolinas.

Thoroughbred racing reacted to the growth of America much like any other business. Tracks were built; some flourished, some died. Newmarket course is no more. Gone also are Jerome Park, site of the first Belmont Stakes, and Union Course. In their places are the famous names of Belmont, Hialeah, Pimlico, Churchill Downs and Saratoga.

TYPES OF RACES

The Kentucky Derby

A confrontation of champions is
the premier attraction in every
sport. In baseball, the two best
teams meet in the World Series;
in football, it's the Super Bowl.
In horse racing, when the best
meet in a stakes race with the
winner taking home a lot of
money, there is drama to whet
the betting appetite.

The Kentucky Derby (run the
first Saturday of every May) is
considered the premier rac-
ing/social event in America. For
one week, the cream of
horse–owning society
congregates in Louisville to bask
in an atmosphere of old
Southern hospitality, soft
conversation and mint juleps,
while the best three-year-old
thoroughbreds in this country
compete for a place in racing
history. There may be other
famous and even richer stakes
races, such as the Belmont
Stakes, Preakness, the
Hambletonian for harness
horses, and the American
Futurity for quarter horses (the
world's richest race), but none
can compare to the splendor of
Derby Day. To win the Derby is
to be anointed; to be crowned
king of the sport of kings. And to
be there and see it happen is a
reflected glory that can be told
and retold forever.

In all three styles, horse races may
be classified as either *claiming* races
or *non-claiming* races.

Claiming races were started when
horse and track owners found that
the most successful way to ensure
large fields (many starters), close
competition, and more wagering
was to have the owners classify their
own horses and sell the winner at a
pre–set price. These "selling races"
became today's *claiming races*. In
order to *claim* (buy) the winner in a
claiming race an individual must
meet the specific requirements set
by the various state racing associa-

tions. A standard requirement is that
you must own a horse running at the
same track.

If a horse wins in a $5,000 claiming
race and is claimed (bought), the
new owner will usually enter the
horse in a higher–priced claiming
race (if he doesn't mind the risk of its
being claimed). This tends to equalize the competition and gives the
owners the opportunity to buy and
sell proven horses. Claiming prices
(*tags*) vary from $1,500 on up. Stymie
was claimed for a mere $1,500 and
went on to win over $900,000. When
an owner feels a horse is ready to
move up, he may then enter it in an
allowance race.

Allowance races, which are non-
claiming races, are for horses that
meet certain criteria regarding previous winning records, amounts of
money won over a specified time, or
other factors, including age and sex.
A horse must show promise (and be
too good to risk losing in a claimer)
to be entered in an allowance race.
When a horse running in allowance
races is ready to move up, it is entered in a stakes race (which is also a
non-claiming race).

MINT JULEP

Put 1½ teaspoons of confectioners' sugar, about 5 fresh mint leaves and a little cold water in a tall glass. With the back of a spoon crush the mint leaves against the side of the glass. Make sure all the sugar dissolves. Fill the glass about ¾'s full with shaved ice, packing it down. Pour in 4 ounces of bourbon and mix. Place in the freezer for about 20 minutes or until frosted and the liquid almost solidified. Garnish with lemon slices and 2 or 3 sprigs of mint which have been dipped in water and then sugar. Add a drop of brandy. Serves one.

Cheers!

Not all the smiling faces you see at the Kentucky Derby belong to winners. And a reason for those smiles is the 50,000 mint juleps that are sold at Churchill Downs on Derby day. Of course, you don't need to be in Kentucky to enjoy the traditional mint julep. So, try this recipe. Here's mud in your eye!

Races such as the Kentucky Derby, the Belmont and the English Gold Cup are all *stakes races* in which only the best compete. The owners put up an entrance fee, and sometimes the track contributes money to enrich the pot, which brings in more horses. (This is called *added money*.) The winner of the race gets most of the money, second and third finishers get proportionately less. Sometimes the fourth, fifth, and sixth horses over the finish line also share in the winnings.

Other non-claiming races include match races and handicap races.

Match races are head–to–head confrontations, usually between two champions. The race is for a large cash prize and to settle, once and for all, which horse is the fastest—at least in that race.

Handicap races are run by horses to whom weight is assigned, based on the racing secretary's judgment of each horses's ability, based on past performance. The better chance a horse has to win, the more weight it will be assigned. (The weight is over and above the weight of the jockey and is carried in the form of lead weights in the saddle . . . hence, the call for speed, "Get the lead out!!!") The purpose of handicapping is to equalize the competition.

Maiden races which may be claiming or non-claiming races, conjure up a picture of shy horses, coyly tiptoeing past the grandstand, but this is not accurate. A *maiden race* is simply for horses who have never won a race.

Short and Sweet

Today, the mass media make superstardom an easier height to attain, even for short people. Steve Cauthen is a case in point. He won the Triple Crown aboard Affirmed on his very first try. During 1977 he rode six winners in one day—three times! At the age of 18, Cauthen was already more famous than Tod Sloan, Isaac Murphy and Jimmy McLaughlin all rolled into one.*

*Turn to page 187 if you don't know who these men are.

Steve Cauthen.

THOROUGHBRED RACEHORSE HALL OF FAME

Thoroughbreds are best known for their earnings—the purses they've won. Here are a few famous names and what their bankbooks look like:

Horse	Years raced	Amount won
Kelso	8	$1,977,000
Forego	6	1,938,900
Round Table	4	1,749,000
Dahlia	5	1,500,000
Secretariat	2	1,316,000
Nashua	3	1,288,000
Damascus	3	1,176,000
Citation	5	1,085,000
Whirlaway	4	561,000
Seabiscuit	6	437,000
Man O'War	2	249,000

Kelso went to the post 63 times. He finished first 39 times, second 12 times and third two times.

Man O'War was such a favorite with the bettors—he only lost one race in his career to a horse named Upset—that on more than one occasion it was necessary to bet a dollar on him to win a penny.

The most money won in any one year was $860,000, by Secretariat in 1973—a year in which Secretariat tied the Aqueduct 1-mile record in the Gotham, broke the 1½-mile record in the Belmont Stakes, broke the 1¼-mile record in the Kentucky Derby, and broke Belmont's 1½-mile grass-course record.

Man O'War.

Jockey Eddie Arcaro on Citation.

HARNESS RACEHORSE HALL OF FAME

For some reason, harness horses seem to engender more human interest than their aristocratic thoroughbred cousins. Whereas money is the root of thoroughbred fame, other, pithier factors contribute to the renown of the cart-pullers. Take, for instance, Dan Patch, the "Man O'War of harness racing." He was never defeated, and held nine world speed records. The human factor was the attachment Dan had for his owner, a Mr. M. W. Savage. Both horse and owner had heart attacks on the same day and died within 24 hours of each other.

Goldsmith Maid, the *grand dame* of harness racing, spent the first eight years of her life pulling a cart on a farm. Someone bought her for about $350 and started her racing. She ran her fastest race when she was 19 years old, earned over $364,000, and died at the age of 28. Greyhound's claim to fame is his exceptional winning percentage: he came in first 71 times in 82 starts. Then there's Hambletonian, the "father" of the breed. Almost every trotting horse today can be traced back to this lover, who sired 1,331 foals from 1851 to 1875.

This is not to say that harness horses don't earn big money too. The leading trotter was Fresh Yankee who earned $1,294,000 in eight years. The leading pacer was Albatross who earned $1,200,000 in only three years.

Standardbred Triple Crowns

The Triple Crown of trotters—The Hambletonian, Kentucky Futurity and Yonkers Futurity—has been won by Speedy Scott (1963), Ayres (1964), Nevele Pride (1968) and Lindy's Pride (1969). For pacers, winners of Little Brown Jug, Messenger Stakes and Cane Futurity have been Adios Butler (1959), Bret Hanover (1965), Romeo Hanover (1966), Rum Customer (1968) and Most Happy Fella (1970).

Greyhound. (United States Trotting Association.)

Albatross.
(United States Trotting Association.)

INAUGURAL SPRING RUNNING MEETING OF THE
Saint Louis Jockey and Trotting Club
Commencing June 4th, 1878; Continuing Five Days.

PROGRAMME.

STAKES AND PURSES.

FIRST DAY.
TUESDAY, JUNE 4, 1878.

FIRST RACE. Hurdle Race, mile heats, over four hurdles. Purse, $250, first horse to receive $200, second $50.

SECOND RACE. "Ladies Stakes," for two-year-old fillies, three-quarters of a mile, $50 entrance, half forfeit, $500, added, of which second to receive $100, third to save stake. Closed with thirty nominations.

THIRD RACE. January Stakes, for three-year-olds, mile heats, $50 entrance half forfeit; $500 added of which second receives $200, third to save stake. Closed with thirty five nominations

SECOND DAY.
WEDNESDAY, JUNE 5, 1878.

FIRST RACE. Groeley Stakes, for all ages, three mile dash, $50 entrance, half forfeit; $500 added, of which second to receive $100, third to save stake. Closed with twenty two nominations.

SECOND RACE. Planters' House Stakes for two-year-old colts, three-quarters of a mile, $50 entrance, half forfeit, $500 added, of which second to receive $100 third to save stake. Closed with thirty one nominations.

THIRD RACE. One mile and three-quarters, for all ages; Club Purse $350, first $250, second $100.

THIRD DAY.
THURSDAY, JUNE 6, 1878.

FIRST RACE. Garneau Cup, value $500 in plate or money, for all ages, mile heats, $50 entrance, half forfeit, second to receive $100 out of stakes, third to save stake. Closed with thirty four nominations.

SECOND RACE. Merchants' Stakes, for three-year olds, mile heats, $50 entrance, half forfeit; $600 added, second to receive $200 out of stakes, third to save stakes; winner of January Stakes to carry 5 lbs. extra. Closed with thirty seven nominations.

THIRD RACE. Two miles, for all ages; Club purse $300, first $200, second $100.

FOURTH DAY.
FRIDAY, JUNE 7, 1878.

FIRST RACE. Lindell Hotel Post Stakes, two mile heats, for all ages, $100 entrance, play or pay; $1000 added, of which second horse to get $200, third to save stake. Closed with eleven subscribers.

SECOND RACE. Mile beats, a handicap for all ages; Club purse $350, first $250, second $50; entries to be made the day before at 12 M., weights to appear at 2 P. M., acceptances to be made through the entry box at the usual time of closing.

THIRD RACE. Mile heats, three in five, for all ages; Club Purse, $500, first $400, second $150.

FIFTH DAY.
SATURDAY, JUNE 8, 1878.

FIRST RACE. Lucas and Hunt Stakes, for two-year-old colts and fillies, one mile dash, $50 entrance, half forfeit; $500 added, of which second to receive $100, third to save stake; winner of the Ladies and Planters House stakes to carry 5 lbs. extra. Closed with thirty seven nominations.

SECOND RACE. Blow Stakes, for all ages, three mile heats; $50 entrance, play or pay; $1000 added, second to receive $200 out of stakes, third to save stake. Closed with eighteen nominations.

THIRD RACE. Consolation purse, for horses that have run and not won during the meeting, if beaten once allowed 5 lbs., if beaten twice, 10 lbs., and if beaten three times and over, 15 lbs.; purse $250, first $200, second $50, one mile and a quarter.

☞The above Stakes Closed February 1st, 1878. ☜ ☞All the distinguished Horses of the South and West are Entered.☜

Ten Broeck, Aristides, Chesapeake, St. Martin, Whisper, Chiquita, Cape Race Largenteen, Vera Cruz, McWhirter, King Faro, King William, Mahlstick Ella Rowett, Incommode, Lizzie Whipps, Bill Bass, Charlie Gorham, Pat K., Himyar, Milan, Pomeroy, Blue Eyes, Kate Claxton, &c., &c., &c.

STAKES, ADDED MONEY AND PURSES
21,450.00 DOLLARS.

J. L. PATTERSON, SECRETARY.

J. L. JANUARY, PRESIDENT.

"A BALK" ON A SWEEPSTAKE.

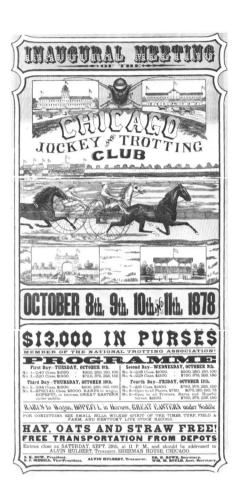

AT THE TRACK

High-Priced Trivia

Some of the following tidbits of information are meant to be memorized and then casually dropped at the track in the form of ". . . Did you know. . . ?" They are bound to increase your stature among your more knowledgeable sporting friends. They could also spur you on to bigger and better betting habits.

• What was the record payoff on a $2 win ticket? $1,883.50 at Latonia, Kentucky, in 1912. The odds were over 900 to 1.

• The record payoff on a $2 Quinella was $3,100.75. The odds? Over 1500 to 1.

• The daily double has always been a longshot. At Detroit Race Course, in 1973, a couple of surprises won the first and second races. Two lucky holders of $2 tickets each took home $19,909.60. These odds were almost 10,000 to 1.

• The world's record payoff on a daily double ticket was back in 1948. A £1 ticket on the daily double cost $2.50. The first horse paid 40 to 1 and was coupled with a 55 to 1 winner in the second race. The one and only winner collected $25,310. (There is no mention of the bookie who sold this ticket and what happened thereafter.)

Your first trip to a racetrack can be exciting and—best of all—rewarding. Or it can be confusing and expensive. When you get there, don't let the other bettors intimidate you. They have not stepped out of the pages of Damon Runyon, and do not necessarily know more about what's happening than you do. A large part of how you feel depends on your preparation, since going to the track to win does require some work.

Make sure you purchase a racing form early in the day or the night before. It's like getting a scorecard ahead of time. (You'll learn how to read this technical document soon.) Having a friend who has some knowledge of betting is a great help. He'll probably be delighted to go with you and show off his expertise in what seems to be a complex subject.

On your way into the track, be sure to buy the track's official program, which tells you the type of race, and the horses running, for each race. Other information in the program includes any last minute changes in the races as well as handy bits of information about the track itself.

Try to arrive early, to give yourself a chance to get the feel of the place, and to find out where everything is. When the time comes to make your moves, you won't have to ask for directions. Asking where the two-dollar betting window is will get you the same response as turning to your neighbor at a football game and asking, "Who's playing?"

The track's official program contains general information about the track itself, as well as information on the races for that day, including the morning line, the horses that have been scratched, and the new numbers that have been assigned to those that remain. It is not as complete a source of handicapping information as the Daily Racing Form. (Courtesy of The New York Racing Association Inc.)

Check out the betting windows. There are several windows for each different type or amount of bet. Each time the man behind the betting window punches out a ticket, the bet is automatically recorded. The total amount bet on any one horse to *win* (first horse over the finish line), *place* (first or second horse over the finish line) or *show* (first, second or third horse over the finish line) determines the odds and is flashed along with other pertinent information over the totalizator board (referred to as the *tote board*). The tote board is located in the infield area within the racing oval, but all tote board information is displayed on flashboards by the betting windows too. If you choose to do so, you can also stay by the betting windows to view the race. Everything going on outside is inside—on closed circuit TV. The betting windows and the tote board are the two most important locations at the track.

For personal viewing of the race, decide where you wish to sit or stand at the track. Most seating and standing room is along the home-stretch, and along the turns at either end of the homestretch. You may choose the grandstand, which entitles you to stand near the rail, or sit in a bleacher seat. When you get up to place a bet at the betting window, reserve your seat by placing a piece of paper on it. Food in the grand-stand area is typical ballpark: hot dogs, hamburgers, french fries, soda and beer.

More luxurious accommodations may be had in the clubhouse, which

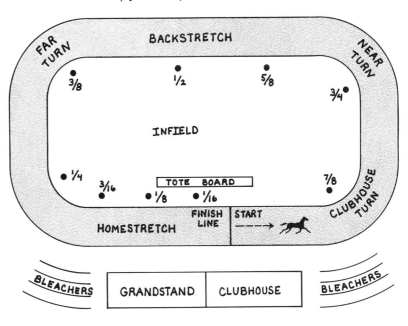

A Typical (Mythical) One Mile Track

7/8 POLE... POINT AT WHICH YOUR HORSE IS LEADING.
BACKSTRETCH... THEY ALL LOOK ALIKE FROM THIS DISTANCE.
FAR TURN... BAD ANGLE FOR JUDGING WHO'S IN FRONT.
3/16 POLE... POINT AT WHICH YOU BEGIN TO HAVE DOUBTS.
1/16 POLE... POINT AT WHICH BREEDING SHOWS (THE HORSES', NOT YOURS.)
FINISH LINE... POINT AT WHICH YOUR DOUBTS ARE REALIZED.
TOTE BOARD... DOCUMENTED PROOF THAT HANDICAPPING IS NOT A SCIENCE.

Points to focus on during a race, here on a one mile track. Pole positions vary according to each track's circumference. Similarly, the starting gate positions vary according to the length of each race.

usually means a reserved seat in an enclosed structure. The lines here are shorter, the food better and the price of admission higher. You can even dine at the clubhouse and see the races from your table. The betting windows are just a few convenient steps away, although a fistful of losing tickets makes the prime rib difficult to digest.

Of course, knowing where to view the race and place your bet is only a part of the picture. Deciding who to bet on is the next important step to take.

SOME BIG RACES

Seekers of high drama in thoroughbred racing can satisfy their appetites for thrills by traveling from track to track to be on hand for the high-stakes races, where the best horses run for big money.

Serious followers of the sport, to whom breeding is more important than betting, can outline a "tour-de-horse" that will take you around the

SOME BIG RACES

The race	The track	Where (and nearest large city)
Kentucky Derby	Churchill Downs	Louisville, Ky.
Belmont Stakes Champagne Stakes Coaching Club Stakes Jockey Club Gold Cup Stakes Man O'War Stakes Woodward Stakes	Belmont Park	New York, N.Y.
Preakness	Pimlico	Baltimore, Md.
Santa Anita Derby Santa Anita Handicap San Juan Capistrano Invitational Handicap	Santa Anita	Arcadia, Calif. (near Los Angeles)
Washington, D.C. International Invitational Stakes	Laurel Race Course	Laurel, Md. (near Baltimore/ Washington D.C.)
Flamingo Stakes Widener Stakes	Hialeah	Miami, Fla.

country and include races featuring the best two-year-olds in Kentucky, or the best four-year-olds on the West Coast, or the best fillies in the South.

Ask the people at the track who are studying the horses instead of the newspaper, and you will be able to compile a list of events that should include many of the following:

The race	The track	Where (and nearest large city)
Bay Meadow Handicap El Camino Real Stakes	Bay Meadows	San Mateo, Calif. (near San Francisco)
Matchmaker Stakes United Nations Handicap	Atlantic City	Atlantic City, N.J.
Gold Rush Futurity	Centennial	Denver, Colo.
Heritage Stakes	Keystone Race Track	Cornwall Heights, Pa. (near Philadelphia)
Haskell Handicap Monmouth Oaks Sorority Stakes	Monmouth Park	Oceanport, N.J. (near Newark)
Ohio Derby	Thistledown	Cleveland, Ohio
Longacre Mile	Longacres	Renton, Wash. (near Seattle)
Fantasy Stakes	Oaklawn Park	Hot Springs National Park, Ark. (near Little Rock)

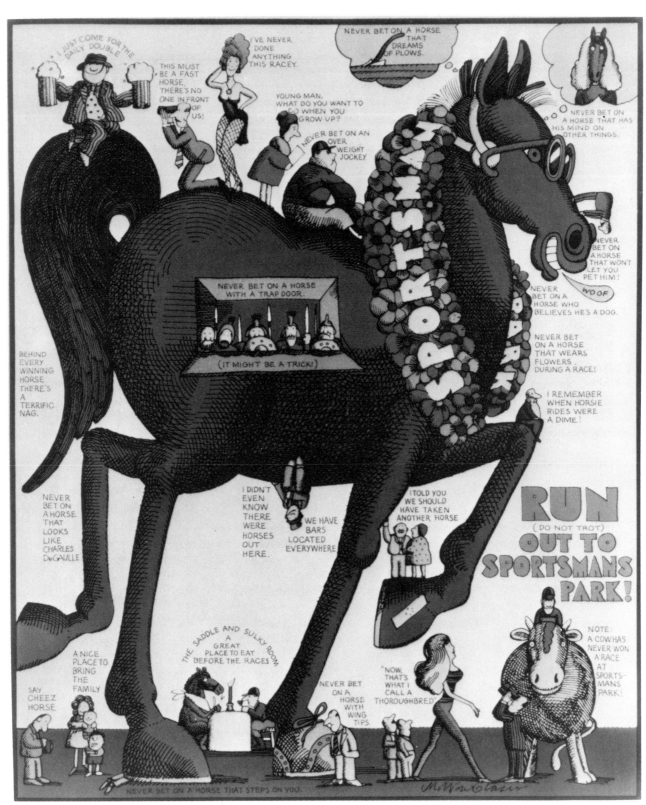

(Courtesy of Sportsman's Park.)

A BEGINNER'S COURSE IN HANDICAPPING

When archaeologists were digging in the suburbs of Herculaneum, they uncovered a wall inscribed: "For the smallest reward, Elvius the charioteer will tell all factions the names of the winning chariots in the races of Rome, and this before the day of the contest. . . ."

Elvius had some secret system for picking winners and was willing to sell his predictions. His modern–day horse–racing counterpart is the handicapper.

Each handicapper has developed his own handicapping system. It is based on the comparison of similar information regarding each horse in a given race for the purpose of picking a winner. Handicapping systems vary in their predictions because handicappers compare and weigh the information differently.

Touts will sell you their predictions (*tout sheets*), and can be found outside every track doing just that. Some of these "seers of the turf" write for newspapers, and their predictions can be bought for the price of a daily paper. Experienced handicappers determine the *morning line* (the first set of odds and estimated payoffs before the race for each horse running) which appears in the track's program.

No one goes to the racetrack without some kind of system. Your system may be the ready–made variety just described, or a system based on a do-it-yourself analysis of the information. If you have any hope at all of

at least holding your own, your system better be based on more than just the "inside" information obtained from a friend at the office.

Since handicapping means predicting the outcome of a race on the basis of comparing information, the better your information is, the better your chances of winning. Getting a

You probably won't find magazines like this one casually strewn about your dentist's waiting room (though it would make the waiting time go faster). Racing magazines like Turf Guide *are aimed at the racing fan and everything about racing— trainers and other backstretch personnel, horses, tracks, races, jockeys, etc.—is covered. Several ads for "sure fire" systems may also appear.*

tip from a reliable source is always nice. Tracking jockeys' wins and losses for your own records is helpful. But the average bettor already has all the information he needs for intelligent handicapping in the *Daily Racing Form*. Published daily, the "Telly" (as many diehards still abbreviate its former name, the *Morning Telegraph*) gives exhaustive data—from the horse's maternal grandsire to a symbolic description of its last ten races (or fewer, if the horse hasn't run ten times). With this information, even the first–time bettor can have a fighting chance of coming out ahead, and surely avoid bets

that are simply a waste of money. The DRF prints an "Explanation of Data in Past Performances" in every issue, so pick up a copy and learn the language of the past–performance charts.

The DRF gives you the information, but you must decide what to make of it. Some factors can be fully evaluated only by the experienced bettor, others depend on plain common sense. What follows here is the nuts–and–bolts of handicapping for the neophyte horseplayer—the key factors used to compare each of the horses in a race in order to make intelligent wagers and avoid bad risks.

The Daily Racing Form gives exhaustive information for each horse running in each race. In this case, it's High Galaxie in the first race at Saratoga. (Copyright © 1978 by Daily Racing Form, Inc. Reproduced with permission of copyright owner.)

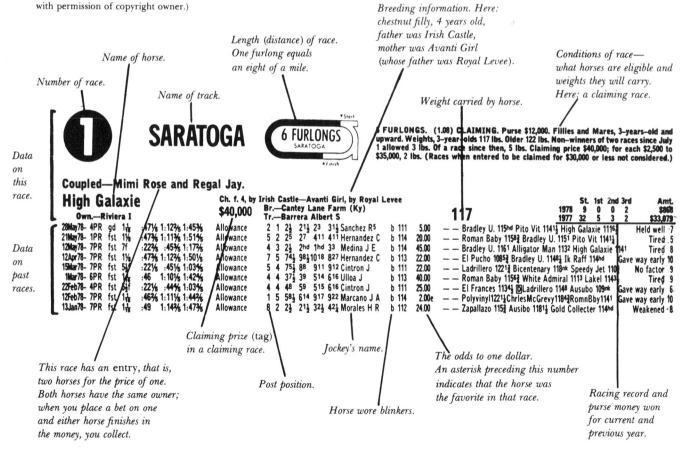

Breeding information. Here: chestnut filly, 4 years old, father was Irish Castle, mother was Avanti Girl (whose father was Royal Levee).

Length (distance) of race. One furlong equals an eight of a mile.

Conditions of race— what horses are eligible and weights they will carry. Here: a claiming race.

Name of horse.

Number of race.

Name of track.

Weight carried by horse.

Data on this race.

Data on past races.

This race has an entry, that is, two horses for the price of one. Both horses have the same owner; when you place a bet on one and either horse finishes in the money, you collect.

Claiming prize (tag) in a claiming race.

Jockey's name.

Post position.

Horse wore blinkers.

The odds to one dollar. An asterisk preceding this number indicates that the horse was the favorite in that race.

Racing record and purse money won for current and previous year.

Day, Month and Year of the Race

This information is important because it tells you whether the horse is making its first start after a long layoff, or has been running at regular intervals. Most professional handicappers advise against *backing* (betting on) a horse that hasn't run in the last 30 days. There are many factors to be evaluated in making your bet, and eliminating an otherwise attractive horse just because he's been away from the races for 31 days isn't always wise. But for the beginner, it's a good rule of thumb.

If the horse has had one race after a long vacation, and that race was a good one, today might be the day to bet on it. Some horses need a race to regain the sharpness and stamina that can't always be acquired in workouts alone.

Number of the Race and Name of the Track

Obviously, the horse doesn't care whether he's running in the first race or the ninth. But it would be significant to a professional if the horse had run in the eighth race at a New York track (Aqueduct, Belmont or Saratoga). This is because the eighth race at New York tracks consistently has the best horses, and a so-so race against horses in the eighth may have been a winning race against those in, say, the sixth race.

Some handicappers will not back a horse making his first start over a track. The thinking is that unfamiliarity with the new track—the footing, the angle of the turns, general surroundings—will hinder the horse's performance. In borderline cases, a horse that hasn't run recently, and has never run over today's track, probably shouldn't be bet.

Straight from the Horse's Mouth

This unique betting system comes to us via an FBI informant who, with a partner, managed to support himself with it. It isn't based on handicapping, your mother-in-law's birthdate, the jockey's weight divided by the phases of the moon or any such nonsense. It's based on the fact that races never start exactly on time—they begin whenever the horses are ready. If a race is scheduled for 1:00 and the horses are at the starting gate at 12:58, they leave at 12:58. During the course of the day, several races might start up early, which means the final race could end early. A "past-post" betting team would then have enough time to place a bet on a race the results of which they already know—but the bookies don't, since there aren't any phones at the track. Team member A positions himself in the clubhouse balcony and signals the results of the race to his confederate, team member B. Team member B "flops a bet" to a bookie, thus betting on an outcome that he knows will happen. Team members A and B split the payoff.

Past-post betting, when you get right down to it, is a way of ripping off the bookies. But, of course, they never complain to the police.

Coupled—Mimi Rose and Regal Jay.

High Galaxie — Ch. f. 4, by Irish Castle—Avanti Girl, by Royal Levee — $40,000 — Br.—Cantey Lane Farm (Ky) — Tr.—Barrera Albert S — 117 — Own.—Riviera I

Number of race and name of track.

Day, month, and year.

(Copyright © 1978 by Daily Racing Form, Inc. Reproduced with permission of copyright owner.)

My dear reader, I am going to give you a little advice. If you feel that you must illustrate the proverb that "a fool and his money are soon parted," I will tell you how to get rid of your surplus cash. Take from the racing calendar for the day the names of all the horses in all the races. Write them all on separate slips of paper, put these in a hat and shake them up. Draw one and bet on that one. You will lose your bet, of course, but you will have had some slight chance to win, and that you will not have by listening to and following the advice of a tout.

(*From* Easy Money *by Harry Browlaski, Searchlight Press, 1911*)

An Understatement

Yes, indeed, I've been known to place a few pilasters on the nose of some spirited nag.

(*W. C. Fields*)

Track Condition

This extremely important factor is usually rather easy to evaluate. Checking the list of past performances, you may notice that a particular horse runs significantly worse (or better) on an *off track* (sloppy or muddy). Some can't *stand up* in the slop, while some *move up* (improve) on a wet track. Before rushing off to the betting window though, make sure that track condition is the only variable responsible for the change of form. An ambitious trainer may have overmatched his horse, and the poor result may not have been due to the sloppy track but to having been outclassed. (See discussion of Type of Race and Class, below.) Distance of the race, blinkers on or off, weight carried, even just bad racing luck—any of these may have been the real reason for a horse's running poorly over an off track. The same variables may have been responsible for a good race despite the slop. But if you can determine that all other things were more or less equal, and the horse has displayed a marked like or dislike for running on a sloppy, wet track, that fact should weigh heavily in your betting decision. Some horses have no preference, and run equally well on wet or dry surfaces.

If a horse shows no slop or mud races in his chart, see if the DRF has given him a *mud mark*. This is a fairly reliable indicator of a horse's ability on an off track. The good mud-runner mark of "X" is rarely given, and always means an absolute tiger in the slop. With increasing experience, you may be able to recognize a horse bred for mud. Mud-loving sires often pass this taste down to their *get* (offspring), and a number of prominent sires are known for this trait. As a beginner, however, stick to what you can see in the past performance charts, and let only a horse's strong preference one way or the other influence your decisions.

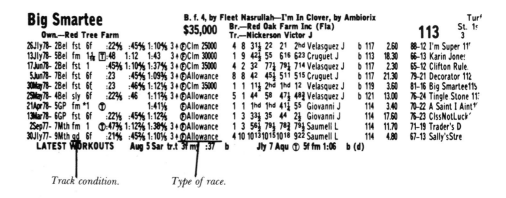

Track condition.　　Type of race.

(Courtesy of Sportsman's Park.)

Tall in the Saddle

The winningest jockey of all, Willie Shoemaker, won over 7,200 races and over $63 million in purses. Willie was, and probably still is, considered the greatest, even though he owns one of racing's less coveted titles: "The Boo Boo of a Lifetime." It happened back in the 1957 Kentucky Derby when, aboard Gallant Man, he thought he had won the race and stood up in the saddle. Alas, it was the 16th pole he had seen, not the finish line. His horse slowed just enough for Iron Liege to pass him and win by a nose.

"Who Am I?"

Who among you has ever heard of Tod Sloan, Isaac Murphy or Jimmy McLaughlin? With the exception of racing aficionados and sports trivia nuts, most people don't know that these men were the riding stars of their day (and their day was not that long ago). Even the name of Johnny Longden, who retired after riding over 6,000 winners and earning over $24 million in purses, is usually met with a frown and a shrug in "Who Am I?" games.

The great Eddie Arcaro rode over 4,700 winners during his career (including two triple crowns) and earned over $30 million in purses. But he's probably better known today as a television pitchman.

Morgan Lives!

Tucked away amidst the rolling green fields, pastures, and woodlands of Vermont, sits the internationally famous Morgan Horse Farm, birthplace and stomping grounds for generation after generation of Morgans—America's first light horse breed. It all began late in the 1700s, with the little colt of thoroughbred and Arabian blood. His name was Figure, and his owner's name was Justin Morgan. Sold and traded right and left, Figure became known as a good-looking, strong, fast, tenacious hard worker—and also, incidentally, picked up a reputation as a great breeding horse.

As his fame grew, he became known by the name of his original owner, Justin Morgan. He was small in stature by most standards but he was unusually strong—with short, wide, deeply muscular back and legs. He moved with a proud, bold, fearless, spirited style and was extremely sensitive to a rider's commands. He ran very fast for short distances—a favorite wager in Vermont at the time. His progeny, to whom he passed on all his good qualities, were quite in demand. In the 1850s, when trotting racing was in its heyday, "The World's Fastest Trotting Stallion" was Ethan Allen—Justin's great-grandson. Though certain changes have been made in the breed to adapt it to modern standards, the Morgan horse's sought-after combination of stamina, vigor and physical conformation has proven, over and over again, to be phenomenally successful.

No standardbred to beat 2:00 for a mile has not had Morgan blood.

Type of Race and Class

On any given day, seven or eight out of nine races at a track might be claiming races, so it is essential to understand the claiming system if one is to handicap intelligently.

In a claiming race, the owner of a horse must put a dollar value on the horse's ability. This tag is the amount a purchaser must pay to claim the horse, and determines the *class* the horse is in. If the horse is entered in a claiming race of too high a tag, it will be beaten by its stronger rivals. If it is entered too cheaply, it may well win but will probably be claimed by another owner who recognizes that the horse can run profitably for a higher tag.

The handicapper uses the claiming system to evaluate a horse's chances on the basis of his performance at various levels of the claiming scale. Common sense tells you that a horse that has run poorly in $10,000 company has little chance

A Morgan Foal, UVM Attraction. (UVM Morgan Horse Farm.)

against $15,000 horses. But even if the horse had won impressively for $10,000, the 50 percent jump to $15,000 is a big one, and it must still prove itself against these higher-priced rivals.

Look closely at the recent claiming levels of every horse in the race. One or more competitors may have won or run well for today's tag; others may be *dropping down* from a higher level in search of a win, or *stepping up* from good races against cheaper horses.

When handicapping claimers, there is one ironclad rule you must follow: bet a horse that has a chance. Stay away from the 50 to 1 shot with the same name as your mother-in-law if the horse has never been close against today's level of competition.

Allowance races unfortunately don't afford the bettor an obvious way of determining a horse's class, the way the tag does in a claiming race. In an allowance race, a horse's class is determined by the purses offered in the races it has run in the past. Since purses of past allowance races aren't indicated in the DRF, the only way to get this information is to go to the track often, and record the purses offered in the various races and which horses were running. (Past programs and DRF's would supply this information too.)

Information from the DRF can, however, give you a suggestion of each horse's class. Firstly, you can see from the DRF which horses are moving up from a claimer. Any horse that meets the conditions set may enter an allowance race, but the

BUYING A RACEHORSE

One way to become a racehorse owner is to buy a share in a winning stallion who is being syndicated. Thirty–two shares are sold, and as part owner, you share in the stallion's earnings (usually stud earnings). Secretariat was syndicated for $190,000 per share in 1973; What a Pleasure holds the record at $250,000 per share in 1976. Less famous syndications may be $20,000 to $30,000 per share.

Another possibility leading to ownership is the yearling auction. The most famous ones take place in Keeneland, Kentucky, in July and Saratoga, New York, in August. You don't get away for under $50,000 for anything with good lines and low mileage, and prices go as high as $700,000. The record price for a yearling was $1.5 million for Canadian Bound, son of Secretariat.

You can become an owner for much less at other, less expensive auctions but the purchase price is just the beginning. It costs $10,000 to $12,000 a year to maintain a horse. Add to that the cost of a trainer ($30 per day plus a percent of the winnings) and a jockey ($35 to ride, $45 for third, $55 for second, $75 for first, and 10 percent of a stakes purse). Then there's the horse doctor, horse dentist, groom, exercise person, walker, and more.

There are no rags-to-riches stories for the racehorse owner. The occasional million-dollar winner is a pleasant surprise to folks who can afford to lose thousands gracefully each year.

A groom's tender loving care. (Courtesy of Sportsman's Park.)

It's a Horse's Life

A thoroughbred's future is usually decided at birth. The owner may decide to keep it or sell it; it may be race–trained or used exclusively for breeding.

Most thoroughbreds are born between mid-February and the end of June. The birth is carefully planned in order to give the little one some growing time before its first birthday, for no matter when a racehorse is born, it is considered one year old on its first January 1. This arrangement makes it less complicated to group horses by age for racing purposes.

The thoroughbred racehorse begins its training as a yearling. This schooling includes getting used to a jockey and riding tackle, learning to get out of a starting gate and learning to avoid looking directly into the camera in the winner's circle. They start racing at the age of two (their second January 1), and many retire as four-year-olds, after a short two–year career. (As many an athlete knows, the legs are the first thing to go.)

Once retired, a thoroughbred has only one career available— breeding. A mare can have one foal each year, but a stallion can sire as many as thirty. When not thus engaged, the retired racehorse must be content to stay in the barn, where it is washed, fed and generally catered to. Or it can lope around the farm, munching grass and putting on a few pounds.

THE WORLD OF THE HORSE OWNER

Owning, racing, and breeding a thoroughbred racehorse is an expensive hobby. The names of Whitney, Vanderbilt and Belmont are synonymous with the sport, and the Jockey Club is not a place where short people come to shoot pool.

The rich and famous owners of thoroughbred racehorses usually maintain, among their other residences, a breeding farm where their four-legged playthings are born, trained, and bred. Each of these racing farms or stables has its own set of colors, which is reflected in the shirts worn by its jockeys. While the owner is off doing rich and famous things, the care and feeding of the horse is left in the usually capable hands of a trainer—who receives a salary, a percentage of the purses and the chance to be photographed in the winner's circle with the owner, the jockey, and the horse.

There are horse farms that are not the private domain of the "horsey set." These farms may consist of one man and his mare on a half acre, or they may be owned by a corporation that "stands a band" of brood mares and stallions on thousands of acres, breeding their own mares to their own stallions. If an owner does not have his or her own farm, there are places available that board mares and breed them to stallions "standing" on other farms. Some farms own or board stallions only, and charge stud or breeding fees to other owners, who bring their mares and leave them until a foal is born.

Most farms sell their yearlings privately or at an auction. Some farms also sell brood mares, stallions, and mature horses. Some may even retain some foals for training and race them under their own colors.

Making money by owning a racehorse is an even longer shot than making money through betting. The "horsey set" is a closed corporation, and successful horse ownership is no guarantee of membership. Acceptance comes through breeding—one's own, not the horses'.

competition is generally tougher than in claiming races. So when a horse jumps from the claiming ranks to allowance company, it should be running as well as it can and have been winning races at, or near, the highest tag at that track. There are no hard and fast rules, but in general, a horse that can't beat claimers isn't worth a bet in allowance company.

Another suggestion of class indicated in the DRF is the average amount of purse money won each time the horse has run in this and the past year. To figure out this average, take the amount of purse money won for each year and divide it by the number of starts for that year. (See page 184, upper right corner of DRF.) In general, the higher this average the higher the class.

Speed Rating and Track Variant

The speed rating and track variant figures simply mean that some tracks are "faster" than others. This can be true even on the same track on different days, or in different races on the same day.

Some tracks are hard and fast, rather like Astroturf, while some have more "give" and are slower because they are deep sand. The sandy tracks, notably Aqueduct in New York, get faster when they get wet—so if there's a shower between races, the times run by the winners of the races before and after can't be compared on a one–to–one basis. The speed rating and track variant figures—which always appear together in the past performance chart of the DRF—permit a more meaningful comparison of running times, either between one track and another, or under different conditions at the same track.

The DRF gives a detailed explanation of these figures if you want to delve into higher mathematics. For the novice it's enough to know that when the speed rating and track variant numbers add up to 100 or more, the horse ran a good race.

Distance, Points of Call, Fractional Times, Weight

The distance of the race, the horse's position with respect to the leader at various points in the race (points of call), the leader's time at those points (fractional time), and the weight carried are all included in the past performance chart of the DRF. They should all be used together, and especially in conjunction with class and track condition, to make a fully informed betting decision.

Each point of call is expressed by a superscript number, which reflects the horse's position with respect to the leader and its length behind the leader at that point of call. A 3^2 at the first point of call, for example, indicates that the horse was in third position, two lengths behind the leader, at the first point of call. (In racing parlance this is expressed as "third by two lengths.") The distance between points of call and, therefore, the fractional times at those points of call, varies with the length of the race. The longer the race the slower the fractional

Lillian Russell, the famed American actress, frequented the racetrack at Saratoga in the 1890s. She was an incredibly successful handicapper, although she insisted that she picked her winning horses by randomly stabbing the program with her hatpin.

A Natural High

Q: When does a jockey ride tallest in the saddle?

A: In the early morning. Jockeys are taller in the morning than at night, just like the rest of us. Sleep lets the body stretch as much as one inch by morning—make that ¾ of an inch for Steve Cauthen.

(*Courtesy of* Systems & Methods)

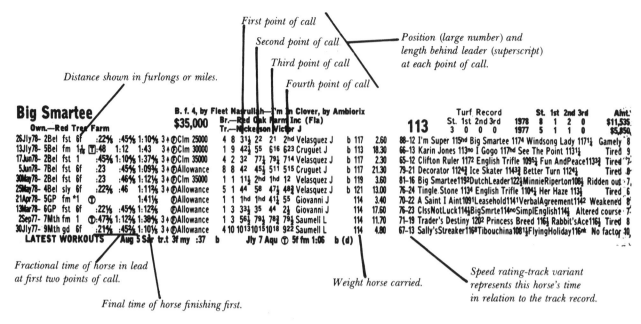

First point of call

Second point of call

Third point of call

Fourth point of call

Position (large number) and length behind leader (superscript) at each point of call.

Distance shown in furlongs or miles.

Fractional time of horse in lead at first two points of call.

Final time of horse finishing first.

Weight horse carried.

Speed rating-track variant represents this horse's time in relation to the track record.

times at points of call will be. (Horses in a long race will, like runners, pace themselves so they'll last out the longer distance.) The final time will also be slower, obviously, for a longer race. When comparing fractional times and final times, among horses, be sure you are comparing races of the same distance.

Another obvious factor that affects running time is the weight carried by the horse. The more weight a horse carries, the slower it will run.

As important, but less obvious, is the effect of class upon running time. There may, for example, be a horse in today's race that has won its previous race, say six furlongs in 1:11, and is now moving up in class. You notice that this horse's 1:11 winning time was faster than any other horse in today's race over the same distance and under the same track conditions. This data would seem to point to a sure winner. But for rea-

sons no one quite understands, a horse who is stepping up substantially into a higher class simply may not run to his physical potential. As some horsemen say, "The class horse comes up and looks the cheap horse in the eye, and the cheap horse blinks." In short, horses can't be counted on to duplicate their previous running times when moving up in class, so never rely on time alone when you're handicapping a race.

Another important way the fractional times at points of call can be used is to observe a horse's running style—whether the horse is a *speed horse* (one who likes to be in front) or a *stretch runner* (one who likes to put on speed towards the end of a race, even from a way back). Neither one of these styles is better than the other although some tracks seem to favor one over the other. Aqueduct, for example, is traditionally a "speed" track—the horse who starts out in front usually ends up in front. In addition, the running styles of all the horses in a race must be considered before one can say which style is better. If there's only one speed horse in a race, for example, the other horses may let it gallop off to an easy lead, and it's likely to have enough energy left in the stretch to hold off the late-running horses. By the same token, if the race is packed with speed horses, they will often kill each other off vying for the lead, forcing very fast fractional times and setting the stage for a stretch runner to overtake the tiring speedsters.

The classic races of the late 1960s between two great horses, Dr. Fager and Damascus, illustrate the above phenomenon. Dr. Fager was the ultimate speedball—he just wanted to run as fast as he could, as far as he could. Damascus, on the other hand, could be *rated*—kept back off the lead to save his energy for one big run at the end. Damascus's trainer knew Dr. Fager's style and would also enter one of his other horses in the race as a "rabbit" for Dr. Fager. This horse's job was to tire out Dr. Fager by forcing him to run too fast in the early stages of the race, which Dr. Fager would do simply because he refused to have any horse in front of him. By the time the field hit the homestretch, Dr. Fager would be used up, while Damascus, though farther back, would still be fresh—and with his strong late run, Damascus could overtake the gallant but exhausted Dr. Fager.

John W. "Bet-a-Million" Gates once threw a costly party for the jockeys of the next day's races. Under the influence of such sumptuous food and drink, they became quite talkative. Based on the information he thus overheard, Gates managed to win $200,000 the next day.

Comment Line

The comment line (sometimes called the *trouble line*) describes in a few words the horse's performance. Most often, the comment line—"Tired," "Early speed," "Trailed"—merely confirms what you can see from the points of call. But look at the horse's race again if the comment reveals some bad racing luck. "Stumbled start," "Bumped," "Checked" (horse's progress was impeded during the race and the jockey had to slow it down), among others, are words that make a veteran handicapper's eyes light up if, despite a problem, the horse ran a creditable race. For example, a

The first three finishers indicates which horses finished first, second, and third, along with the weights they carried and the margins (distance) separating them.

Comment line.

High Galaxie — Own.—Riviera I

Ch. f. 4, by Irish Castle—Avanti Girl, by Royal Levee
$40,000 Br.—Cantey Lane Farm (Ky)
Tr.—Barrera Albert S

117

	St.	1st	2nd	3rd	Amt.
1978	9	0	0	2	$868
1977	32	5	3	2	$33,079

28May78-	4PR	gd	1 1/16	:47⅕	1:12⅖	1:45⅗	Allowance	2	1	2½	21½	23	31½	Sanchez R5	b	111	5.00	— —	Bradley U. 115hd Pito Vit 1141½ High Galaxie 1116½	Held well 7
21May78-	1PR	fst	1⅛	:47⅗	1:11⅗	1:51⅘	Allowance	5	2	25	27	411	411	Hernandez C	b	114	20.00	— —	Roman Baby 1158¾ Bradley U. 1151 Pito Vit 1141½	Tired 5
12May78-	7PR	fst	7f	:22⅘	:45⅗	1:17⅖	Allowance	4	3	2½	2hd	1hd	33	Medina J E	b	114	45.00	— —	Bradley U. 1161 Alligator Man 1132 High Galaxie 1141	Tired 8
12Apr78-	7PR	fst	1⅛	:47⅗	1:12⅖	1:50⅕	Allowance	7	5	74½	98½	1018	827	Hernandez C	b	113	22.00	— —	El Pucho 1085¾ Bradley U. 1148¼ Ik Raff 114hd	Gave way early 10
15Mar78-	7PR	fst	5½f	:22⅕	:45⅕	1:03⅗	Allowance	5	4	75½	88	911	912	Cintron J	b	111	22.00	— —	Ladrillero 1221¾ Bicentenary 118nk Speedy Jet 110¾	No factor 9
1Mar78-	6PR	fst	1 1/16	:46	1:10⅕	1:42⅘	Allowance	4	4	37½	39	514	616	Ulloa J	b	113	40.00	— —	Roman Baby 1156¾ White Admiral 1113 Lakel 1143½	Tired 9
22Feb78-	4PR	fst	5½f	:22⅕	:44⅘	1:03⅗	Allowance	4	4	48	59	515	616	Cintron J	b	111	25.00	— —	El Frances 1134½ [D]Ladrillero 1148 Ausubo 109nk	Gave way early 6
12Feb78-	7PR	fst	1 1/16	:46⅖	1:11⅕	1:44⅖	Allowance	1	5	58½	614	917	922	Marcano J A	b	114	2.00e	— —	Polyvinyl1221½ChrlesMcGrevy1184¾RomnBby1141	Gave way early 10
13Jan78-	7PR	fst	1 1/16	:49	1:14⅖	1:47⅗	Allowance	8	2	2½	21½	32½	42¼	Morales H R	b	112	24.00	— —	Zapallazo 115¾ Ausibo 1181½ Gold Collecter 114hd	Weakened 8

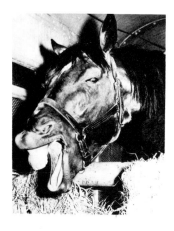

The First Movie Star?

We all know that stop–action photography is *de rigeur* at racetracks. But did you know that a late-1800s racing bet inadvertently led to the invention of the motion picture?

The $25,000 bet, between the then-governor of California and some friends, was whether a galloping horse ever has all four hoofs off the ground simultaneously. To settle the bet, which had been going on for years, the governor decided to hire the photographer, Eadweard Muybridge, who set up several cameras alongside a racetrack. As the horse ran past, individual timers tripped the camera shutters in sequence, forever settling the argument. Muybridge then went on to invent the zoopraxiscope, an early form of motion picture projector, to display his photographs. By the way, they showed that a horse has one foot on the ground at all times.

horse stumbles leaving the gate, and at the first point of call it is in last place in a race of ten: 10^{25}. Then the calls are 6^{15}, 4^{10}, 3^5. A decent third–place finish, but ordinarily not a performance to get excited about. However, when you realize that the horse nearly fell down at the start, and made up 20 lengths on the leader in the course of the race, you could certainly ask yourself what this horse would have done if it had broken cleanly. It may be worth a couple of dollars to find out.

If you want to learn more about handicapping, pick up one of the books listed in the back of this one. But bear in mind that, even for han-

dicapping whizzes, it is extremely difficult to win money consistently by betting on horses. As an old saying goes, "You can beat a race, but you can't beat the races."

Only a tiny fraction of the millions of people who bet on horses win with enough regularity to support themselves, and to be called professionals. These fortunate few are aided by years of experience, an intuitive "feel" for picking winners, or maybe reliable inside information from jockeys, trainers, or exercise riders. Don't be discouraged if your first few picks don't line your pocket with gold. In handicapping, there is no substitute for experience.

(Courtesy of Sportsman's Park.)

(Courtesy of Sportsman's Park.)

A DAY AT THE RACES

To see how one handicapper would actually use the information in the *Daily Racing Form*'s past–performance charts to decide which horse he should bet on, follow this race. The horses shown were entries in the first race–a claiming race, at Saratoga on August 9, 1978. The notations point out the most important factors to consider for each horse shown.

It seems to be a tossup between Byline Girl, Mimi Rose, and Regal Jay. For some mystical reason, our handicapper friend just doesn't feel that Regal Jay will win today. Byline Girl, what horse people call an *honest horse* (one who never runs a bad race), might be a good choice if the odds were rather long, say 9 to 1. He decides to go with Mimi Rose, because her recent races look better than Byline Girl's.

Curious to know the results? Regal Jay, Byline Girl, High Galaxie. Close, but no cigar. That's why our handicapper hasn't quit his job as a lawyer.

Another bad sign: she's had a 4-month layoff since her last race.

Won 5 out of 32 races in 1977 + earned a lot of money – over $33,000.

High Galaxie

Own.—Riviera I

Ch. f. 4, by Irish Castle—Avanti Girl, by Royal Levee
$40,000 Br.—Cantey Lane Farm (Ky)
Tr.—Barrera Albert S

117

	St.	1st	2nd	3rd	Amt.
1978	9	0	0	2	$868
1977	32	5	3	2	$33,079

28May78-	4PR	gd	1 1/16	:47⅕	1:12⅖	1:45⅗	Allowance	2	1	2½	21½	23	31½	Sanchez R5	b 111	5.00	— —	Bradley U. 115hd Pito Vit 1141½ High Galaxie 1116½	Held well	7
21May78-	1PR	fst	1⅛	:47⅗	1:11⅗	1:51⅘	Allowance	5	2	25	27	411	411	Hernandez C	b 114	20.00	— —	Roman Baby 1158¾ Bradley U. 1151 Pito Vit 1141¼	Tired	5
12May78-	7PR	fst	7f	:22⅖	:45⅗	1:17⅖	Allowance	4	3	2½	2hd	1hd	33	Medina J E	b 114	45.00	— —	Bradley U. 1161 Alligator Man 1132 High Galaxie 1141	Tired	8
12Apr78-	7PR	fst	1⅛	:47⅗	1:12⅖	1:50⅕	Allowance	7	5	74½	98½	1018	827	Hernandez C	b 113	22.00	— —	El Pucho 1085¾ Bradley U. 1148¼ Ik Raff 114hd	Gave way early	10
15Mar78-	7PR	fst	5½f	:22⅕	:45⅕	1:03⅘	Allowance	5	4	75½	88	911	912	Cintron J	b 111	22.00	— —	Ladrillero 1221¾ Bicentenary 118nk Speedy Jet 110¾	No factor	9
1Mar78-	6PR	fst	1 1/16	:46	1:10⅕	1:42⅘	Allowance	4	4	37½	39	514	616	Ulloa J	b 113	40.00	— —	Roman Baby 1156¾ White Admiral 1113 Lakel 1143½	Tired	9
22Feb78-	4PR	fst	5½f	:22⅕	:44⅘	1:03⅘	Allowance	4	4	48	59	515	616	Cintron J	b 111	25.00	— —	El Frances 1134½ [D]Ladrillero 1148 Ausubo 109nk	Gave way early	6
12Feb78-	7PR	fst	1 1/16	:46⅖	1:11⅕	1:44⅖	Allowance	1	5	58½	614	917	922	Marcano J A	b 114	2.00e	— —	Polyvinyl1221¼ChrlesMcGrevy1184¾RomnBby1141	Gave way early	10
13Jan78-	7PR	fst	1 1/16	:49	1:14⅖	1:47⅗	Allowance	8	2	2½	21½	32½	42¼	Morales H R	b 112	24.00	— —	Zapallazo 115¾ Ausibo 1181½ Gold Collecter 114hd	Weakened	8

All previous races indicated were run in Puerto Rico... not known for tough company – and this horse didn't win any of them.

Ran a respectable last race; came in 3rd.

Byline Girl

Own.—Girdner P K

B. m. 5, by Make Money—Haida, by Indian Hemp
$35,000 Br.—Michelson E M (Cal)
Tr.—Lake Robert P

113

Turf Record						St.	1st	2nd	3rd	Amt.
St.	1st	2nd	3rd		1978	11	3	1	4	$40,594
1	0	0	1		1977	16	4	4	5	$34,885

16Jly78-	3Bel	fst	6f	:22⅖	:45⅕	1:10⅘	3↑ⒻClm c-25000	6	2	22½	34½	36	36¾	Velasquez J	b 117	*1.20	81-13	Quaker Queen1174½Solomon'sSeal1172¼BylineGirl1171¼	Weakened	8
10Jly78-	2Bel	fst	6f	:22⅗	:46	1:10⅖	3↑ⒻClm 40000	6	1	42½	42½	44½	37¾	Velasquez J	b 113	*1.80	82-15	Full Flight 1094 Mimi Rose 1143¾ Byline Girl 113no	Lacked rally	6
24Apr78-	6Aqu	fst	6f	:22⅗	:46⅕	1:10⅘	ⒻHandicap	4	1	31½	32	2½	2¾	Hernandez R	b 113	*2.20	88-20	Flag Of Leyte Gulf 114¾ Byline Girl 1132¾ Ali Trace 1093½	Gamely	7
6Apr78-	8Aqu	fst	6f	:23	:46⅖	1:11⅕	ⒻHandicap	1	1	11½	1½	2½	31¾	Hernandez R	b 113	*1.30	85-23	Dalton Road 122nk Power 1101½ Byline Girl 1134	Weakened	6
1Apr78-	6Aqu	fst	6f	⊡:22⅕	:46	1:12⅖	3↑ⒻAllowance	3	3	21½	11½	12	11¾	McKnight R E7	b 112	3.20	85-17	Byline Girl 1121¾ Regal Jay 1212¾ [D]Native Fruit119hd	Ridden out	7
28Mar78-	8Aqu	fst	6f	⊡:22⅗	:46	1:11⅘	ⒻHandicap	2	5	21	33	44½	48½	Hernandez R	b 114	3.60	79-17	Spot Two 1172½ Dutch Leader 1091½RegalJay1104½	Crowded early	5
12Mar78-	8Aqu	fst	6f	⊡:22⅘	:46	1:11	3↑ⒻCorrection H	7	7	54	67	614	615	Hernandez R	b 113	3.80	77-13	Bold Brat 1187 Tetrarquina 120¾ Dalton Road 1212	No factor	7
18Feb78-	8Aqu	fst	6f	⊡:22⅗	:46⅘	1:13	3↑ⒻBerlo H	5	3	43	54	52½	3¾	Hernandez R	b 112	5.60	81-20	Tetrarquina 116no Notably 113¾ Byline Girl 112¾	Rallied	8
13Feb78-	8Aqu	fst	6f	⊡:22⅗	:46⅖	1:12⅖	Allowance	2	4	21½	31½	31½	54½	Hernandez R	b 115	4.70	81-25	Petrograd115¾LoadedorBusted115½BoldndStormy115½	Weakened	8
27Jan78-	4Hia	fst	6f	:22⅗	:46	1:10⅗	ⒻClm 40000	9	2	31½	31	12	16	Velasquez J	b 116	*.60	90-20	Byline Girl 1166 Delidust 116no Minnie Riperton 1162	Ridden out	12

LATEST WORKOUTS Aug 1 Sar 6f fst 1:12⅖ h — Jly 6 Bel 5f fst 1:02 h — Jun 29 Bel 5f fst 1:02 b — Jun 23 Bel 5f fst 1:01⅖ h

Finished in the money 7 times out of last 10 races. Won another $40,000 claiming race (Jan. 27).

Has been the favorite in last 4 races.

Has not run at this track for at least 10 months.

Dropping down in class from allowance company to today's $40,000 claiming race.

Mimi Rose

Own.—O'Brien T

B. m. 5, by Night Invader—Dana's Rose, by Third Brother
$40,000 Br.—C L O Training Center Inc (Fla)
Tr.—Smith Sidney J

117

	St.	1st	2nd	3rd	Amt.
1978	5	0	2	0	$9,240
1977	19	3	1	1	$42,950

17Jly78-	8Bel	my	7f	:22⅗	:45⅘	1:23⅖	3↑ⒻAllowance	5	2	1hd	42	615	624	Rodriguez J A	b 117	14.10	61-16	Flying Above 122no Pressing Date 1221¾ Blowfish 1173	Gave way	6
10Jly78-	2Bel	fst	6f	:22⅗	:46	1:10⅖	3↑ⒻClm 40000	2	4	1½	1hd	1hd	24	Rodriguez J A	b 114	2.60	86-15	Full Flight 1094 Mimi Rose 1143¾ Byline Girl 113no	Weakened	6
4Jly78-	7Bel	sly	7f	:22⅘	:46	1:25	3↑ⒻAllowance	1	2	11	12	11	22¾	Rodriguez J A	b 115	15.10	74-13	Our Mims 1222¾ Mimi Rose 115½ Sans Arc 1152¾	Gamely	5
12Mar78-	2Aqu	fst	6f	⊡:22⅘	:46⅕	1:11⅗	ⒻClm 40000	3	1	1hd	2hd	22	64	Gonzalez B	b 117	3.30	85-13	Power 117nk Ali Trace 1171 Caroline K. 1172½	Tired	9
18Feb78-	5Aqu	fst	6f	⊡:22⅘	:46⅗	1:12	Clm 40000	5	5	64½	44½	57½	56¼	Gonzalez B	b 108	11.80	81-20	ReallyCooking115hdKintla'sFolly1081¾Itsgoodlife1171½	No mishap	9
21Dec77-	4Aqu	sly	6f	⊡:22⅖	:46⅕	1:12⅘	3↑ⒻClm 40000	3	6	69	68	611	614	Vasquez J	b 117	4.10	69-26	Do's Melody 1152¾ Lady Whig1131¼MushMouse117½	Disliked slop	6
5Dec77-	8Aqu	my	6f	⊡:22⅖	:46⅕	1:11⅗	3↑ⒻHandicap	4	1	44	57½	511	57¼	Gonzalez B	b 107	2.80	82-16	Gurkhas Band 117nk Keep It Secret 105nk One Sum 1133	Tired	5
2Dec77-	8Aqu	sly	6f	:22⅕	:45⅕	1:10⅖	3↑ⒻAllowance	2	3	3½	31½	33½	54¾	Vasquez J	115	12.40	86-18	Royal Dux 1152¼ Ring O' Bells 1131 Illiterate 1151¼	Tired	6
18Oct77-	8Aqu	fst	6f	:22	:44⅘	1:09⅖	3↑ⒻAllowance	2	5	42¼	23	25	56½	Vasquez J	b 115	6.50	89-12	Beyond Reasoning 1155¼ Ordination115hdIlliterate115½	Weakened	8
5Oct77-	4Bel	fst	6f	:23⅕	:46⅖	1:10⅗	3↑ⒻClm 40000	4	3	3½	1hd	12	11¾	Vasquez J	b 117	6.40	89-14	Mimi Rose 1171¾ Perto 1172 Ali Trace 115¾	Driving	6

LATEST WORKOUTS Aug 3 Sar 5f fst 1:04 b — Jly 1 Bel 5f fst 1:01 h — Jun 24 Bel 5f fst 1:01⅕ h — ●Jun 13 Bel 6f fst 1:14 h

Finished so badly that something very unusual must have happened in this race; should probably discount this race.

In last $40,000 race, came in 2nd by 4 lengths to a horse that carried 5 lbs. less – and beat Byline Girl, another contender in this race.

Ran 0 for 9 in 1978; 1 for 8 in 1977. This horse just doesn't like to win.

Princess Polly — Own.—Hooper F W

B. f. 3, by Crozier—Polly N, by Quibu — **$40,000** — Br.—Hooper F W (Fla) — Tr.—Fenstermaker L R — **112**

	St.	1st	2nd	3rd	Amt.
1978	9	0	0	3	$7,340
1977	8	1	1	2	$11,020

31Jly78-	2Sar	fst	6f	:22⅘	:45⅘	1:10⅗	ⒻClm 35000	6	4	635	63½	54	33½	Cordero A Jr	b	116	7.90	83–15	My First Word 116¾ Better Turn 1162¾ Princess Polly116¾	Rallied	7
13Jly78-	5Hol	fst	6f	:22	:45	1:10	3↑ⒻClm 32000	1	7	66½	65¾	43	35	Gonzalez R M	b	112	36.60	82–16	Ms. Nudini 1163 Hello Hostess 1202 Princess Polly 1122½	Rallied	7
4May78-	6Hol	fst	1	:46⅖	1:11⅘	1:38⅗	ⒻClm 32000	4	5	44	43½	45	35¼	Snyder L	b	116	12.20	68–20	Le Shona Tov 1165 WestwardSal121nkPrincessPolly1161½	Fair try	7
20Apr78-	1Hol	fst	6f	:22	:45⅗	1:10⅘	ⒻClm 32000	2	10	912	96½	87	89½	Pierce D	b	116	11.10	73–20	Oh You Kid 1163¼ Le Shona Tov 118¾ Splashem 1112½	No factor	10
31Mar78-	5SA	gd	6½f	:21⅗	:44⅖	1:16⅖	ⒻClm 32000	5	8	98¼	68	52¾	42½	Pierce D	b	116	9.20	85–13	Agree 118¾ K. O. Kelly 1161½ Le Shona Tov 118nk	NO mishap	9
17Mar78-	1SA	fst	6f	:21⅖	:44⅖	1:09⅘	ⒻClm 40000	7	10	911	69	47	57½	Pierce D	b	116	62.70	82–16	Hempen'sLove1146DonnforSure1161Terrsto'sDrm122½	No mishap	10
10Feb78-	7SA	my	6f	:22⅖	:46	1:11⅗	ⒻClm 40000	7	7	86¼	65	66	56	Pierce D	b	116	35.20	75–25	Beautification 1163 Hoisty Can Fly1161½WestwardSal1141	Outrun	8
1Feb78-	7SA	fst	1	:46⅖	1:11⅖	1:37⅘	ⒻAllowance	9	7	87	99½	813	811	Cordero A Jr	b	114	49.50	69–20	[D]Equanimity 1162 Mint Castle 1151 My Buck 1133½	No factor	9
21Jan78-	7SA	fst	6f	:21⅘	:44⅘	1:10⅖	ⒻAllowance	6	6	69¼	69	57½	58	Cordero A Jr	b	114	13.00	79–15	Palmistry 1195 Envisioned 1131½ Queen Yasna 1131½	No threat	6
14Nov77-	2Aqu	fst	6f	:23⅖	:48⅕	1:13⅖	ⒻClm 40000	4	8	53¾	76	44½	34¼	Velasquez J	b	116	4.80	72–28	Sue Me Not 1161¼ Queen By Night1143PrincessPolly1163¾	Rallied	8

LATEST WORKOUTS Jly 22 Hol 7f fst 1:29⅘ h — Jly 7 Hol 4f fst :50 h — Jun 30 Hol 4f fst :50⅕ h — Jun 24 Hol 3f fst :36⅘ h

Hasn't run since March, for a 5 month layoff. But this trainer has been known to bring back winning horses after a long layoff.

An entry (and favorite) in last race, but coupled horse could have brought down the odds in last race. This horse should go at 8 or 9 to 1; anything less than 5 to 1 means "smart money" is being bet because of "inside information" (like a great latest workout).

Hasty Snob * — Own.—Sommer S

B. m. 5, by Aristocratic—Hasty Jane, by Hasty Road — **$37,500** — Br.—Polinger M (Md) — Tr.—Martin Frank — **115**

Turf Record	St.	1st	2nd	3rd		St.	1st	2nd	3rd	Amt.
	2	0	0	0	1978	4	0	0	0	
					1977	21	4	7	4	$64,560

12Mar78-	2Aqu	fst	6f	⊡	:22⅘	:46⅕	1:11⅗	ⒻClm 40000	7	5	99¾	911	811	88½	Graell A	b	117	*2.00e	80–13	Power 117nk Ali Trace 1171 Caroline K. 1172½	No factor	9
3Feb78-	8Aqu	fst	1 1/16	⊡	:46⅗	1:12	1:44⅖	ⒻAllowance	2	7	713	59½	55½	55¼	Graell A	b	119	11.00	88–13	Spring In Tokyo 1152¾ Dr. Mary Lou119hdAbystar1152¼	No factor	7
27Jan78-	6Aqu	fst	6f	⊡	:22⅘	:45⅗	1:11⅗	ⒻClm 35000	3	10	1210	1117	912	911	Hernandez R	b	117	2.60e	78–17	Caroline K. 1174¾ Corbatera 106nk Reflection Pool 114½	Outrun	12
6Jan78-	8Aqu	fst	6f	⊡	:22⅖	:46⅕	1:12	ⒻHandicap	1	8	89	78	63	55	Graell A	b	107	18.80	82–20	Dalton Road 119nk One Sum 1142 Keep It Secret 105nk	Mild bid	8
22Dec77-	4Aqu	my	1 1/16	⊡	:48⅖	1:14	1:48	3↑ⒻClm c-35000	7	5	32½	3½	1hd	21¾	Amy J	b	117	3.00	73–23	Sir For Her 1061¾ Hasty Snob 117¾ Jac A Mac 1111¼	Gamely	8
6Dec77-	6Aqu	sly	1 1/16	⊡	:48	1:13⅕	1:45	3↑ⒻAllowance	5	3	42	32	52¼	56¼	Cruguet J	b	117	4.90	84–15	Casquette 1152¾ Spring In Tokyo 115hd Naples 117¾	Tired	7
28Nov77-	6Aqu	gd	1		:46⅘	1:11⅗	1:37⅖	3↑ⒻAllowance	1	2	1hd	11½	1½	1no	Cruguet J	b	117	2.10	79–21	Hasty Snob 117no Passage Way 115nk Dr. Mary Lou 1151	Driving	4
29Oct77-	6Aqu	fst	1		:49⅗	1:13⅘	1:38⅖	3↑ⒻAllowance	5	5	53½	44½	46	33¼	Cruguet J	b	117	5.20	71–15	Book Of Ruth 114¾ Aunt Bud 1172½ Hasty Snob 1171¼	Rallied	6
4Oct77-	7Bel	fst	7f		:23⅖	:47⅕	1:24⅕	3↑ⒻAllowance	1	6	52½	42½	52½	42½	Maple E	b	117	7.20	78–20	Tiger Heart 114¾ Aunt Bud 117hd Squander 1141¾	No rally	7
27Sep77-	8Bel	gd	1 1/16		:47⅘	1:12⅖	1:43⅘	3↑ⒻAllowance	2	4	42	1hd	2½	22	Maple E		117	6.00	81–17	I Gogo 1132 Hasty Snob 1173 Aunt Bud 117½	Weakened	5

LATEST WORKOUTS Aug 1 Sar 6f fst 1:13⅕ h — Jly 21 Bel 5f fst :59 h — Jly 9 Bel 3f fst :36 h — Jly 3 Bel 3f fst :36⅕ b

Good last workout.

Has outside post position, an advantage at Saratoga (every track has a bias).

Regal Jay — Own.—Seidt M

B. f. 4, by Poppy Jay—Regal Hint, by Pointer — **$40,000** — Br.—Karutz W S (Ky) — Tr.—Smith Sidney J — **117**

Turf Record	St.	1st	2nd	3rd		St.	1st	2nd	3rd	Amt.
	1	0	0	0	1978	12	1	2	1	$25,520
					1977	22	5	6	3	$53,340

17Jly78-	7Bel	my	1		:45⅗	1:10⅕	1:36⅖	3↑ⒻAllowance	1	6	512	613	618	623	Cruguet J		117	22.70	63–16	Mrs. Warren 117hd Tingle Stone 1124½ Dr.MaryLou1173	No threat	8
27Jun78-	8Mth	fst	6f		:22	:44⅘	1:10	3↑ⒻMWashngtnH	2	5	61¾	78	75¼	611	Cauthen S		117	4.10	79–16	Sharp Belle1151¼PlainandFancy1182¾Watchfulness1155	No threat	8
8Jun78-	7Bel	sly	6f		:22⅗	:45⅘	1:11	3↑ⒻAllowance	3	2	52	55½	44½	43½	Velasquez J		117	13.30	83–19	Akita 114no Keep It Secret 1103 Linda's Sister 119½	No rally	7
30May78-	4Bel	fm	1	Ⓣ	:46⅗	1:11	1:35⅗	3↑ⒻAllowance	3	1	42½	715	721	725	Velasquez J		121	10.10	67–10	Fia 1171 Imaflash 117hd Tokamak 1171¾	Tired	7
25May78-	7Bel	sly	1 1/16		:47⅗	1:12⅗	1:44⅘	3↑ⒻAllowance	4	1	13	11½	1½	1¾	Velasquez J		121	2.70	78–24	Regal Jay 121¾ Milina 1213¾ Star Gala 1107¾	Driving	5
14May78-	6Aqu	sly	6f		:22⅗	:46⅗	1:11⅘	3↑ⒻAllowance	1	2	43	42½	44	44¼	Miranda J7		114	*1.90	80–26	Linda's Sister 121no Hey Nancy 113nk Sallys Flight 1104	Tired	6
4May78-	8Aqu	fst	6f		:22⅖	:44⅘	1:09⅕	ⒻHandicap	8	1	44	48	711	712	Velez R I		107	23.80	85–16	Gladiolus 109½ Bold Brat 1224¾ Small Raja 121hd	Tired	9
27Apr78-	8Aqu	fst	6f		:23⅖	:47	1:11⅗	3↑ⒻAllowance	6	1	1hd	11	32	43	Velez R I		121	2.80	82–25	Perto 1212¾ Marston's Mill 108nk Crewzette 116no	Weakened	7
13Apr78-	8Aqu	fst	7f		:23	:45⅘	1:23⅗	3↑ⒻAllowance	2	4	11½	11½	12	24	Rodriguez A M5		116	2.90	79–23	White Star Line 1134 RegalJay1162NativeFruit121no	Second best	6
1Apr78-	6Aqu	fst	6f	⊡	:22⅕	:46	1:12⅖	3↑ⒻAllowance	4	5	65½	52½	32½	21¾	Velez R I		121	8.30	83–17	Byline Girl 1121¾ Regal Jay 1212¾ [D]Native Fruit 119hd	Rallied	7

LATEST WORKOUTS Aug 2 Sar 5f fst 1:00⅖ h

Has only won one race in last 10, but could find excuse for every loss...for example: she never ran at this track; 17 July—didn't like mud and was outclassed; 27 June—had to be shipped to N.J. & some horses don't like to be shipped. Only race with no adverse circumstances is 25 May—and she won this race.

Good speed rating-track variant (totals 102). Also, the 2 horses that came in 1st are very nice—so she ran in good company and came in 4th which is not bad.

PLACE YOUR BETS

When the handicapping is done, and you are as sure as you will ever be that you know who will win—when reason, logic and faith are all on your side—it's time to risk your money. Actually, you are handing your money to the state racing association, which holds it until it is time to pay it back to the winners. You may wonder how the track knows how much to pay the winners, or who in fact, figures the odds. The answers are all part of the *pari-mutuel system*. Here's how the system works:

When you place a bet on a horse, you are (in effect) becoming a small part of a large betting pool, and your bet affects the ever–changing odds. As the betting tickets are punched out, the *totalizator* (or *tote*) automatically records the amount and bet, and figures out the odds. The information then appears on the totalizator board (*tote board*) for bettors to see. Contrary to popular opinion, it is you, the betting public, who set

the odds—not the track. (The term pari-mutuel actually means "to wager among ourselves.") In plain arithmetic, odds are an expression of how much is bet to win on each horse against the total amount bet to win (*win pool*) on all the horses.

The morning line, which appears in the track program, is the first set of odds to appear on the tote board before a race, and is established by professional handicappers. But these odds change constantly as bets are made. The payoff is based on the final odds established before the race is run. So the bettors establish the favorite, not the track; and the track could care less if a longshot or a favorite wins. Its take is the same. (Big money bet away from the track, at OTB or with bookies, does not figure into the odds because it does not come through the pari-mutuel system.)

Here's how the pari-mutuel system figures the odds and the payout:

HOW THE WINNING ODDS ARE FIGURED

	There are three horses in this imaginary race, and the following amounts are bet:	The first thing the totalizator does is add up the win pool.	It then deducts a commission (around 15 percent) for the track and the state.	The net remaining win pool is divided by the amount bet on each horse, to arrive at a payoff.		The payoff is then translated into odds.	Payoff amount won, minus "breakage," on a $2 bet.
HORSE	Amount Bet to Win	Total Win Pool	15 percent Commission	Net Remaining Win Pool	Quotient	Win Odds Shown on Tote Board	Winning Ticket Pays
Alley Oop	$12,000				÷ 12,000 = 2.41	2 to 1	$4.80 + $2 = 6.80
Belly Up	14,000	$34,000	$5,100	$28,900	÷ 14,000 = 2.06	2 to 1	4.10 + $2 = 6.10
Charlie	8,000				÷ 8,000 = 3.61	4 to 1	7.20 + $2 = 9.20

Notice that some amounts are rounded down to the nearest ten cents. Should Alley Oop win, therefore, each holder of a ticket would win $2.40 for each dollar bet—or $4.80 on a $2 bet. The $2 bet is also returned to the bettor, for a total payoff of $6.80. Alley Oop had a total of $12,000 bet on him to win. Therefore, the most that could be paid out to winning ticket holders is $28,800 ($2.40 for each dollar, or $2.40 × $12,000). The net remaining win pool was $28,900. That $100 difference is called *breakage*, and comes from the rounding down of each payoff to the nearest ten cents. Breakage is returned to the state and to the track . . . sorry.

THE TOTE BOARD

The tote board is the scoreboard *cum* cash register of the racetrack. It is the balance sheet and financial statement of each race, brought to you in flashing lights in front of the grandstand and in smaller displays near the betting window. The board computes its information as bets are made at the betting windows, and each ticket sold is recorded by the totalizator machine. Here's what to look for:

Before each race the current odds (probable payoff) for each dollar bet on each horse in that race are posted. These odds change as the public bets, and the changes are reflected on the tote board. Final odds appear on the tote board just before each race, and after the race.

Race number

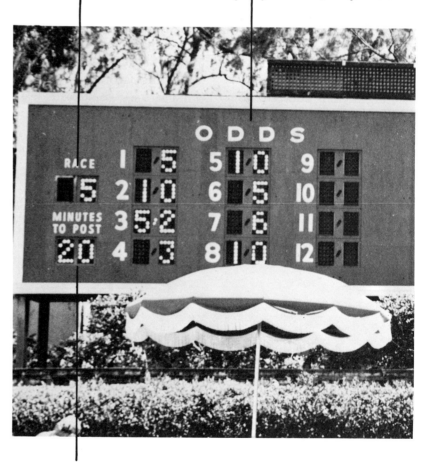

Time (in minutes) to the next race.

The "official" sign is posted after a review of the race finish and foul claims by track officials. Photo finish cameras are used to settle claims of foul.

The order of the first four horses to cross the finish line.

The payoffs that win, place and show horses returned to the holders of $2 tickets.

If there is a photo finish, dead heat, inquiry, or objection, the appropriate word will be posted here.

(S. J. Stidham Photographer.)

Jockeys

"What percent of winning is the horse and what percent is the jockey?" This question will never be fully resolved. But the ability of the person in the saddle is considered sufficiently significant to make millionaires of a select group of people who, if not for a special talent, might have lived their lives in the reflected glory of diminutive giants like Napoleon.

The jockey, who sits atop a half-ton animal that runs at 40 miles an hour, makes up in certain mental and physical attributes what he or she lacks in sheer size. Genetics may have decided that the body will be small, but other powers must accompany the small body. A jockey needs a sense of balance, timing, coordination, judgment, hands that can communicate with a horse and the ability to live with a constant battle to keep the weight down.

All in a day's work for jockey Ernesto Sarmiento, as he weighs in after a victory at Sportsman's Park. He is wearing three pairs of goggles: it was a muddy track that day and when one pair got caked with mud it was pulled down, and a fresh pair was there to take its place. (Courtesy of Sportsman's Park.)

Spectacular Bid winning the Flamingo Stakes. (S.J. Stidham Photographer.)

JUST ANOTHER DAY AT OTB

Nestled snugly between a supermarket and a pizza parlor on a street in the borough of Brooklyn in New York City is an example of a new neighborhood phenomenon, the Off Track Betting (OTB) office.

This particular office is not unlike many of the hundreds of others that have opened in recent years. Perhaps the clientele here is somewhat different in that the office caters to a higher percentage of housewives than its mid-Manhattan counterparts. It is not uncommon to see a baby carriage or grocery cart parked by the front door for several minutes while a housewife stops by to fill out her little betting slip and take two dollars out of the grocery money.

We asked several of the "regular" customers about their betting habits, with the following conversation being somewhat typical:

"Good afternoon, madam. We've noticed that you stop by here quite often. Have you been doing it for a long time?"

"I'm sorry, you must be mistaken. This is the first time I've ever come in here."

"What made you stop in today?"

"I had to place a bet."

"Do you bet often?"

"My husband asked me to bet for him."

"Does your husband bet often?"

"He goes to the track on Saturday."

"I see, so this is a special occasion."

"Somebody gave him a tip at work, so he called me and told me to get the bet down."

"Do you ever go to the track?"

"Once or twice to the trotters."

"Do you find having this OTB office here a convenience?"

"It's easier than looking for a bookie. I . . . listen, I'm in a hurry."

"One final question. Does the fact that your husband might be throwing away his money bother you?"

"Listen, there's no way I can blow this one. I studied the sheets since last night. Blue Devil is a shoo-in in the first, and I bet him three times to win. But just in case, I boxed him with 4 and 6 so I'm covered, and then I wheeled him with six others in the second race so I got almost a sure hitter on the DD. See you around."

(Eugene Grossman–OTB.)

THE BETTING WINDOWS

What to Look for on Your Ticket

This ticket is a six-dollar combination on number 7 in the third race at Churchill Downs on May 2, 1978.

The bettor invested six dollars, in the hopes that horse number 7 would come in first, second or third.

This is the same as making three two-dollar bets (one each to win, place or show).

Number 7 finished out of the money. (That is why we still have the ticket.)

It is important to familiarize yourself with the betting windows. Over each window is a sign that tells you the kind and amount of bet you can make at that window. Do not overlook the possibility of getting on the wrong line. Know what you want to bet, make sure you're on the right line.

While on line, do not be distracted by any conversation going on around you. Be prepared to tell the man behind the window (ticket seller) the correct information and check the ticket he gives you, as he might make a mistake.

Don't be ashamed of your bet. Say it loud and clear so the ticket seller can hear it. To be accurate, place your bet by number, not by the horse's name. For example, "Number 4 to win."

If you wish to bet six dollars at the two dollar window, you would buy three two dollar tickets. For example, "Number 4 to win, three times."

Types of Bets

Betting can be as creative as handicapping, and the number and types of exotic bets available differ from track to track. At one end of the spectrum there is the simple two dollar ticket to win. At the other end

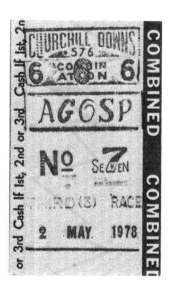

What Happens to Your Two Dollars

Whether you place your bet at the track or at an OTB office, eager hands divide the spoils. If you get through a bookie, there are fewer hands . . . but they seem larger and stronger.

All legal bets are "held" by the State Racing Association and are divided as follows:

	At the track	Through OTB	Through a bookie
Amount returned to track for expenses and to be paid to winning horses	$ .10	$ .02	—
State tax	.20	.04	—
City tax	—	.20	—
OTB expenses	—	.16	—
Returned to bettors	1.70	1.68	1.70
	$2.00	$2.00	$1.70

Are you curious about the 30 ¢ that is missing from the final column? There are some things we are all better off not knowing.

TYPES OF BETS

Type of bet	What you are betting	What must happen in order for you to collect
Win	One horse to finish 1st	Horse must win.
Place	One horse to finish 1st or 2nd	Horse must win or place. (You collect place payoff in either case.)
Show	One horse to finish 1st, 2nd, or 3rd	Horse must win, place, or show. (You collect show payoff in any case.)
Combination	One horse to finish 1st, 2nd, or 3rd	Horse must win, place, or show. (If horse wins, you get win, place and show payoffs. If horse finishes 2nd, you get place and show payoffs. If horse finishes 3rd, you get show payoff.)
Exacta	Two horses in one race to finish 1st and 2nd	Horses must finish 1st and 2nd in exact order you pick.
Quinella	Two horses in one race to finish 1st and 2nd	Horses must finish 1st and 2nd but not in any order.
Triple	Three horses in one race to finish 1st, 2nd, and 3rd	Horses must finish 1st, 2nd, and 3rd in exact order you pick.
Big Q	Four horses—two in one race, two in next race—to finish 1st and 2nd	Horses must finish 1st and 2nd in exact order you pick, in their respective races.
Daily Double	Two horses—one in first race, one in second race—to finish 1st	Each horse must come in 1st.

there is the exotic "Big Q," which is a two-race, four-horse combination (see above). You may purchase as many different tickets on each race as you desire, but bear in mind that in general, the more exotic the bet, the less chance there is of winning.

You may wonder why anyone would bet that a horse would come in second or third, especially if all the handicapping information points to a winner. The answer is simple—prudence, caution, conservatism, insecurity, fear, parsimony, intelligence or any combination of the above.

Sorry, Wrong Number

There is a story told by pari-mutuel employees about the clerk who punched out the wrong ticket. Someone asked for number 4, and the clerk punched out number 5.

After correctly issuing a number 4 ticket, the clerk was left with an unwanted ten-dollar ticket on number 5. The clerk waited, hoping someone would ask for a number 5 ticket. However, no one did, and he was left with his ten-dollar mistake, which he rectified by putting ten dollars of his own money into the register, and pocketing the ticket.

Yes, you guessed it—number 5 won and paid 100 to 1. The butterfingered clerk collected $1,000.

Simple Systems

Some of these have a kind of logic; others are just plain silly. They're offered here for those with a spirit of adventure.

● For each horse, add the first number of the morning line to the jockey's weight (given in the track program). Bet the second-lowest figure to win and place. (From a New York cabdriver.)

● Add together each horse's first three points of call in the last three races of this level. Bet the horse with the lowest total. A variation stipulates that the horse must also have come in at least third, by no more than three lengths, in races at this level run in the last three months. (From a yet-to-be-discovered actor.)

● Progress through the alphabet while going down the list of horses in a race. If the first letter of a horse's name coincides with a letter of the alphabet, bet him—for example if the fourth horse's name is Derring-do. (From an anonymous donor.)

● Add together each horse's earnings in all the races of this level within the last year. Divide by the number of races to find the average. Bet the horse with the highest average. (From a tout.)

● Close your eyes and stick a pin through the track program or racing form. Bet the horses the pin thinks will win. (From Lillian Russell.)

Favorite Betting Systems (In More Ways Than One)

As you know, handicapping is a complex system that the serious or professional horse player uses to pick winners. But there are other, simpler systems the rookie bettor can use to try to separate the winner from the losers.

One of the most popular of these systems is betting the *favorite* (the horse that the betting public has estimated to be the winner). For some this means observance of the commandment, ''Thou shalt bet the favorite to win only.'' For others it means: bet the favorite to win across the board. Does either one really work? Yes, and no—as you will see. If you were to bet on every thoroughbred race run on every track in the United States for one year, you would discover that the favorite will, in three races out of ten, actually turn out to be the winner. And that's not all. You would also find that these very same horses would finish in the money (that is, no worse than third) in six out of every ten races.

What betting the favorite means in terms of dollars and cents is that you will win *more often* than if you had bet the longshots, but you will win *less money each time.* Will you win enough to make the investment pay off? The only way to find out is to go to the track and test the system.

What Happened One Year at Saratoga

If you can't bet on every race at every track, you can go to one *race meeting* (racing season at one track) and show up every day to bet on the favorite in every race. All you need do is take a month off from work and go to, say,

"Win, place, show, win, place, show, win. . .''

picturesque Saratoga, New York, in August, to test the theory.

In 1977 the Saratoga meeting had a total of 216 races. Let's say you bet two dollars on the favorite to win in each race, for a total of $432. And, you also bet six dollars on the favorite across the board (two dollars to win, two dollars to place, two dollars to show). This last little investment amounted to $1,296, for a total bet of $1,728. Here's what would have happened:

SARATOGA 1977: HOW THE FAVORITE FINISHED IN 216 RACES

	1st	2nd	3rd	Out-of-the-money	Total
Number of finishes	76	42	27	71	216
Total winnings paid for across-the-board $2 bets	$395.80	$242.90	$427.90	—	$1,243.60
Total winnings paid for $2 bets to win	$395.80	—	—	—	$395.80
Percent of races won	35%				
Percent of in-the-money races	67%				

Your horses actually performed slightly better than the national average for winning and finishing in–the–money. . . . Nevertheless:

	Money invested	Money won	Money lost
To win	$432.00	$395.80	$36.20
Across the board	$1,296.00	$1,243.60	$52.40

So much for that system? Maybe, but there are always exceptions that prove the rule, and big money winners (and favorites) like Secretariat and Forego do just that.

A Tale of Two Horses or, the Exceptions that Prove the Rule

Two of the big winners of recent years were Secretariat and Forego. If the theory of betting the favorite was applied to these outstanding thoroughbreds, what would have been the results?

Secretariat liked to win big ones: more than half of his starts were in races with purses over $100,000. During his two-year career, he came in first 11 times in 12 major stakes races, and came in second once. If you had bet two dollars on him to win each of those big races, you would have invested a total of $24 and you would have made a profit of $29.50.

When the new record books are printed, Forego will be listed as the number two horse in lifetime earnings, just behind Kelso. In the four years since he became a big favorite in 1974, he came in first a total of 24 times out of 36 races. If you had bet $72 that he would win those races, you would have made a profit of $92.20.

Neither set of winnings would have been a big deal, but, then again, you wouldn't have lost.

	Secretariat	Forego
Number of years raced	2	6
Number of *starts* (total races run)	21	57
Number of 1st, 2nd, 3rd finishes	16-3-1	34-9-7
Number of out–of–the–money races	1	7
Total earnings	$1,316,800	$1,938,900
Percent of races won	76%	60%
Percent of in–the–money races	95%	88%

(Courtesy of Sportsman's Park.)

IN THE HOMESTRETCH

We offer the following suggestions in much the same way as one might say, "take care of yourself"—it's a polite thing to do even though there's a good chance it will be ignored. If past experience is any example, you'll probably get annoyed at not "reading" your first race, and immediately switch to a system for picking winners that is a combination of gutsy nerve, groping guesses, blind faith, and foolish optimism. However, the following is good advice, if you can take it:

• *Do* set a budget and stick to it. Decide how much you can afford to lose on the day, and when you reach that limit, QUIT! *Don't* try to get even on the last race.

• *Do* wait as long as possible to place your bet. Contrary to popular rumor, the payoff is based on the final odds, not the odds at the moment you bet.

• *Don't* let long odds scare you away if you have determined that a horse is a real contender; go ahead and bet him if you like him. Incidentally, 12 to 1 odds are long, but can be considered. Odds of 50 to 1 are very long, and should be avoided.

• *Don't* feel you have to bet each race. Bet the ones that you think you have "read."

• *Don't* look down on place and show bets. A return of 3 to 2 on your investment is better than bank interest—and a lot more exciting.

Remember that there's no substitute for experience. This means not only long years of handicapping but, equally important, seeing race after race in person. Only by seeing a race can you know, for example, that a horse had traffic problems that weren't reflected in the DRF; you might bet him next time out when you wouldn't have on the basis of his chart alone.

Finally, go to the races to have fun, not to get rich. It's no fun to lose, but the information in this book should help you lose less often than most people. Stay within your budget, use your head—and then scream your lungs out when you see your horse come from ten lengths behind at the top of the stretch to hit the wire nose—to—nose with three other horses. Win or lose, that's fun!

The Origin of the Pari-Mutuel System

In 1865, a Frenchman by the name of Joseph Oller devised the first mechanical system to sell lottery tickets on horse races. This system was not complicated, but the purchaser had no choice regarding the horse. It took M. Oller four more years of tinkering before he came up with a machine that issued tickets on the horse of one's choice.

Obviously, a machine that sells tickets and figures the odds competes with the bookmaker. The machine had no friends in the French government, but the bookmakers did, so M. Oller's system was banned. Having nothing better to do with the machine, M. Oller shipped it off to America, where it was installed in Churchill Downs. Again, the bookmakers objected and the machine was returned to France, where in 1887, the government finally relented and pari-mutuel betting became the official system.

It took a few more years for the Americans to change their minds, and this well-traveled machine once again crossed the Atlantic in 1908 to be established as the only legal form of betting in the state of Kentucky. Similar laws were enacted in every state, with New York falling into line in 1940.

Pari-mutuel, on-track betting, off-track betting and bookmaking all compete for the same dollar. What they do with the dollars differs.

What Are the Odds?

Greyhound handicappers give a slight edge to the number 1 dog on the inside track so that the outside dog, number 8, has, if nothing else, his track position against him. On June 10, 1977, somebody forgot to tell that to the dogs. It happened in the 12th race at Sodrac Dog Track in South Dakota. The finish? 8–7–6–5–4–3–2–1!

Nothing Doing!

Take a deep breath before reading this item about a recent chase at Amada (Arizona) Greyhound Park. In the ninth race on the July 12, 1978 matinee, the number 7 dog, Nothing For Her, paid *nothing* to win. It seems that the crowd, including Nothing For Her's owner and trainer, thought nothing of her chances—nary a soul bought a ticket on Nothing For Her. But win she did, and with no win payoff in the race all the win pool money wagered on the other dogs went into the place pool for the overlooked number 7 greyhound.

(*Courtesy of* Systems & Methods)

SPEED IS THE NAME OF THE GAME: GREYHOUND RACING

The greyhound is one of the oldest of dog breeds, and it is bred for one thing, SPEED! Baying hounds ran the deer to ground in Egypt over 3,000 years ago. Today a descendant of that same hound chases a mechanical rabbit to its own frustration and to the excitement of thousands of people in 12 states here in the United States.

The English took up the sport where the Egyptians left off, and ran the dogs after all manner of game . . . a fox hunt without horses, or red jackets, or stewed kidneys for breakfast. People, being people, began to bet on which dog would catch the fox. Eventually, someone had the idea of having the dogs chase after a mechanical lure, and concentrating solely on the betting. People had grown bored with seeing the stuffed fox or rabbit caught by the fastest dog in every race. They wanted to see the lure get away, as it did occasionally in real life.

So, as the French did with the pari-mutuel system when they couldn't sell it at home, the English sent dog racing to America in 1919. For the next ten years, nothing very exciting happened to dog racing. Then, in 1932, several dog tracks requested permission to install pari-mutuel betting. We were about to make use of both European castoffs. The canine bookies started barking; they took the track owners to court, and won their case. (The judges undoubtedly preferred handmade odds to machine-made bullets.) However, several years later the dog tracks did obtain the right to install the pari-mutuel system.

By comparison, today's greyhound would have little success in running the gazelle to ground as its ancestors did in Egypt. The dogs are fast, but they lack stamina. Races are short, and vary from five-sixteenths to seven-sixteenths of a mile: it takes the dogs 30 to 45 seconds to cover the distance. This time includes the bumping that is so much a part of the race. Unlike thoroughbred racing, where males and females each have their own events, greyhounds compete in mixed company. (This might be the cause of the bumping.)

Betting the Dogs

There are usually three classes of dogs, and the pooch handicapper keeps abreast of the movement of the racers from class to class in much the same way that the horse handicapper keeps track of performances in claiming races.

An owner will run his dog every three or four days, and the informed bettor gets to know his bow-wows quite well. Dog handicapping is a more convoluted science than horse handicapping, and some rather weird systems have evolved.

We have heard a tipster say, ". . . if it's a girl in the first post position, bet her. She's closest to the rabbit, and if she bats her eyes or wiggles her tail coming out of the traps, she's also running for her life. . . ."

Someone claims that a female in the first post position will always win, because the male dogs would never run past her marvelous smell. However, the simplest system we have discovered is: ". . . bet the dog that's just relieved himself . . . he's running light. . . ."

(Hollywood Greyhound Track.)

The Mechanical Rabbit

The idea of the mechanical rabbit goes back to the 1800s in England, when racing dogs were trained to chase after a stuffed hare, mounted on a rail and drawn along ahead of the pack via a pulley and crank system.

On more than one occasion, the thrill of the chase was interrupted by a forearm cramp, which led to utter confusion and an explosion of flying cotton.

It was not until the early 1900s that Oliver P. Smith perfected and tested his mechanical hare at a dog track in California.

The means of propulsion of this little creature has been a reflection of the evolution of man's discovery of sources of power. First, there was power supplied by man himself. It was the power of the human arm. Next, after the discovery of electricity, this power source energized our little, floppy-eared runner. Can it be that somewhere, in a modern laboratory, someone is perfecting a nuclear bunny?

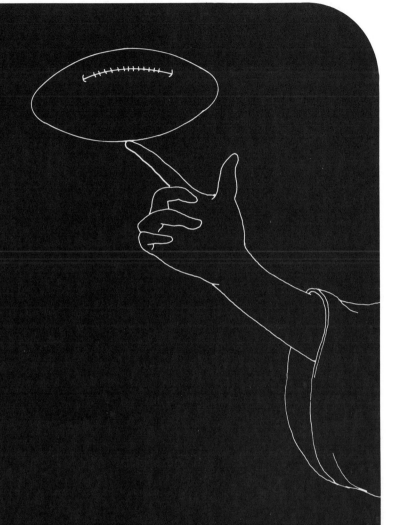

A SPORTING CHANCE

MEET YOUR MATCH

Damon Runyon once said, "All life is 6 to 5 against." He must have been a sports bettor. Not only are your chances of winning sports bets pretty slim, but unless you're betting with a licensed Nevada bookie, or at a racetrack or jai alai fronton, the bet's illegal.

Even an informal small money bet made between friends is against the law, though law enforcement officials don't bother too much with social bettors. The law is more concerned with the people who receive some sort of remuneration—commission or salary—from wagered money. (When bookies are busted, it's the bookies and not their customers who are prosecuted. If a bookie's customer should go to trial, he faces the same minor charges that betting with a friend would bring.)

Yet, sports betting is big business. All over the country money changes hands between friends after every World Series; office football pools flourish; bookies make a very good living; major newspapers even carry information that can be used for sports betting.

Like all bettors, the sports gambler lives in a world of heightened awareness, however narrow. The nine-to-five daily routine is forgotten when you've bet five dollars on the Super Bowl, and the added excitement is worth a lot more than the five dollars. Every fumble, every foul shot, every suicide squeeze . . . they all take on added significance when your money is on the line.

Actually, betting is the logical extension of a long-time involvement with sports. If you're the average sports bettor, you've been exposed to sports all your life: you've grown up having certain teams as favorites; you're familiar with the players and may identify with some; you might even play the game yourself. What then could be more natural than for you and a friend to come to a little verbal agreement about whose favorite team will win? It's a way of competing, both in reality and by association. The winning bettor derives great satisfaction from the fact that not only did his team win, but he knew that it was going to, and what the margin of victory would be.

Most social sports betting is not done to make money, but because the bettor enjoys the game, follows the action throughout the season, and has favorite teams and players.

POINT SPREADS OR BETTING LINES

Most sports betting today relies on a marvelous invention called the *point spread*, which theoretically makes the competing teams' abilities equal. There hasn't always been a point spread, however. At one time there was only one way to bet: man to man, team to team, even up. Couched in football terms, what this came down to was a simple, straightforward wager along the lines of, "the Packers will beat the Giants—my ten dollars against your ten dollars says so." This sort of betting works out fine with evenly matched adversaries, but when there's a mismatch—an inevitability in this less-than-perfect world—there will be problems. This inevitability of inequality first gave birth to the odds (which as you know by this time is a mathematical way of expressing the probability against something happening—in this case, against a certain team winning). Let's say that by some strange quirk of fate, Notre

Dame is scheduled to play Vassar College. Although this is clearly the mismatch of the century, imagine further that the experts have figured Notre Dame as the 5 to 1 favorite. What this means is that on a ten-dollar bet for Vassar (the underdogs), you would collect $50 if they won ($10 × 5 = $50), and the original $10 you bet would be returned. A bet on Notre Dame to win would pay you two dollars ($10 × 1/5 = $2) and your ten-dollar investment would be returned if they were victorious. For most favorite-betting fans, that's hardly worth the trouble. Something else was needed—the point spread, which makes equals out of unequals and makes sports betting unique. It consists of either points added to an underdog team's final score, or points subtracted from the favorite team's final score. These point spreads are computed by experts, using various handicapping systems. As an illustration, let's take another

The Inventor of the Point Spread

Most experts agree that Charles K. McNeil is the man who invented the point spread. Like Mozart, Da Vinci, and other obvious geniuses, McNeil showed considerable early promise. At the age of five he was already making up calendars three years in advance.

After graduating from the University of Chicago in the late 1920s, he took a job teaching mathematics at a private school in New York City. His salary paid his rent, but his real passion was gambling, especially on football. Though he didn't bet much he was extraordinarily successful. So successful that the bookies got curious and began to ask questions.

McNeil explained to them how he made his selections on the basis of a point spread. The bookies apparently hung on every word, for soon the "revolutionary" point system devised by this mild–mannered math teacher was being used throughout New York City.

The point spread makes equals out of unequals.

A team that is riding high on a streak is said to have momentum. *(UPI.)*

football match-up, this one within the realm of possibility: the New York Jets vs. the Miami Dolphins. If Miami is quoted as a 14-point favorite over New York and you bet on Miami, they would have to win by more than 14 points for you to win your bet. If they win or lose by 13 points or less, you lose. If they win by exactly 14 points, all bets are off and no money changes hands. (In the streets, bookies call this situation a *push*.) For the Jets bettor to collect, his team must either win the game or lose by no more than 13 points. That is, if the Jets come within 13 points of the Dolphins' score, he goes home a winner.

There will be fluctuations in the point spread, or line, right up until game time—fluctuations which reflect injury reports, changes in the weather, rumors of recent clubhouse discord . . . everything that can possibly affect the outcome of the game. Some such changes may be reflected in the football line that is published in newspapers the Tuesday before a weekend game. (Other sports lines appear in newspapers on the day of the game.) To illustrate how such factors alter the line, assume that the Dallas Cowboys will play against the Washington Redskins on Sunday. On Tuesday, the Cowboys open as 5-point favorites. But on Wednesday the Cowboys announce that Tony Dorsett, their star running back, is injured, and will not play in the upcoming game. The point spread will now diminish in favor of the Redskins, since Dorsett is a central part of the Cowboys' offense. The Dallas team, once 5-point favorites, might drop to 4- or even 3-point favorites.

HANDICAPPING SYSTEMS

Perhaps the single greatest problem—and the single greatest joy—a bettor faces is in deciding upon the accuracy of the point spread his betting friend (or bookie) is offering him. How can you assess the abilities of opposing teams or players, and thus decide on how large the difference in their final scores will be? Use a handicapping system, just like the experts do. The point spread is a way of expressing an opinion, based on a specific system that attempts to predict the outcome of a game. When you place a bet, you are, in effect, comparing two handicapping systems—yours against the opposing bettor's—and hoping that the final score will prove that yours is the better system.

The key factors that a handicapping system assesses are like the pieces of a puzzle. Once you've put them all together, you have an overall picture of how a team is likely to perform. The better your system, the closer your picture will resemble reality. Wagering without a system—using intuition alone, for example—is bound to make you a loser. With a system, your chances of winning increase.

There are many ways for the sports bettor to find a system. Advertisements for sports handicapping services and power rating systems (see pages 228–229) can be found in newspapers and sports publications. They disseminate their information, for a price, via weekly publications or the telephone. Most of these services are for the football bettor, but there are several that handicap basketball and baseball too. They do the figuring for you, and give you the results of their particular system for picking winners and point spreads. But you can derive a lot more fun and satisfaction by doing your own handicapping.

One piece of advice: no matter what system you use, remember that the ideal handicapping system for the occasional bettor involves assessing modest amounts of information about a team or a player. The idea is not to find the guiding principle of the universe, but to interpret certain key factors that will help you bet as intelligently as possible.

The Educated Bettor

The type of information you need to handicap consists basically of knowing the teams' strengths and weaknesses, and the conditions under which the upcoming game will be played. You then decide how important each factor is—how it will influence the outcome of the game. The best way to get most of this information is first-hand—by watching as many games as you can (this includes exhibition and pre-season games too). Become well acquainted with the teams, and keep up-to-date records of your observations. Unless you enjoy the game itself, and know it well, you have no business betting and expecting to win.

Beware of handicapping your favorite team, and betting on a team just to show your loyalty or confidence. It often results in favoring a team just because you want them to win.

Always keep your eyes and ears open for reports about games you've missed. But realize that other people's interpretations can be biased. So ingest the comments of newspaper sports columnists, TV and radio sportscasters and friends with a grain of salt. Objective data on a team's past performance may be found in publications such as *Sporting News*, *Sports Illustrated*, and *Sports Eye*.

Finally, realize that even the best handicapping system in the world won't eliminate the risk involved in placing a sports bet. You're dealing with flesh-and-blood human beings, and they are less predictable than cards or dice.

If you are a rookie bettor, or a faithful loser, make imaginary bets on paper for awhile. (This cuts down on losses to an amazing degree.) If you don't at least break even on paper, don't expect to win in the real world either. But, add a dash of common sense to the guidelines in this section and you'll at least have a sporting chance.

Don't discount the emotional factor. It can inspire a team to greater heights than what their playing capabilities appear to be.

The Pleasure Principle

Never get beaten by your system or become a slave to it—whether it's one you have adopted or created. Beating the bookies, the point spread, and the vagaries of fate are difficult enough. If a system is too complex and takes too many diverse factors into account, the sports fan will lose a lot of the pleasure of handicapping. If the "slumping pitcher" or the "hot quarterback" system hasn't been working for you lately, rethink your position. Systems were born to be revised.

WHAT'S YOUR LINE?

Most major newspapers publish sports lines as a service to their readers; sportscasters generally parrot the newspaper line. These sports lines are intended to represent the actual differences in strength (in whole numbers) between two teams, and are not for betting purposes. However, they can be used for bets. These lines may be figured by Jimmy "The Greek" Snyder, whose column appears in numerous newspapers; they may "unofficially" originate with the sports editor's bookie; or they could be based on the *official line,* which comes out of Las Vegas.

The official line originating from Las Vegas is used by bookmakers all over the country. It is based on information from various regional experts who furnish their opinions to Las Vegas. A small group of Nevada experts are permitted to adjust the line according to any flaws and weaknesses they see. The result is the official line, which the legal bookmakers in Nevada post. Use is made of half-points, and the line is used for betting purposes. Actually, the whole purpose of this line is to attract betting on both teams, regardless of whether it is an accurate handicap or not. Local bookies use the official line—for which they pay a hefty sum each week—and adjust it for local conditions, and to balance their books.

Another line is the power line, which is explained on pages 228–229.

Bob Martin

If you have $10,000 or even $25,000 to risk on the outcome of a football game, and you'd like to keep it legal, Bob Martin is the man to see. His love affair with gambling began over four decades ago, and in the mid-1960s he made it legal. This renowned authority on sports gambling has come a long way from his native Brooklyn—he's now in charge of the sports betting at the Churchill Downs Sports Book on the Las Vegas Strip. There are others who set prices and betting lines in Las Vegas, but Bob ("Mr. Oddsmaker") Martin is credited with setting the preliminary odds that are sent out to other bookies all over this country. That, combined with the size of the bets he accepts, makes him a very high-class bookie indeed.

The Latest Line

Giants done in early by costly mistakes in loss to Cards at St. Louis, have capability to beat Redbirds and silence boobirds in home finale . . . But for being live playoff hopeful while Browns are out of it, Jets would not be favored; go with Browns to prevail before home crowd.

PRO FOOTBALL

Favorite	Pts.	Underdog
St. Louis	3	GIANTS
JETS	1	CLEVELAND
ATLANTA	3	Washington
Dallas	4	PHILADELPHIA
NEW ENGLAND	11½	Buffalo
Houston	2½	NEW ORLEANS
Green Bay	1½	CHICAGO
DENVER	8	Kansas City

MIAMI	6	Oakland
SAN DIEGO	3	Seattle
SAN FRANCISCO	3½	Tampa Bay
(MONDAY)		
LOS ANGELES	6	Cincinnati

PRO BASKETBALL

Favorite	Pts.	Underdog
MILWAUKEE	7½	San Diego
LOS ANGELES	8½	Atlanta
SEATTLE	4½	San Antonio

HOCKEY

Favorite	Goals	Underdog
BOSTON	2½	Minnesota
Buffalo	½-1	Toronto
RANGERS	1-1½	Philadelphia
MONTREAL	1-1½	Islanders
CHICAGO	1½-2	Detroit

Home Team in CAPS.

(Reprinted by permission of the Chicago Tribune-New York News Syndicate, Inc.)

FOOTBALL— THE SUPER SPORT

From a gross dollar volume standpoint, football wagering is the king of sports betting.

Football has the dubious distinction of being the sport upon which the most money rides. The Super Bowl is the biggest single betting event in the country (outside of baseball's World Series, which consists of several games).

HANDICAPPING FOOTBALL

Its been said that the best thing about football is the information the game generates—enough to keep even the most ardent handicapper happy. Not all the information is of equal value, however. Solo tackles per game, or yards per completion, for example, are interesting, but hardly useful to the bettor. Here are the most important factors for you to keep your eye on. Many of these same factors are used for handicapping other sports events as well.

Final Scores vs. the Point Spread

Your team may be having a miserable 3 and 11 year. Nevertheless, it is possible that in spite of their losing record they are constantly beating the point spread. Take the New York Jets of 1977. They were crushed by nearly every opponent, but they still almost always beat the point spread published in the newspapers.

You should keep track of all final

scores in relation to the point spread. In time you should see trends developing—which teams are underrated, which are overrated, and which teams beat the point spread. If you had been doing that in 1977, you could have won a bundle on the Jets.

Weather and Climate

This is one of the most overlooked sports betting angles. Warm-weather teams—like the Miami Dolphins—always have a tough time of it when they're playing in a cold-weather climate—like in Minnesota. A team that trains in the sunshine never quite gets used to subarctic conditions. Fumbles are more frequent, as are incompletions and other lapses.

It goes the other way too, of course. When the Minnesota Vikings, accustomed to subzero temperatures, have to play in balmy weather, say 85° F.—as in Miami or New Orleans—they're also bound to lose some of their drive and energy.

Mud, rain, and wind can also radically affect the outcome of a game, but more so for a speedy or passing team than for a plodding, strong-running, "three yards and a cloud of dust" team. If the game is to be played in an area that's prone to bad weather, wait as close to game time as possible to make your bet.

The weather is only one of the factors that can change the point spread of a game.

Injuries

A bettor must know a team's offensive and defensive strengths before he can judge how severely an injury will hurt its chances. Key injuries that will significantly affect the final score aren't always as obvious as you might assume.

A ball-control team can even lose its quarterback and still be a powerhouse. As long as its running backs and offensive linemen are healthy, it can still do the job. If a throwing team should lose its quarterback, star wide receiver or pass-catching tight end, however, it could be irreparably crippled.

Nobody Does It Better

How does Danny Sheridan, just about the best sports handicapper around, do it?

"My entire approach is based on one assumption: that football is 99 percent emotion. The average fan will think I'm nuts, but I totally ignore comparisons of opponents' offenses, defenses, quarterbacks, injury reports, and so on. . . . What I look at is this: Everyone agrees that with few exceptions, team A can beat team B on any given day. I carry it a step further and try to see if that given day is about to arrive . If I think that's the case—and it usually has to do with a team's emotional outlook—then I'm not afraid to go up against the conventional wisdom.

"Two years ago, for example, Oklahoma had the greatest college team in the nation, and they were playing at home against the University of Kansas. At game time, Oklahoma was a 25–point favorite, and . . . they'd just come off a road trip during which they'd slaughtered schools that had already beaten Kansas. What the odds-makers didn't appreciate was how completely Oklahoma was looking past Kansas to their game with Nebraska the following week. Kansas, meanwhile, had been pointing toward the Oklahoma game all season. So I picked Kansas. . . . Even my subscribers thought I was out of my mind—until Kansas won, 23 to 3."

(Danny Sheridan in "Picking Winners" by Lawrence Linderman, from Esquire, *December 1977. Used by permission.)*

Star players aren't the only ones to watch for injuries. Losing three or four men from the starting line-up can turn a Super Bowl contender into an also-ran, because those might be the guys who do their jobs consistently well—but quietly. Football is, after all, a team sport.

Replacing a competent veteran with a rookie can often lead to disaster in a pressure situation. You should have a good idea of how strong a team's bench is; you never know when one of those guys will be needed.

Emotion

Never discount this crucial factor. Those dinosaurs that play pro football are very emotional animals. Did the Rams humiliate the Saints earlier in the year? Did they accuse the Saints of not being able to beat Our Sisters of Mercy Convent? If so, look for inspired football the next time they clash.

The Importance of the Game

Ask yourself who the teams played last week, who will they play next week? The answers will help you gauge how hard the team will play. If a team has already clinched a play-off spot, it's not going to go all-out to beat an inferior team. If a team is fighting for a play-off spot, it will. When two teams are struggling to stay out of last place, bet the underdog—they'll fight hard to avoid that spot at the very bottom.

A team that has just won a pivotal game against an arch rival might be

In all team sports the bettor should be concerned with the whole team, not just the star players. (Bill Smith.)

down (drained) the following week. A team facing a big shootout in the near future might be "looking ahead," and therefore *flat* for this week's opponent.

The Schedule

Travel is another determining factor. The discerning bettor pays a lot of attention to a team's schedule. Sometimes jet lag determines the score to a greater extent than the talent in the field. This doesn't apply to short hops, as when Philly plays Washington; it concerns long hauls, that can crush even the finest football team. Paying attention to the schedule will tell you when a favored team may be just too tired to play at its peak.

Home Field Factor

Closely connected to the schedule is the home field factor. Playing on the home field is not as important in football as it is in other sports, because the increased use of artificial turf has resulted in more uniform playing surfaces.

Nevertheless, a three-season study by one group of statisticians resulted in some interesting findings: When two teams were evenly matched and there was no point spread (called a *pick'em*), the home team won about three times more often than the visiting team. When the spread was from 1 to 3 points, the visiting team won almost three times as often as the home team. When the point spread was between 7 and 9½, the visiting team won almost twice as often as the home team. And, when the spread was between 12½ and 14½, the visiting team lost almost twice as often as it won. These findings are only the result of a three-season study, and this year's season may not conform, of course. Keep your own records to see if this season seems to be moving along the same lines.

Clubhouse Disharmony

Do the players complain about their coaching staff, the meddling front office, or the size of their salaries? Is there racial discord on the team? If you read about such things in the papers, take note. Remember—unhappy teams don't play very well.

BETTING

In an informal bet, you either give points or take them. If, based on your handicapping system, you think that your team will win by more than 14 points, you offer to give 14 points to an opposing bettor's team. If he agrees to the spread (thinks your team will win by less than 14 points) you shake hands, and the bet is on. If, however, he wants more than 14 points, the two of you haggle and bargain until you arrive at a mutually satisfactory point spread. When you finally come to

Losers are immortalized in the words of country songwriter Glenn Sutton's lyrics to "The Football Card":

The Football Card
Well, the gamblin' bug bit a lot of men
But what it's done to me is a rotten sin
I was on the job and workin' hard
When a man comes along with a football card.
And said try your luck boy, all your friends have won
I've bet myself clean out of house and home.
Cuz there ain't nothin' this side of hell
Like tryin' to pick a winner in the NFL
So I played the thing for a week or two
And got a little behind like most folks do.
Especially when your luck is goin' wrong
And started doublin' up
That's when they popped me, son.
Well, I lost my furniture on a Denver bet
And Oakland got my new Corvette
And the Rams are the reason I cashed five hot checks.
The Cardinals took my bank account
And the Redskins got a similar amount
That I borrowed from a finance company on a 90 day note.
Then Dallas put me in a hell of a fix
I gave up 7 and they won by 6
You'd think that Staubach personally hated me.
The Green Bay Packers were doin' fine
Til they had to go into overtime
And when you got plus 1, you're dead when they win by 3.
Then, along come the Baltimore Colts
For another stack of the cool 'C' notes.

terms, the bet is made at even money: if you each put up five dollars, you stand to win five dollars.

Betting with a bookie is basically the same, except you're not betting even money. For single games (*straight action*), the odds are usually 11 to 10. Whether you bet the favorite or the underdog you must in effect put up $11 in order to win $10. If you win the bet you get back $21—the $10 winnings plus your original $11 bet. If you lose the bet, you owe the bookie $11. On a *parlay*, where you bet a single wager on two games, the odds are usually about 12 to 5. So if you bet $5 and both teams win, you get back $12 plus your original $5 bet; if one team loses you lose your $5 even if your

It seems I can't win no matter what I try.
Bert Jones might be their franchize
But the way he bloodshot these old eyes
Is enough to make a grown man sit and cry.
Well, the Pittsburgh Steelers left no choice
But for my poor wife to file for divorce
On the simple grounds of football cruelty.
Then I heard somewhere that the Bears were hot
So with them I took another shot
And you guessed it pal, the Falcons beat 'em 40 to 3.
Then Seattle and the cool Jim Zorn
Made me wish I'd never been born
I even let Tampa Bay take a shot at me
But I've got the Bengals and the Chargers to thank
For the losses that drove me to rob that bank
Even the cop that arrested me
Looked like a referee.
Now here I sit with a stupid grin
And the jury's just now comin' back in.
And the foreman and the judge are lookin at me real hard
And I know in my heart what they're gonna say
They gonna put me away where I can't play
That American Dream of tryin' to beat that Football Card.
Football, I can't win.
I think I'll give it one more shot in the playoffs
Maybe I can win the Superbowl
Football I hate it. I love it. Mercy.

© Flagship Music Inc (BMI), Nashville, Tenn.

other team wins.

Though the odds are the same for all bookies, the point spreads, or line, they offer the bettor may be different. A bookie changes the spread in order to "balance" his "books." The spread theoretically balances the teams' strengths, but this noble aspiration is somewhat mitigated by the bookie's real goal in life: to attract bets in relatively even amounts on both sides. In effect, this is the same as balancing his books on any one game. For instance, in any two-team confrontation, the bookie may want precisely half his action to be on each team. If one team is being heavily bet and the other ignored, however, he will adjust his point spread accordingly, to make the lightly–bet team more attractive. If, for example, the favorite is being heavily bet and the point spread is 7, the bookie may change it to 8. This makes it more difficult for the favorite to beat the spread, and should attract more underdog bettors.

The reason for this balancing act is known as *vigorish* or *juice*—the 10 percent extra on the losing wagers a bookie needs to stay in business. He doesn't care which team wins: as long as his customers win and lose equal amounts, he collects his 10 percent extra from the losers. He is assured of this percentage by accepting bets at 11 to 10 odds (sometimes quoted as 5½ to 5). This means when you bet $100 and win, you come out $100 ahead. But when you lose, you pay the bookie $110. The extra ten dollars is the *vig* —the bookie's commission for his services—and it's paid only on losing bets. For every $200 wagered ($100 wagered and won by bettors plus $100 wagered and lost by bettors), the bookie will earn a ten dollar profit if his books are balanced. It may not seem like much, but sports betting in general caters to the affluent, and usually involves big money.

A bookie may also change the point spread to avoid the *push* (when the final score hits the point spread exactly). To do this, he simply adds a half-point to the spread. While half-points do not exist in actual final scores, half-points are very real for the bettor. Say, for example, the spread is 4½ and the final score is 14 to 10. If you had bet the underdog, you would have won the bet, because the favorite won by less than 4½ points.

The Inside Dope on Inside Information

They don't call it inside dope for nothing—for you are a dope if your bet is based on information supplied by a clubhouse worker or any other such little "birdie." Just think—betting is the bookies' business. What makes you think that any inside information that falls into your hands doesn't get to them too? Bookies have access to several lines—the early line from legal bookmakers in Nevada and other regional bookies being just two sources. The only inside info you can really bet on is that bookies will hear about any change in the odds before you do.

FINDING A BOOKIE

Much wagering, particularly on the World Series and the Super Bowl, is conducted between friends. One likes the Steelers, the other likes the Cowboys; there's a handshake, and the deal is done. This is fine for the occasional bettor, but for the dyed-in-the-wool sports gambler it just won't do. He places his bets with a bookie.

People find a good "sports accountant" the same way they find a good doctor or lawyer—by word of mouth. The recommendations of friends and relatives are paramount. Inveterate bettors feel that the sinister image of the bookmaker is inaccurate, and view him as a man of integrity. Of course, there are exceptions, but as a rule they feel that a book must be as good as his word or he wouldn't be able to stay in business. He must, after all, build up a bond of trust with his clients, since most sports betting is done on credit.

In many cities, the sports accountant works on the *call back* system. Bettors call his answering service—most often a housewife trying to earn a little extra money—and leave their names and numbers. In time, the book calls back from a pay phone. The client asks for the prices (odds and point spreads) on the games that interest him, and if anything sounds appealing, the bet is made. "Settle-up Day" is

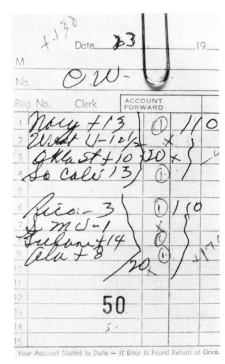

A bookie's typical wager slip.

usually Tuesday, and takes place at some pre-arranged place between bettor and bookie.

In this age of consumerism, if a bettor isn't satisfied with his book—the spreads are too high, the call-backs are too slow, etc.—he can shop around for another. Bookmaking is a service industry in the most classic sense.

No One Really Knows

How many bookies are there? How many bettors? Statistics are highly unreliable.

First of all, most people will not admit to gambling since it is illegal in most states. On the other hand, politicians tend to overstate the size of the "gambling menace," especially around election time. As for law enforcement agencies, you rarely read about the candy store bust—it is always the "multi–million dollar betting combine" when you see it in the headlines.

As close as the FBI and the IRS can estimate, there are at least 300,000 bookies in the United States. As for the amount of action they handle, the most conservative figure cited is $40 billion annually ($50 or $60 billion is probably more like it). That's about the size of the Gross National Product of a fairly well-off, industrialized nation.

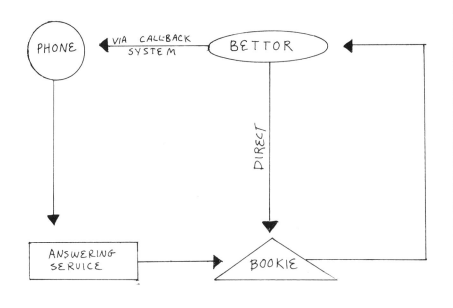

POWER RATING SYSTEMS*

Some handicapping services call themselves *power rating systems*, or *lines*. You'll find advertisements for them sprinkled liberally throughout sports magazines and newspapers. The originators, who use computations worthy of the latest space launch, start out by comparing previous points scored by and against two competing teams. As shown in the example below, Team A has a winning average of 5⅔ points; Team B lost by an 8-point average. So Team A would enjoy a spread of 13⅔ points over Team B. But that's not the end of it. The

originators—many of whom use computers—add or subtract points according to certain factors. For instance, being the home team might be worth five points; an injury on a team could mean two less points; four points might be subtracted from a team's point spread because of team discord.

Bookies never use such power lines, but are aware of them because their customers may be influenced by them. (The bookie bases his line on the official one handed down from Las Vegas.)

Just to satisfy curiosity, a

comparison of a newspaper's betting line, a power rating line, and the actual point spread at game's end for the 1974 College Football Bowl Games appears on the next page.

Notice that the betting line came within two points of the actual point spread in only two games—the Peach Bowl and the Fiesta Bowl. The power rating line fared even worse—it was within two points only in one game, the Rose Bowl. The average difference between the betting line and the final point spread was about nine points; the power rating, twelve points.

TEAM A

Game	A's score	Opponent's score	Difference
A vs. C	31	26	+ 5
A vs. D	24	10	+14
A vs. E	17	19	− 2
		Total point difference}	+17
		Average point difference}	+ 5⅔

TEAM B

Game	B's score	Opponent's score	Difference
B vs. C	13	33	−20
B vs. D	14	10	+ 4
B vs. E	6	14	− 8
		Total point difference}	−24
		Average point difference}	− 8

Courtesy of R. Phillip Hacker, Federal Bureau of Investigation.

1974 COLLEGE FOOTBALL BOWL GAMES

Game	Betting line	Power rating	Actual point spread
ASTRO-BLUEBONNET BOWL North Carolina State		3	
vs.			
Houston	2½		0
SUN BOWL North Carolina			
vs.			
Mississippi State	6½	13	2
PEACH BOWL Texas Tech			
vs.			
Vanderbilt	1	10	0
FIESTA BOWL Brigham Young			
vs.			
Oklahoma State	10	14	10
GATOR BOWL Texas U.	7	3	
vs.			
Auburn			24
SUGAR BOWL Florida			
vs.			
Nebraska	12½	17	3
COTTON BOWL Penn State	3½		21
vs.			
Baylor		3	
ROSE BOWL Ohio State	6½		
vs.			
Southern California		3	1
ORANGE BOWL Alabama	10½	13	
vs.			
Notre Dame			2

College Football

Handicapping games on the college level is much the same as handicapping pro football. (The early betting line comes out the Tuesday before the game, but may go up and down all week long.) But it may be more difficult to get objective information, as home team newspapers like to make the local team look better than they really may be.

Additionally, the emotional factor becomes even more influential than in the pro games. With traditional rivalries, such as Michigan vs. Ohio or USC vs. UCLA, the point spread is rendered meaningless because emotion has such unpredictable power. In these situations, some say you should lean toward the underdog, who usually has the most to prove, and more often than not beats the point spread. Playing a game on the home field makes this factor even more important. A home underdog is a prime candidate to beat the point spread. Homecoming weekends are even worse—with the players' parents, girlfriends, friends, and professors watching. Imagine what that does to their will to win!

ON THE REBOUND

College Basketball

What goes for the pros generally goes for the college teams too. In one sense, however, the coach in college basketball is more important than in pro games. He's in the position of taking good high school material and maybe making it great. And for all the pros to see. He has great influence on the players, who are in a malleable, transitional state, and who aspire to the heights that a pro has already achieved.

The point spread in college basketball is likely to be inaccurate because of two factors: the number of games per season—4000 college basketball games—which means a lot of factors to consider (college football plays 600 games per season); and a lack of information, since most printed information comes from the publicity departments of the schools.

Many experts also believe that home court advantage means more on the college level than on the pro level. They argue that professionals are accustomed to travel and strange surroundings; unlike college teams, the pros are less likely to be distracted by an unfamiliar court and have probably played on the opponent's home court before anyway. Finally, the pros' play is their business—and they mean business.

Each year basketball gets a little bigger, and so does the betting action on it. That's because the game is rather heart-stopping for the bettor—leads can change more than 20 times in a single game. Point spreads are given in major newspapers, but even the best-figured line can be wrecked by a last–minute foul shot.

HANDICAPPING

Basketball handicapping is the same as football handicapping. In figuring out the point spread, some of the same factors as those in football are taken into consideration: injuries, final scores vs. point spreads, importance of the game, and the schedule. Factors unique to basketball include the following.

Streaks

No other professional sport is so prone to streaks. Wins and losses tend to come in bunches. A team can play atrociously for the first half of a season, and then come on like gang busters for second half. As the players say, it's just a matter of

(UPI.)

230

"putting it all together." So pay attention to win/loss records. Chart them from the start of the season, and see if a pattern develops. Is one team on a streak? Is another in one of its periodic tailspins? In 1977, for example, the New Jersey Nets were indescribably awful for most of the season. But with 15 games to play, they suddenly caught fire. If you had been charting their progress, you could have made a pile of money.

Sports bettors are not necessarily interested in winning—but they are interested in winning by points.

Home Court Factor

If two teams are evenly matched, the home team will usually win the game. But figuring out what part that home court advantage plays is a very tricky business, since it varies from year to year. Some seasons, nearly all teams seem to get clobbered on the road. Other seasons, road victories and home victories are in about the same ratio.

To complicate matters, different teams react differently to the home court. From 1977 to 1978, Portland was virtually unbeatable at home. During this same period, the New York Knicks were patsies at home— they seemed to freeze in front of their vociferous fans. Only if you compare the win/loss records for both home and away games will you know which teams have a definite home court advantage.

The Emotional Factor

Some have labeled this the "hungriness factor." Every season there will be one or two teams that feel they have something to prove. Their talent may be mediocre but they'll win many games on hustle and drive. Like the 1977 Atlanta Hawks: picked by the experts to finish last, they actually made it to the play-offs. The only way to discover these good investments is to keep records of how each team does against the point spread.

Bookies Hate College Basketball

What bookies hate above all else is dishonesty. It's true they don't report all their income to the IRS, but they do pay off on time and they trust their clients will do the same. They don't like college basketball because, as most insiders suspect, "fixing" may exist, especially in the smaller conferences.

It's nothing flagrant. A player will not deliberately miss a shot. But he will allow his opponent to drive around him and score. He will commit stupid fouls. There are a lot of ways to shave a point and sabotage a point spread. Even referees have been mentioned in terms of fixing. By calling foul shots and controlling the tempo of the game, they can play as much a part in the final score as a player.

College basketball fixing, say the cognoscenti is going to be our next national scandal.

It is not, however, the immorality of the dishonesty that the bookies hate—it just means bad business, because it interferes with the vig.

BETTING

Basketball bets are basically the same as football bets. Nothing in basketball, however, approaches the level of betting that takes place for a Super Bowl.

PROS AND CONS OF LEGALIZED GAMBLING

State governments are faced with this dilemma: should they legalize—and therefore be able to tax and benefit from—gambling?

Should they, in effect, sanction an activity that many officials regard as immoral, in order to reap monetary rewards and increase their revenues? Here, in a nutshell, are both sides of the question, as outlined in a 1973 government bulletin:

Pros

1. Gambling, it is alleged, is a universal instinct, which cannot be eradicated.

2. State laws against illegal gambling are difficult and expensive to enforce.

3. Since many persons will gamble despite prohibitive laws, practice diverges from law. This results in hypocrisy and widespread violation of the law.

4. If gambling is legalized, the courts might be more willing to enforce statutes against illegal forms of gambling.

5. Lotteries and taxes on gambling are a relatively painless way to raise public funds.

6. Undesirable persons who have entered gambling and given it a bad name can be forced out.

7. The impulsive gambler exists whether or not gambling is legalized.

8. Gambling provides employment for about 420,000 people.

Cons

1. Gambling creates no economic goods and no wealth, and is a parasite.

2. Gambling operates on a one–sided percentage basis which makes it impossible for bettors as a class to benefit.

3. At best, gambling distributes wealth from the many to the few. A Massachusetts study showed that four out of five who could least afford to gamble purchased lottery tickets.

4. If gambling is considered undesirable, legalization makes gambling more accessible to more people and promotes it.

5. Legalized gambling may increase certain types of crime such as counterfeiting, robbery, and embezzlement.

6. Legalized gambling will not eliminate illegal kinds of gambling. People will continue to patronize bookies who furnish credit; bettors may also prefer bookies because they can place a large bet without affecting the payoff prices and the odds—when a longshot wins, the bettor using a bookie can make two to three times as much as he would have if he had bet at a track.

7. Off-track betting will not eliminate or weaken the numbers game because the payoff percentage is considerably smaller, ticket outlets are not readily available or convenient for those who play numbers, drawings are too infrequent, and tickets cost too much.

8. Gambling, like other "natural instincts," may be controlled and regulated in the public interest—illegal gambling flourishes because of political corruption and protection rather than as a result of natural instinct.

Baseball betting is second only to football in popularity. There are betting lines, as in football and basketball, but there are no point spreads.

HANDICAPPING

Handicapping in baseball is done with the odds. If, for example, the New York Yankees are favored over the Los Angeles Dodgers in the World Series, the line may be Yankees 7 to 5. Basically, the odds reflect who the favorite is, but they are also used for betting purposes to determine how much must be bet in order to win a certain amount. In addition to the handicapping factors already mentioned, consider these.

The Pitcher

Connie Mack once said that pitching was 70 percent of the game. It's probably closer to 90 percent. A winning pitcher, like Tom Seaver or Nolan Ryan, can turn any team into an instant favorite. But a pitcher's performance should be looked at in relation to the whole team. A pitcher who devastates most teams just might have no success against one particular team.

And what if the star pitcher is injured? The relief pitcher in the bull pen takes over—so take a look at those guys too. A "stopper" like Sparky Lyle is every bit as crucial as that flashy starter.

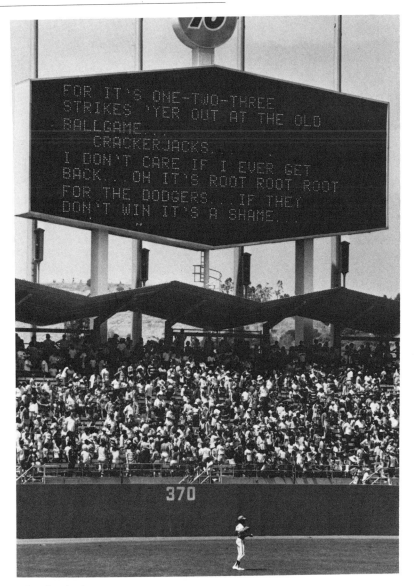

(Robert Landau.)

The pitcher's capabilities account for 80 to 90 percent of the game. Here, Dodger pitchers Doug Rau (number 31) and Charlie Hough (number 49) stretch out in pre-game exercise drills. (Robert Landau.)

Gimmick Bets

A hustler—sometimes occupying the bleacher seat next to you—may try to tempt you with a gimmick bet, which is essentially a guessing game.

• In *run pools*, you bet 50¢ for a very slim chance of winning a $150–$200 payoff. You select four or five teams you think will score the most runs in the coming week, and must be correct in all choices to win the bet.

• In *six hit pools*, you select three players who you think will together total six or more hits in one day. Only one game in a double header counts. Winners are paid off at 8 to 1.

• To play *Big Eight* (also called Over/Under), you pick a team and bet that it will score either over eight runs or under eight runs in a game. If the team scores exactly eight runs, all bets are off. The odds for this type of bet are usually 9 to 5 (you bet five dollars to win nine dollars).

• *Homers* is the most difficult of gimmick bets to win, but if you do the payoff is an enormous 279.5 to 1. Bettors select three players who they think will each hit one homer in a single day. Only single games of double headers count, and bettors must specify which of the two games they are counting beforehand.

The Team's Hitting

Some of baseball's most feared sluggers are streak hitters—Graig Nettles is one of them. He'll strike out a lot, and then hit four or five homers in as many games. When a streak hitter is really on fire, he can singlehandedly carry a ball club—so look for the man with the hot hand.

The Playing Field

No two ballparks are alike. In Boston's Fenway Park, for example, the Red Sox are deadly because of the short left field fence they know so well. In Yankee Stadium, where left field is known as "Death Valley," the Sox are at a great disadvantage. Shots that would be homers in Fenway Park are just routine outs in Yankee Stadium. Chicago's Wrigley Field is also notoriously conducive to hitting homers. On artificial turf, infielders must be not only sure-handed, they must be fast, since grounders take off like rockets.

Win/loss records must be viewed in relation to the playing field factor.

BETTING

Unlike football, in baseball you bet on a team to win and the number of runs they win by is usually immaterial. If they win, you win.

When one places a bet with a bookie, the payout depends on the bookie's price line, which is an extension of the odds—usually from

EVERYBODY INTO THE POOL!

The charm of the betting card, also called a *pool,* is that it's so easy to use. Most betting cards are for football, but you'll also find them for basketball, baseball, and soccer. You simply circle your picks (they cost one dollar minimum each) and if you pick three games correctly, you get back five dollars. The only problem is that the pool operator's advantage is outrageously high—37½ percent for picking 3 winning teams, and it may be around 90 percent for picking 10 winning teams. And in case of a tie, you lose your dough—at least with a bookie you would get it back. Another sobering thought: when pools are run privately—by, say, your fellow office workers—the odds against your winning are bad, but at least they're fair. When run by outsiders for commercial gain, the odds can easily be rigged; no one knows exactly how much has been put into the pool—except the pool operators. So payoffs often fall far short of what they should be. The difference is pocketed by the operators.

One-hundred-square sheets are even worse bets than betting cards. When you buy one, in effect you are assigned two numbers from one to ten. Let's say the Chiefs are playing the Raiders, and you are given the numbers 3 and 8. This means that the Chiefs will have to score 3, 13, 23, 33, 43 . . . some number that ends in 3. And the Raiders will have to score a number that ends in eight . . . 8, 18, 28, 38, and so on. If you should luck out on a dollar bet, you would get back $99—not a bad return for your money. But the odds against your winning are 99-1, and an operator would deduct his profit from your winnings so you would actually be getting only about $60.

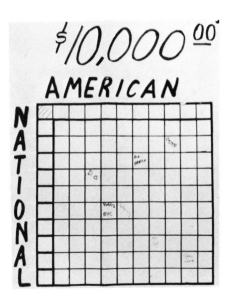

A baseball pool card for $100 per square.

The "Black" Sox Scandal of 1919

The year was 1919 and the Chicago White Sox were heavily favored (4 to 1) to beat the Cincinnati Reds in the World Series. White Sox first baseman Chick Gandil got the idea to throw the Series— "put it in the bag," as they used to say.

Gandil convinced seven other White Sox front–line players to go along. It wasn't hard to do because they were all united in their hatred of Charles Comiskey, the tight–fisted tyrant who owned the White Sox. Comiskey had the most awesome team in baseball, yet he underpaid his players.

Gandil first approached Joe "Sport" Sullivan, a noted Boston gambler, for the fix fee; then he tried William T. "Sleepy Bill" Burns. Neither could meet the $80,000 fee so Gandil turned to the legendary Arnold Rothstein—"The Big Bankroll" himself. Fixing the World Series was too big even for the likes of him and he also turned down the plan. However, one of Rothstein's lieutenants was enchanted with the idea, and gave Gandil and friends the go-ahead—which is precisely what they did.

When the facts finally came to light, the White Sox became the "Black" Sox to their fans. The eight ballplayers of easy virtue were banned from baseball forever—and never received a penny for their trouble. Rothstein's lieutenant never had the money to back them up.

Soccer

Soccer is the world's most heavily bet sport, and the fastest growing sport in this country. In Europe and elsewhere, soccer wagering is done primarily on a pool basis: bettors put up their money—usually a small sum—and try to pick the outcome of 15 to 20 games. The odds against success are astronomical (for instance, 20 games can end over 1,000,000 ways not counting ties), but so are the payoffs. Right now, most of the United States action is of the even–up variety between fans. (There's not enough betting action for the bookies yet.)

When picking the favorite, keep track of many of the same factors used in football but pay particular attention to the weather. Wind and rain can alter the results. The playing field is also important. Some are grass, some artificial turf. A team's unfamiliarity with the playing surface is more than enough to beat that thin line between victory and defeat. Finally, consider past performance. Soccer results are amazingly consistent. If the Cosmos whipped the Rowdies last time out, they'll probably do so again.

Las Vegas—that the bookie is using for that game. The odds depend solely upon who the starting pitcher for the game will be (information announced the day before the game), and if another pitcher starts, bets may be cancelled—unless you have specified you want "action" regardless of who starts.

The price line represents the difference between how much the favorite bettor wins, and assures the bookie of making a profit; assuming he has balanced the books and has attracted an equal number of bets on both teams. For example, a bookie might say the line on the next game is 120-140. A bettor on the favorite must wager $140 in order to win $100; a fan of the underdog must wager $100 in order to win $120. The difference between what the bookies pay each type of bettor if they win is the bookie's profit, or vigorish. In this case it is $20, and is

known as a 20¢ line. The bookie's profit margin is less on a 10¢ line, the other common price line.

Friendly bets on baseball games can eliminate price lines and be based on the odds, which are published in the newspaper. If you bet on the favorite to win, you *lay odds;* the underdog bettor *takes odds.* As in football betting, the parties may go through a negotiating stage until both sides are happy with the odds. If the odds agreed upon are 7 to 5, the favorite bettor wagers seven dollars in order to win five dollars; the underdog bettor puts up five dollars in order to win seven dollars. When one team is a heavy favorite, friends may agree to give the underdog a certain number of runs (like a point spread). The bets made are even money; each bettor puts up the same amount and stands to win the same amount.

Professional soccer in Buenos Aires. (United Nations/P. Teusher.)

IN THE RING

The scandal-ridden history of this sport is blamed for boxing's fall from popularity as a betting sport. The estimated annual handle on boxing matches has declined from a high of about $500 million in 1946—the year Joe Louis defended the championship against Billy Conn and Tami Mauriello—to the current total of less than $1 million a year.

Still, many people who don't bet on other sports wouldn't dream of missing out on some of the excitement that a major bout generates, especially when a charismatic figure like Muhammad Ali is in the ring.

Hemingway's Bout with Boxing

The short story "Fifty Grand," by Ernest Hemingway, explains why boxing is unpopular among bettors and bookies.

The story revolves around Jack Brennan, a boxer who bets on his opponent, Jimmy Walcott, to win. Walcott, informed of the plan, tries a little fancy footwork of his own and lands a foul blow that ought to have disqualified him and given Brennan the fight. But Brennan ignores the painful blow and insists upon continuing the match. He delivers a foul punch of his own and loses the fight—but wins $50,000. Although it wasn't easy for him to lose while appearing to want to win, Brennan explained how he did it: "It's funny how fast you can think when it means that much money."

Muhammad Ali in training. (Mitchell Rose.)

What Ever Happened to Wrestling?

Up until about 60 years ago, championship wrestling matches were serious affairs that were heavily bet. Eclipsed by boxing's fast action, and equally fast rise in popularity, wrestling limped into retirement. When it did eventually resurface, it was more "sportacular" than sport—carefully rehearsed tumbling and rolling, acrobatic feats, gimmicks, ring–shaking body slams, and verbal bouts with the audience and referees.

It went beyond mere "fixing." Everyone knew it was pure showtime and, in activity at least, it mattered very little who won or lost; it was how they played the game that counted. "Good guys" were matched against "bad guys"; among them were masked marvels, Gorgeous George (platinum blond hair and matching gold lamé outfits), Ricky Star (he daintily tossed red roses to his audience between pirouettes), and Haystacks Calhoun (it was sufficient for him to just stand there and be BIG).

Just about the only place you'll see high–quality, pure wrestling matches these days is in the Olympics. Otherwise, this 4,000-year-old, once–noble contest between beautiful, strong, perfect bodies is nothing more than show biz in the guise of sport.

HANDICAPPING

Aside from blind faith, there are a number of actors to take into consideration when deciding which boxer to bet on.

According to one expert, the first rule of thumb is: bet the champion. Temper this maxim by considering the opponent's experience, age, recent history, and present physical condition.

In general, an experienced fighter has the edge over a greenhorn, but his reflexes may not be what they used to be either. Ali lost to Frazier in 1971 because he had been out of the ring too long. And it didn't help that Ali didn't take Frazier's challenge seriously enough to train thoroughly, either. Personalities are important in boxing, because a boxing match is a one-to-one confrontation. The emotional factor comes into play, and should be considered. And never underestimate the power of a boxer with a good knock-out punch: even a superior fighter who outclasses his opponent can be felled by a good knock-out punch if he leaves himself open or if his opponent can penetrate his defenses.

BETTING

Private bets in boxing usually follow straight odds. In the famous Ali-Frazier bout of 1971, Frazier was the 7 to 5 favorite. If you had a bet on him to win, you would have put up seven dollars and won five. Bets on Ali would have been five dollars, and if he had won, bettors could have been seven dollars richer.

As with baseball, boxing bets with bookies use a split line. So if you had bet Ali, you would have put up five dollars to win six dollars from the bookie.

(UPI.)

It's estimated that $3½ million is wagered every weekend on NHL action. And that figure can only increase, as the sport becomes more and more popular.

HANDICAPPING

Like the point spread in football and basketball, hockey's lines are usually quoted in terms of goal spreads—the number of goals by which the favorite must win in order for its backers to collect. Here are some things to look for before you take the plunge.

Home Ice Advantage

Skating on home ice is definitely a plus in hockey, and usually accounts for half a point in the goal spread. The reason for this is two-fold: the players get more pumped up when playing before their fans; and the officials, though loathe to admit it, are often intimidated by the noisy fans (who can be as violent as the players themselves), so they are more apt to call penalties against the visiting team.

Goaltending

Next to the home ice advantage, the quality of the goaltending should weigh most heavily in your handicapping system. A good goalie can often make a woebegone team into a winner. Goals scored against a goalie and *shutouts* (when the goalie prevents the opposing team from making any goals) should tell you who's hot and who's not.

Shots Per Goal

An interesting slant to the game of hockey is the number of shots required to score one goal. According to one expert, who kept tabs on 400 games, the best teams will score one goal for every eight shots taken. One in twelve is average for the worst teams. Additionally, the team with the highest number of shots-on-goal also won or tied a higher percentage of the games.

Then there's the short-handed goal, which occurs when a team has less skaters than the opposing team because it has been penalized. A team that scores a short-handed goal has an almost 80 percent chance to go on and win the game. Teams that score regularly in this manner, like the Islanders, are very dangerous for opposing bettors.

When a team has one more player than its opponent, it's called a *power play*. The teams that score lots of power play goals also win a lot of games. So the smart bettor likes the big power play teams, especially when they are matched against teams that are highly penalized.

BETTING

Hockey betting is like football and basketball betting, with bettors using a goal spread instead of a point spread. But the goal line differs from football and basketball in that it is split, and a double quotation is made. For example, the favorite-team bettor may give up 2½ pucks (meaning they must win by 3), but the underdog-team bettor only gets 2 pucks (meaning they must either win or lose by less than 2). The advantage for the bookie is great here. If the underdog loses by 2 pucks, the bookie collects all the favorite bets, but makes no payments to the underdog bettors. Winning one side and pushing the other can happen quite often due to low scoring games.

SPORTS SEASONS

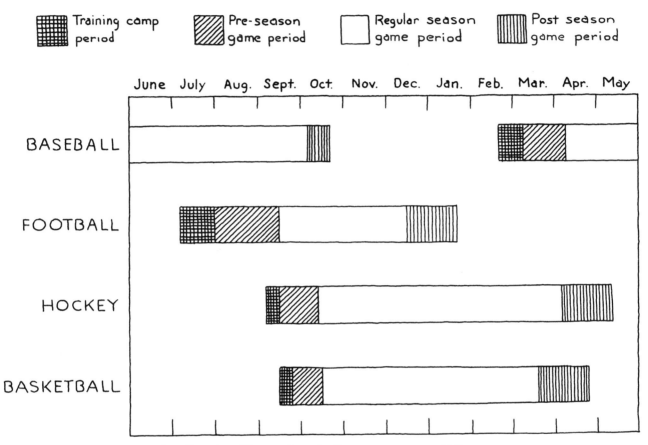

The serious sports bettor can be kept busy all year long. The approximate time from pre-season games until the final game is: baseball—225 days, football—175 days, hockey—240 days, basketball—215 days.

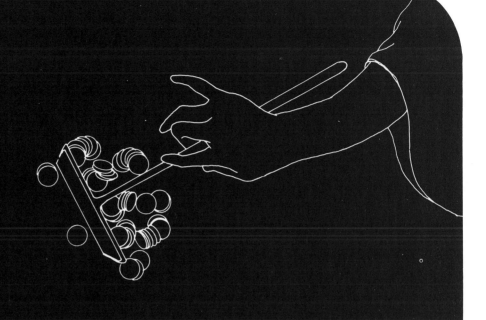

CASINOS—
IN THE
BIG TIME

ALL THAT GLITTERS

Most people who have never been inside a gambling casino can close their eyes and create a picture of what it's like. Movies, books, and television have taken us there many times.

Your first visit may live up to all your expectations, or you may be disappointed. Much depends on where you go, and what you expect to see.

There are places where the glitter, glamour and sophistication of beautiful people in evening clothes is still the norm, and there are casinos where casual is the word and evening dress is reserved for the employees.

At one time, casinos were the playground of only the rich and famous. Today, they are a business in competition for a share of the entire leisure market and you are a much-sought-after potential customer.

The casino operators want your first experience to be fun because they want you to come back. If you have enjoyed playing the games and watching the people, you will. If you happen to lose a little money while having fun, well, next time you might win. That's what it's all about, isn't it?

But it's not fun to stand around wishing you knew what everyone else was doing. Which game should you play? Try them all. It won't be long before you find a favorite. Some of the games are easy—just play and hope for the best. Others require skill, and offer a challenge. Some games offer a better chance of winning than others.

In the pages that follow you will learn the basics of the most popular casino games. Some, like craps and blackjack, may be familiar to you from friendly neighborhood gatherings. But casino rules differ from the home–grown variety. In addition, there are rules which vary from one casino to another (*house rules*). But once you understand the basics, changes in the house rules will pose no problem. You'll also find words of caution about foolish betting when the odds are stacked against you.

Learning these basic rules and avoiding the enticing traps will not turn you into a professional gambler. But you don't have to be one to enjoy the games.

Be a cautious player instead of a foolish bettor or a timid spectator, and you will enjoy yourself and go back again and again.

(Las Vegas News Bureau.)

INSIDE INFORMATION

The world of casinos is governed by strict, precise regulations. One rule which rarely changes from game to game or from casino to casino is that all bettors are playing against the casino, also called *the house.* Since casinos are in business to make money, they must collect more from losing wagerers than they pay out to winners, if they want to stay in business. This doesn't mean that you'll be cheated, however. (A crooked casino is rare these days, but you're sure to avoid any hanky-panky if you stick to the larger, well-established ones.) Casinos assure their profits with the *house percentage* (also called the *house edge,* or *house advantage*) they give themselves.

As explained in Section One, the odds against winning are a mathematical way of expressing a bettor's risk. For example, the actual or correct odds against a single number winning on one spin of the roulette wheel are 37 to 1. Logically, if you wager $1, you should stand to win $37 (plus your original $1 bet). But if casinos paid winners at the correct odds, they would ultimately make no money, because in the long run things tend to even up. For every dollar wagered and lost by their collective customers, the casinos would, in the long run, return one dollar in winnings. That's no way to run a business, so casinos change the correct odds slightly—sometimes not so slightly—in their favor.

In roulette, for example, casinos give 35 to 1 odds. So, if you win on a $1 bet, you'll win $35. The house percentage is $^2/_{38}$ or $5^5/_{19}$ (5.26) percent. This means that you will average a loss of $5^5/_{19}$¢ for every $1 bet. The casino, in the long run, is making $2 for every $38 bet.

Casinos apply this house percentage in varying degrees to all the games they offer. Therefore, they will always be the winners in the long run.

Casinos require players to make bets with chips, not cash. Casino chips come in denominations of $1 (usually white or yellow), $5 (usually red), $25 (usually green), and $100 (usually black). In most casinos you buy chips either at the playing ta-

To London . . .

To East Coast residents of the United States, London is almost as convenient a gambling spot as Las Vegas and more exciting than Atlantic City.

The 23 casinos in London are all located, by law, in private gambling clubs. To enjoy the privileges of gambling you must be either a member or the guest of a member. But you can easily become a member by filling out an "Intent to Game" form, which will be processed in 48 hours.

To gamble in a sedate atmosphere, try the Clermont, Crockfords, or Ladbrokes where you'll find yourself surrounded by antiques and oil paintings, and up to your eyeballs in "class." These clubs are located in townhouses or historic mansions, with excellent dining rooms and small casinos that cater to "high rollers."

Bigger, noisier, and busier casinos—like the Playboy Club, Palm Beach Club, or International Sporting Club—are also available to the tourist by membership.

Vicki Lawrence's interpretation of a gambling casino.

bles, or at the main cashier's cage. (Usually you cash in the chips at the cage too, although some casinos —particularly those in the Caribbean—let you cash them in at the playing tables as well.) Some casinos forbid players to take chips from one table to another—players either cash them in, or trade them for different chips before moving on to the next table.

The mandatory use of chips definitely affects the way you play, and is a clever move on the part of the casino operators, who apparently know human psychology. Tests have proven that people bet and tip more freely when substitute money is used. Chips lend an extra measure of make–believe to what is, after all, only a game.

Casinos reinforce the loss of a sense of reality: there are no windows or clocks in the gaming rooms. The time of day—even whether it's day or night—loses importance and influence over the players' actions.

Another way casinos encourage betting is this common practice: if you win three dollars on a one-dollar bet, the dealer will pay you off with a five-dollar chip, and take change for the house by sliding a one-dollar chip off your stake. If you're buoyed by your last win, you're likely to make your next bet that five-dollar chip instead of your usual one-dollar bet.

Players should also be wary of drinking too much while gambling. Many casinos offer free or inexpensive liquor so players will loosen up and bet more freely.

It is wise to determine how much you can realistically afford to lose before you get any chips. This amount should be thought of as part of your expenses, the same as your hotel room, meals, etc.—the cost of lively entertainment. Once the figure has been established, do not exceed it. You can keep your bankroll alive for a long while by betting intelligently. Make small bets, and don't expect to win. If you do win, use the house money (winnings) to extend your playing time or increase the size of your bets.

LAS VEGAS CASINOS

Las Vegas casinos fall into two categories: the plush and the not-so-plush.

The famous hotels along the Strip offer not only the plush casinos but dining in theater-restaurants with beautiful shows and big-name talent and sports and convention facilities. Such non–gambling activities were originally offered gratis; to lure the gambler in and keep him there awhile. These facilities are self-sustaining now, for no one needs to be lured to Las Vegas any longer. The hotels on the Strip—luxurious and classy to some, garish and brash to others—seem to follow the philosophy that the fancier the surroundings, the more money people will be willing to risk.

On the other hand, downtown Las Vegas hotels and casinos still offer deals—like a free phone call or free photograph, or a free dollar's worth of nickels for the slot machines—to attract the gamblers. And it's the masses they're after, offering penny slot machines and 25¢ craps tables. These are the not-so-plush casinos, and they come right to the point—they just want you to gamble. Food, shows, and the like are just distractions, as far as they're concerned.

The Strip.
(Las Vegas News Bureau.)

Downtown Las Vegas during the annual Mint 400 Desert Race.

Strip Hotels and Casinos

Hacienda Hotel
Dunes Hotel
Caesars Palace
The Castaways
Frontier Hotel
Silver Slipper
Stardust Hotel
Circus Circus
Tropicana Hotel
Aladdin Hotel
MGM Grand Hotel
Flamingo Hotel
Sands Hotel
Desert Inn Hotel
Riviera Hotel
Landmark Hotel
Thunderbird Hotel
Sahara Hotel
Las Vegas Hilton
Showboat Hotel
Royal Inn
Royal Las Vegas
Holiday Inn Center Strip
Paradise Hotel
Holiday Inn
Jockey Club
Marina Hotel

Downtown Hotels and Casinos

California Hotel
Carousel Club
El Cortez
Four Queens
Fremont
Golden Gate Casino
Golden Nugget Casino
Horseshoe
Las Vegas Club
Lady Luck Casino
The Mint Hotel
Nevada Hotel
Union Plaza Hotel
Western Hotel

ANYONE FOR TWENTY ONE?

The object of casino blackjack is to get a card-count higher than the dealer without exceeding 21. If this sounds familiar to you, it's because that is also the object of the private blackjack game. (See pages 100–106.) Many of the rules are the same also, but there are major differences, too.

In casino blackjack the house is always the dealer and the table is arranged for a maximum of six players. Aside from the dealer, the house also employs a *pit boss,* who acts as a kind of blackjack overseer. Among other duties, the pit boss observes the action for any cheating on the part of the dealer or any player and referees occasional disputes.

Cards are dealt from a box–like device called a *shoe.* Unlike a private game, where one 52-card deck

is used, as many as eight decks—410 cards—can be used, but four decks are common. Multiple decks are used to make card counting a difficult, if not impossible task.

In the casino, players must bet before any cards are dealt, and although there are betting limits, they differ from table to table. (The minimum bet in most casinos is two dollars.) Make sure you check the minimum betting limit before you sit down.

The dealer's decision to stand or hit is determined by the house rules. Usually he must stand if he holds a count of 17 or more, and must hit if his total is 16 or less. Counting the ace as 1 or 11 is also usually predetermined for the dealer.

Bets are placed in the betting

Blackjack. (Las Vegas News Bureau.)

squares directly in front of each player, then the deal begins.

Two rounds of card dealing follow. Each player receives one card in each round, starting at the dealer's left and continuing clockwise. The players' cards are either face up or face down depending on the house rules, while the dealer always gets one up and one down. (In European casinos the dealer takes his second card only after all the players have played out their hands.) Players may look at their cards as soon as they are dealt. The first player to the left of the dealer is in the pressure seat, because he makes his hit-or-stand decision first. The game moves quickly, so some say a beginner should try to sit as far to the dealer's right as possible, to give himself more time to make his decision. This also gives the player more cards to see in case he is keeping track.

If the dealer has a natural he has won. He exposes his cards immediately, and collects the bets from all the players except those who also hold a natural. If a player holds a natural too, he exposes his cards and keeps his bet. (He doesn't win anything.) If a player holds a natural and the dealer doesn't, he exposes his cards immediately, and he wins his bet plus whatever amount the house pays for a natural, usually at 3 to 2 odds. From this point on, the active players (those who have not held a natural) decide, in turn, whether to stand or to be hit. If a player goes bust after taking more cards, he exposes his cards and loses his bet to the house.

When all the players have stood or gone bust, the dealer plays his hand.

If all the players have gone bust, the dealer collects all bets and need never show his hand. If there is at least one active player, the dealer exposes his face-down card and stands or hits as the house rules dictate.

If the dealer goes bust, he has lost to every active player, and pays them even money. If he stood at a total which is higher than that of an active player, he has won, and collects that player's bet. If he stood at a total which is lower than that of an active player, he has lost, and pays that player even money. If his total ties with a player's total, no one wins, and the player's bet is returned to him.

Players may double down if they wish. As in a private game, this is voluntary on the player's part, and

In casinos, cards are dealt from a shoe, which holds several decks of cards. Its use saves time and allows more hands to be played between shuffles, and it makes card counting very difficult for the players. Some casinos are going back to using a hand-dealt single deck as a come on, but they shuffle it frequently. (From Dealing Casino Blackjack, *by Thomas F. Hughes, Thomas F. Hughes Publications.)*

Practice Makes Perfect

There is no better place to prepare yourself for that first trip to a casino than in the privacy of your own home.

To make the home experience more authentic, there are several games now on the market that let you turn your home into a casino. For about ten dollars you can buy a craps and blackjack table layout, dice, cards, instruction book and play money. A small roulette wheel with a felt cloth that resembles an authentic layout costs a little more. Call a few friends, lay out the craps or blackjack table, or the roulette wheel, and you're ready.

Another way to learn casino blackjack and baccarat is through the use of a programmable computer. Unisonic Manufacturers makes a pocket as well as a desk model; both cost around $50. The computer displays your hand and the house hand, and you play against it using casino rules. It even reshuffles the cards at a certain point in the game, programs the size of your bet, and keeps a running total of your bankroll. Texas Instruments also makes a Las Vegas-style baccarat computer (TI-59).

Your TV set can also help turn your den into a casino with the electronic TV gambling games that are available.

A player indicates that he is standing with the first two cards dealt, by placing them under his bet.

If he is not satisfied with the two-card total, he indicates he wants to be hit by scratching the table with the two cards.

When a player being hit wants to be hit again, he scratches the table with his fingers.

When a player being hit wants to stand, he waves his hand over the cards.

(Above photos from *Dealing Casino Blackjack*, by Thomas F. Hughes, Thomas F. Hughes Publications.)

Cards are the Devil's Books.

(English proverb)

cannot be forced by the house. A player indicates he is doubling down by turning both of his cards face up and doubling his bet. The dealer then gives him one card, face down.

Players may also split a pair, by turning both cards face up and placing a bet on the second hand. The play proceeds with the two separate hands.

Players may also add an insurance bet, which means that they are taking 2 to 1 odds that the dealer's down card is not valued at ten. When the dealer asks who wants to make an insurance bet—it can be made only if the dealer shows an ace—the bettor wagers up to one-half his original bet and collects if the dealer has a natural.

Some casinos allow a player to *surrender,* or give up before the hand is played after comparing his two cards with the dealer's up card. In this case a player loses half of his bet. Casinos may not allow players to surrender if the dealer shows an ace.

Following are suggestions for hitting or standing, doubling down, and splitting a pair. They do not guarantee consistent winning, but will give the conservative player a better chance to win.

Caveat Card Counter

Casinos discourage card counters by dealing multiple–deck games. Suspected counters are distracted by dealers speeding up the game, or needless noise and chatter. Nevertheless, some players have become so proficient at card counting that casinos have banned them from playing there.

WHEN TO HIT AND WHEN TO STAND

If you are dealt	And the dealer shows	You should
2 through 11	2 through ace	Hit
12	2 or 3	Hit
12	4, 5, 6	Stand
12	7 through ace	Hit
13, 14, 15, 16	2 through 6	Stand
13, 14, 15, 16	7 through ace	Hit
17 through 20	2 through ace	Stand
18 through 20— soft count (ace is 11)	2 through 7	Stand
19 through 20— soft count	8 through ace	Stand
21 (black jack)	2 through ace	Smile

WHEN TO SPLIT A PAIR

If you have a pair of	You should
Aces	Always split.
2's, 3's, 6's	Split if dealer shows 7 or under.
4's	Split only if dealer shows a 5.
5's, 10's	Never split.
7's	Split if dealer shows 8 or under.
8's	Always split.
9's	Split unless dealer shows 7, 10, ace.

WHEN TO DOUBLE DOWN

If you are dealt	You should
17, 18—soft count (ace is 11)	Double down if dealer shows 3 through 6.
14 through 16—soft count	Double down if dealer shows 4 through 6.
12, 13—soft count	Double down if dealer shows 5 or 6.
11—hard count (ace is 1)	Always double down.
10 (if allowed)—hard count	Double down if dealer shows 2 through 9.
9 (if allowed)—hard count	Double down if dealer shows 2 through 6.

Edward Thorp's System

The most famous of all system players is Edward O. Thorp, mathematics professor, computer expert and author of *Beat the Dealer.* His system is based simply on counting the 10-count cards (10s, jacks, queens and kings). The greater the proportion of 10-count cards to non-10-count cards left in the deck, the better your chances of winning.

In this system, the player must convert the ratio of 10-count to non-10-count cards to a decimal. Thorp's computer came up with a table which assigns a decimal number to every possible hand combination (your total hand vs. what the dealer shows). If the 10-count vs. non-10-count decimal is higher than the decimal assigned to your hand (from Thorp's chart) you hit—otherwise you stand.

When Thorp took his chart to Las Vegas and began to clean up, the casino owners quickly requested that either he or the chart go. To this day, people sitting down at a blackjack table and taking out a chart are asked to leave.

The House Advantage in Blackjack

There is no true number that represents the advantage the casino enjoys over the player at the blackjack table. The variables involved make the number impossible to arrive at.

Odds and probabilities change each time a card is dealt from the deck. Players do not play mechanically; they alter strategies, thereby changing the odds on winning or losing.

The famous man-about-gambling, John Scarne, once went through a complex series of mathematical computations which proved that if all blackjack games were played with a single deck of cards, and both the house and the player did the same thing every time they had a certain count, in the end the house would win approximately 6 percent more often than the player.

This advantage will diminish if the player is experienced, cautious and consistent. Conversely, it will increase if the player is unknowledgeable, imprudent and inconsistent.

Blackjack Systems

All blackjack systems are based in some way on the player's ability to count or remember certain cards. The house has, in most cases, taken this advantage away from the player by using multiple decks, which makes counting very difficult.

Simply counting 10-count cards or high- vs. low-count cards will give you some indication of what to do. If there are a lot of 10-count cards left before the deal, or more high than low cards, then bet heavy—because your chances of winning are greater. This is the simplest of systems, and merely moves the odds slightly in your direction.

Another system recommends remembering each card as it is played, and doing mental arithmetic. Every card from 2 through 7 is counted as a plus-1, every card from 9 through ace is counted as a minus-1, and 8's don't count at all. Before the next hand is dealt, check your total. If you have a minus total, it means more low than high cards are left in the deck, and you should bet light. If you come up with a plus total, it means more high than low cards are left, and you should bet heavy.

BANK CRAPS—CALL THE ROLL

DEALER

DEALER

BOXMAN

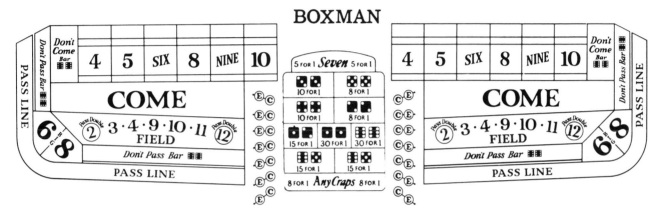

STICKMAN

A bird's-eye view of the craps table.

The casino crap table resembles a small, felt-covered stadium where emotions run high, voices are raised, hands are clapped and one may unashamedly root against the house. The crap table is the best place in the room to have fun. And it offers the most attractive odds af any casino game. With informed betting, you can extend the life of your bankroll—and your fun.

But, more often than not, this green felt sporting field is approached with trepidation. The action looks fast, the betting looks complex, and the other players look like experts as they manipulate their chips, doubling bets or pulling back winnings between rolls.

The basic game is a simple one and its procedures depart from those in private craps (see pages 48–53) only in that the casino banks all bets. Players do not play amongst themselves, only against the house. When a player loses a bet, the house collects; when a player wins, the house pays out.

Players stand around the crap table, with as many playing as there is room to accommodate. Several casino employees monitor the action:

• The *dealer* handles paying the winners and collecting losing chips. Dealers can move come bets and place the place bets for the players. (Players place line bets, come bets, field bets, big 6 and 8 bets.)

• The *boxman* takes cash and gives chips in return, and rules on disputes.

253

• The *stickman* retrieves the dice after each roll and gives them to the roller. He's the only one beside the roller allowed to handle the dice. He also places and pays off the player's proposition bets in the center of the layout.

Players must place their bets before the dice are rolled. When all bets have been made, the stickman gives the dice to the roller, who must throw them right away.

Bets are placed in the appropriate box on the crap table, and the betting is the only complicated part of the game.

SMART BETS

Although the house percentage varies from casino to casino, the following bets are among the best buys in most casinos:

• **Pass.** Before the dice are rolled, the roller or anyone else at the table may put his bet on the pass line. This indicates that he thinks the roller will win—roll a 7 or 11 on the first roll rather than a 2, 3, or 12 (*craps out*); or make his point before rolling a 7. This bet must be made before the roller's very first throw, or before his first throw after he has won or lost.

• **Don't Pass.** Here the opposite prevails, and the bettor feels that the roller will not win. If either a 2 or 12 is rolled (a casino will "bar" one or the other, and whichever one is not barred is a winner just like a 3), the roller loses but, in most casinos, the "Don't Pass" bettor ties and his money stands or may be removed. If the roller rolls a 3 on his first roll, or craps out before making his point, the don't pass bettors win. If the roller fails to make his point (rolls a 7 before repeating his point number) the don't pass bettor wins too.

• **Come.** The come bet is fun and exciting. It is as dramatic as having the dice in your own hands. This bet may be made prior to every roll after the shooter's come-out roll by having one or more chips placed in the come box. It means that whatever the dice do on that roll is considered the first roll for the bettor. If the roller is trying to roll an 8, you bet the come line, he rolls a 6, and the 6 now becomes your point. If he had rolled a 7 he would have lost, but since this counts as the first roll for you, you would have won. If he had rolled a 2 it would mean nothing to him, but since 2 on the first roll is craps, you would have lost. As long as he keeps rolling, your come bet is alive, and you may place additional come bets before each roll. Since you could have many chips on the table representing many bets going for you at one time, it's like being in several games at once. (The dealers keep track of your bets but you must still call upon your own powers of concentration. If you should win a bet, they usually let it ride in the come area—you have to take it away yourself if you don't want to bet.)

Smart Bets

You can tell the difference between a smart bet and an unwise bet by what the house edge is. The smaller the house edge, the smarter the bet. The house edge varies from casino to casino but ranges from about .59 percent for a smart odds bet, to about 16.0 percent for an unwise "any 7" bet. Here are some average house edges on smart bets:

• Pass and Come—1.41 percent

• Don't Pass and Don't Come—1.40 percent

• Pass with Odds—.84 percent

• Pass with Double Odds—.59 percent

• Don't Come. This is like don't pass, except that you are betting that a 7 will come up before a certain number, or that the shooter will roll craps on the next roll.

The smart bets—pass, don't pass, come and don't come—are usually even money bets. You can make them even smarter bets by increasing the payoff and making them odds bets.

Odds Bets

After placing your initial bet, and anytime a point has been established by the shooter, you may double that bet by making an additional bet (the amount depends upon the number you are taking odds on) "behind" the first bet. Now, in fact, you have two bets riding on the same outcome. Should you win, the original bet is paid off at even money, and the second bet is paid at the true odds for the point made. The points 4 or 10 usually pay 2 to 1; the points 5 or 9 pay 3 to 2; and the points 6 or 8 pay 6 to 5.

Odds bets should not be tried until you are comfortable and familiar with the basic game. Since odds bets are not shown on the table, they require nodding agreement between the bettor and the dealer.

Place Bets

You can *place* a bet on any point number by announcing it to the dealer. The payout depends upon the odds against throwing the number before a 7. Placing the 6 or 8 pays 7 to 6 and is a good bet, as the

Craps. (Las Vegas News Bureau.)

house edge is only 1.5 percent. Poor bets are the 4 and 10, which pay 9 to 5 (the house edge is 7 percent). The 5 and 9 pay 7 to 5 with a house edge of 4 percent—not bad, but not good either.

Buy Bets

These are like place bets, except you "buy" the number you bet on in order to get true odds and so avoid the house edge. You must, however, pay a 5 percent commission. The odds on bought numbers are: 2 to 1 for the 4 and 10; 3 to 1 for the 5 and 9; 3 to 2 for the 6 and 8. A player who wants to take extra odds would be wise to make place bets on 5, 6, 8, and 9, and buy the 4 and 10.

A Hazardous History

People have played games using dice or a reasonable facsimile of marked cubes for thousands of years. Dice is sometimes called "rolling the bones" because the first dice were animal bones. At one point, in medieval Europe, dice games were forbidden as the devil's work. The stigma associated with dice games probably originated at that time.

The dice game called hazard, which was probably invented by the Arabs, became the most popular game in England during the 18th and 19th century.

Hazard was very much like modern craps. If you rolled a 2 or 3 on your first roll, you lost. These numbers were called "crabs," and the word appears to have been later distorted to "craps."

The Ivory League

Are you a high school graduate? Do you have a flair for arithmetic? Are you reasonably articulate? Do you have normal dexterity? Are you able to stand on your feet for eight hours at a stretch? Are you a night person? Do you like to dress up every night and go out? Do you mind working for low starting wages with no guarantees of advancement?

If the answers to all of the above are yes, then perhaps you qualify for one of the schools (licensed by the state in which they operate) engaged in the preparation of casino workers, such as dealers, croupiers, and stickmen. There is no overabundance of these skilled workers because only a few of these schools are currently in operation. As more states pass gambling legislation, there undoubtedly will be a shortage of qualified casino personnel.

Tuition in these schools ranges from $600 to $1200 for a six- to eight-week course, and there are no scholarships.

The curriculum starts with basics and proceeds to advanced courses in the theory of blackjack, roulette, and craps. In the more technical areas there are card shuffling, dealing and chip manipulation, which includes counting and stacking. The "laboratory courses" include actual play under nearly authentic conditions.

Graduates may work in the United States or anywhere in the world where casinos are located. Knowledge of the local language is mandatory for work in foreign casinos.

Starting salary is low and tips are not guaranteed. The allure is the lifestyle.

UNWISE BETS

These bets are poor risks, and should be avoided:

Proposition Bets

These are the Seven, Any Craps, and Hard Way bets shown in the center of the table.

● Hard Way. Players are betting that the dice will deliver the numbers they bet on with doubles; and that the doubles will appear before the roller throws a 7 or *soft number* (his number, but not doubles, such as a 6 formed by 4-2). The house edge is high, usually running between 9 and 11 percent, depending on the number.

● Seven. Players are betting that a 7 will appear on the next roll. The house edge is around 16 percent.

● Any Craps. Players are betting that the next roll will be a 2, 3, or 12. The house edge is around 11 percent.

Big 6 or 8

Players are betting that a 6 or 8, whichever they put their money on, will appear before a 7. The house edge is around 9 percent. (You can get an identical bet at a house edge of only 1.5 percent by placing the 6 or 8, as mentioned above.)

Field

Players are betting that on the next roll any one of the field numbers will appear: 2, 3, 4, 9, 10, 11, or 12. The payoff is even money. Also in the "field" are 2 and 12, which pay double. (In some casinos either the 2 or 12 pays triple.) This sounds like a fair bet, but the experts claim it's a poor risk, because the house edge is over 5 percent for the field.

BANK ON BACCARAT

This is the casino game seen most often in the movies. The media have presented the game as one of mystery and glamour. Actually, it is the simplest card game played in the casino.

The word "baccarat" means "zero" in Italian, while chemin-de-fer, which is a version of the same game, means "railroad" in French. There is also a third version, called baccarat-en-banque. In all versions, the object of the game is to get a card-count of nine. The major differences among the three concern whom you are betting against—the other players or the house. The odds, however, are the same.

Chemin-de-fer and baccarat-en-banque are more popular in European casinos, while baccarat is favored in the United States. In most casinos the American version is called Nevada-style baccarat.

Baccarat. (Las Vegas News Bureau.)

HOW TO PLAY NEVADA-STYLE BACCARAT

Nevada-style baccarat may be played by one to seven people at the small baccarat tables, and up to twelve people at the larger tables. Rules vary from casino to casino, and are posted by the tables, but the basic play remains the same. The minimum and maximum bets are also posted by the tables. The minimum bet is usually at least ten dollars, reinforcing baccarat's traditional image as a big money game.

Two hands of two face-down cards each are dealt from a shoe containing six or eight decks of cards. One hand is the bank hand, the other is the player hand. (There is only one bank hand and one player hand, no matter how many people are playing.) Each player must decide before the hands are dealt which of the two he will bet on to win, and indicate his choice by placing his bet in the appropriate box on the table.

This is one casino game where the deal does not permanently remain with the house. The shoe passes counterclockwise around the table. A player retains the deal until a bank hand loses. However, the dealer does not have to bet on the bank hand. If all players bet on the same hand, the deal passes to the house.

It doesn't really matter which hand a player bets on to win. Everything depends upon chance, and the play is governed by hard, fast rules. Neither hand has an advantage, and winners are paid off at even money. The house insures its profit by taking a 5 percent commission (called

The typical "big table" layout has space for up to 12 bettors. Players are assigned numbers from 1 to 12, depending upon the seat they choose. Bets for the bank are indicated by placing chips on the bank numbers, in the proper boxes on the table. Bets on the player are placed just over the line in the player boxes.

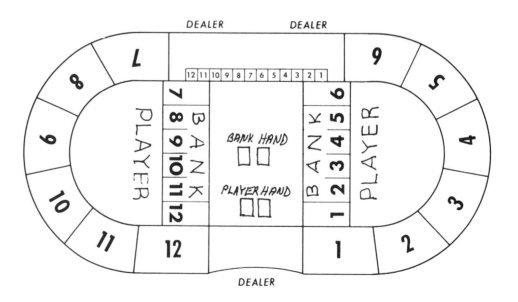

CHEMIN–DE–FER

In Nevada-style baccarat, the house always holds the bank, paying off winners and collecting from losers. In chemin-de-fer, one of the players holds the bank and is designated the banker.

At the start of the game the bank is auctioned to the highest bidder, and after that it rotates around the table. If a player does not wish to be the banker, the bank moves to the next player.

The banker decides how much he will bet and puts that amount, in chips, on the table. The other players may cover as little or as much of the total bank bet as they wish, starting with the first player to the right of the banker. If the first player covers the entire amount, he says, "banco." Then the other players must wait until the game is finished and hope for a chance at the next game.

When the betting is completed, the banker tells the dealer to begin. As in bacarrat, two face-down, two-card hands are dealt—one for the banker, and one for the players. The banker and the player (one player representing all) look at their cards and immediately turn them over if a hand totals a natural eight or nine.

The player hand goes first. If his card count is zero, one, two, three or four, he must draw another card (as in Nevada-style baccarat). If the count is five, he has the option to stand or draw. (There are no options in baccarat.) If the count is six or seven, he leaves them face down and does nothing more. (In baccarat he would turn them face up.)

Whatever the player hand has done, the cards remain face down (except natural eight or nine, or the card he has drawn).

The bank hand stands or draws by the same rules as baccarat, with two exceptions. If the bank hand totals three he may stand or draw if the card drawn by the player is a 9. (In baccarat he must draw). If the bank hand totals five, he may stand or draw if the card drawn by the player is a 4. (In baccarat he must draw.)

Baccarat-en-Banque

This European version of baccarat is played mostly in French casinos. In the 1920s a Greek syndicate operated virtually every baccarat table in Europe and they imposed no limit on betting. The player is dealt two hands and he may bet on either or both. The house is dealt one hand. The bank rests permanently in the hands of the house or a concessionaire.

The play starts the same way as in Nevada-style baccarat, and the same rules govern the players' hands. The bank may draw or stand as he wishes with no rules. As in chemin-de-fer, no one shows his hand until the bank is finished playing (unless a player has a natural). If a player has bet the same amount of money on both of the player hands, and one wins and the other loses, it is considered a tie; otherwise, each of the two player hands are considered individual bets and win or lose as such.

vigorish) out of the winning bank hands. If players should bet the bank hand and win, the house will put in a marker against their seat number in the amount of the commission they owe. If you win ten dollars betting on the bank hand, for example, you owe the house fifty cents. Even if you eventually lose all your money, you will still owe the house commissions on your previous winning bank hands. Players

Las Vegas Poker

Poker – loving gamblers can find plenty of action in Las Vegas both downtown—at Bingo Palace, Fremont, Golden Nugget, and Union Plaza, to name a few; and on the Strip—at Aladdin, Caesar's Palace, Dunes, Flamingo, Hilton, MGM Grand, Sahara and Stardust, among others. Action there is not the friendly social game type—players are strictly out for blood. If you don't win consistently in your own friendly games, stay away from the Las Vegas poker tables.

settle up with the house either before they leave the table, or during a break while the cards are shuffled. The house dealer will let the players know what they owe.

Once all the players have placed their bets on the table and the two hands have been dealt, the play begins with the dealer turning over the cards.

The winning hand is the one that comes closest to a count of nine. A third card may be drawn, to help the count of either hand. Whether or not a third card is drawn depends on the count of each hand as dealt. The rules for drawing a third card for a player hand are shown (they are also posted at the baccarat table).

Aces count as 1; 2-spot through 9-spot cards count their face value; 10-spot and picture cards count as zero. Counts over nine take the value of the single-unit digit. A hand of 13, then, would have a value of 3; a hand of 10 would have a value of 0.

A two-card hand that totals exactly nine—(ace-8), (2-7), (3-6), (5-4), (10-9), (picture card-9)—is called *la grande*. A two-card hand that totals exactly eight—(4-4), (3-5), (2-6), (picture card-8), (ace-7)—is called *la petite*. These are the two best hands—*naturals*—and are usually winners without having to draw a third card. In the case of a tie, no one wins and bets are moved to the tie box to be used for the next game.

NEVADA-STYLE BACCARAT RULES

If the player hand totals	The player hand must
0, 1, 2, 3, 4, 5	*draw* a card
6, 7, 8, 9	stand

If the bank hand totals	The bank hand must
0, 1, 2	*draw* a card
3	*stand* if player's third card is 8; otherwise *draw* a card.
4	*stand* if player's third card is 1, 8, 9, 0; otherwise *draw* a card.
5	*draw* if player's third card is 4, 5, 6, 7; otherwise *stand*.
6	*draw* if player's third card is 6 or 7; otherwise *stand*.
7, 8, 9	*stand*

If the player hand is a two-card "natural" 8 or 9, the bank automatically loses.

PLAYING THE SLOTS

The standard slot machine is a sturdy but complex mechanism with hundreds of parts and springs. Out of the 8,000 possible symbol combinations that can appear, only some are winners. How often these winning combinations appear is determined by the casino owner and, once set, this house percentage never varies over the long run, unless the machine is reset. (This would require the dismantling of the machine by an experienced mechanic.) But the house percentage may differ from machine to machine. Unfortunately, there is no way a player can determine which slot machines give out the highest percentage of returns.

In other words, the house is the only consistent winner, and there is nothing a player can do to increase his chances of winning. The best betting advice is to stay away from these "one-arm bandits."

However, most first–time visitors to American casinos don't heed this advice, and admittedly it is difficult, because the slots are everywhere. Probably a majority of the slots today can take up to five coins, and by feeding in more coins the player may either increase the potential payout, or the ways the symbols can line up to form a winning payout. If you are unfamiliar with the slots ask a change girl for help. Here, however, are the simple how-to's of working a slot machine:

1. Get change from the change booth. Sometimes there are only quarter machines, but each coin denomination is usually represented.

2. Put your money in the slot.

3. Pull the handle.

That's it. No strategy, nothing to learn. The game is 100 percent luck, and everyone has the same chance of winning.

Payouts vary from about 75 to 98 percent. It may not seem so if you are constantly losing, but on an average, a machine will give back 90 percent of the coins it takes in, leaving the house with a 10 percent cut. New players frequently think that their winnings are only the coins that spill out into the payout hopper. Actually many machines don't pay out the entire jackpot into the hopper. You must stay with the machine and call a change girl to get the rest of your money.

Watch the experienced players

(Courtesy of Nevada Gaming Schools, Inc. Photo by Mike Nichols.)

Of all casino games, the slot machine is the only all–American product. The handle was pulled for the first time in San Francisco in 1895. Charles Fey, the inventor, leased his machines to bars and split the winnings. The machines were similar to today's, and were set to return 86 percent of the coins they received.

The product was improved by Hubert Mills of Chicago, who flooded America with his machines until about 1930, when there were hundreds of thousands of them in use all over the country.

In those days slot machines were considered the devil's work, and it became popular for a politician to have a picture of him appear in the newspapers wielding an ax to a machine.

Today, in Nevada and New Jersey, these machines are considered to be businesses and are taxed as such. The state of Nevada collects $40 per year for each machine. County and federal taxes are charged too. Clark County (Las Vegas) collects $250 per machine and the Federal Government collects $250 per machine. Therefore, each machine pays a base figure total of $540 in taxes, and an additional percentage of its gross winnings go back to the tax collectors.

In 1976 the machines in Nevada earned a net amount of $440 million after paying out winnings.

What appears to be the penny-ante part of casino gambling, because it deals mostly in coins, is actually one of the biggest moneymakers and compares with the take from the craps and blackjack tables.

operate, then emulate them. Just six to ten pulls with no return, and they move on to another machine. Where casinos abound and competition is keen, the house must maintain at least a few machines with a high percentage payout if it wants players to keep coming back.

The "cold" machine cannot be warmed up by feeding it. It is cold because it is set to be stingy. If you are playing a cold machine (you can't really determine this unless you play the machine a reasonable amount of time), leave it and find one that is in a more generous mood. Regardless of the mathematical logic, there are people who think they can induce a machine to spill its guts merely by gorging it on silver. If, in the middle of this feeding technique, they run out of change, don't try to move in on their territory. Tradition and temper demand that you allow a player to continue at his machine without interruption after he has gotten more change.

Beware, too, of the illegal machine. This machine, usually found in private clubs, is set for a house advantage of 30 percent.

Anatomy of a Slot Machine

The coin unlocks the handle which, when pulled downwards, starts the three reels inside the machine moving. Twenty different symbols are pictured around each reel. A timer determines how many revolutions each reel makes, and activates a rod-like device that drops on the ratchets of each reel. The left reel stops first, then the middle, and then the right one. As each one stops, a symbol appears at the pay line "window" of the machine. Whether the machine gives up its coins depends upon which symbols appear. How many coins they pay out depends on the house percentage. The usual fare is fruit (plums, oranges, melons, cherries, lemons), bars, and bells.

Since each reel can stop in any one of 20 positions, there are 8,000 possible combinations.

(Courtesy of Nevada Gaming Schools, Inc. Photo by Mike Nichols.)

ROULETTE— ROUND SHE GOES

Roulette may not be quite as old as the invention of the wheel, but it comes close: the ancient Greeks and Romans were reported to have played a game of chance using the revolving wheel of an overturned chariot. The symbol of the wheel of fate may be found in the art of the Chinese, the Aztec Indians and the American Eskimo. Some of the art depicts a vertical wheel surrounded by horizontal worshippers; evolution has brought us the horizontal wheel attended by vertical worshippers.

The European wheel, as first introduced, contained 36 numbers plus a zero as it does in today's European casinos. The game first appeared in America in the gambling houses of New Orleans. Americans eventually added a double zero; therefore, the American wheel contains 38 pockets.

The *croupier* (the man or woman in charge of the game) keeps the

Roulette. (Courtesy of Four Queens, Las Vegas, Nevada)

large horizontal wheel with its 38 pockets turning slowly. The players, who sit around the table, place their chips on the table in position to indicate the number(s) they think will win. There is a minimum and maximum number of chips you may bet, and they are posted at the table.

When all the players have made their bets, the croupier spins a small wood, ivory, or plastic ball along the rim of the big wheel. As the momentum of the ball slows down, the ball falls onto the surface of the wheel and bounces into one of the 38 pockets. The number of that

pocket is the winning number. There are only 11 different types of bets and 8 different payoffs. In Europe, where there are 37 pockets, if the ball falls into the zero pocket all bets are held, and the wheel is respun. This results in a mathematical house edge of 2.70 percent.

In America, where there are 38 pockets, if the ball drops into either the zero or double zero pocket, the house wins all (except those bets placed on zero or double zero). This advances the house edge from 2.70 percent to 5.26 percent, and is the major reason why most players shun

Until the development of the Las Vegas resort casinos in the 1940s, gambling took place in clubs. Here, the Old Northern Club, before machine gambling came in. (Gladys Frazier Collection, University of Nevada, Las Vegas Library.)

the roulette wheel in American casinos.

Look around the casino. Compared to the lively crap tables and card tables, the roulette wheel is usually a quiet place. Even though the odds are poor, the liability is somewhat offset by other advantages (such as being able to sit down). And roulette is the simplest game to learn and to play.

HOW TO PLAY ROULETTE

The layout	What you are betting	The payoff*

Five numbers (0 or 00 or 1 or 2 or 3) ----------------------------- 6 to 1
Low (1 through 18) -------------------- Even
Two numbers (5 or 6)----------------- 17 to 1
Three numbers (7 or 8 or 9) ------------------------------------- 11 to 1
All even numbers ---------------------- Even
All red numbers ----------------------- Even
Six numbers (13 or 14 or 15 or 16 or 17 or 18)-------------------- 5 to 1
All Black numbers --------------------- Even
Second twelve numbers (13 through 24)------------------------- 2 to 1
All odd numbers ----------------------- Even
One number (30)----------------------- 35 to 1
Four numbers (29 or 30 or 32 or 33)------------------------------- 8 to 1
High (19 through 36) ------------------ Even
One column (3 or 6 or 9 or 12 or 15 or 18 or 21 or 24 or 27 or 30 or 33 or 36)--------------- 2 to 1

*Although the odds on payoffs vary with the type of bet, the house edge remains 5.26 percent, except for the five-number bet where the house edge is 8 percent. The five-number bet should, therefore, be avoided.

Each player uses a different colored chip. This is each player's color as long as he sits at that wheel. The number of chips placed on the board indicates the amount of that bet. And the placement of the chip on the board indicates your bet.

The System

In the late 1800s a wealthy Englishman named Joseph Jaggers decided to beat the roulette wheel at Monte Carlo. He directed his "staff" to record every turn of every wheel for weeks. Then he analyzed the results.

One wheel seemed to deliver certain numbers more often than it statistically should, so Mr. Jaggers sat down at that wheel and won £60,000.

The house realized it had a biased wheel and immediately repaired it. The house also instituted a policy of balancing each wheel daily. Any opportunity to mechanically "read" the wheel disappeared.

Today, there are more sophisticated systems which take into account the speed of the wheel, the speed of the ball as it rotates, mathematical probabilities, minimum maturity sequences, and many other scientific inputs.

There are some systems that defy classification. An example is illustrated in the story about the man who sat at a roulette table in Las Vegas. He was playing slowly and cautiously, and he was winning. Before placing a bet, he would take a small pill box from his coat, lift the lid and look inside. Someone finally asked him what he was doing, and the player allowed his curious companion to peek inside the box. There he saw that the small space was painted partly in red and partly in black. In the box a roach crawled about. The bug's position when the player flipped the lid dictated the next play.

The serious, up-to-date system player may make use of various means, but no true system has ever been devised.

The global gambling directory includes:

Argentina	Korea
Austria	Lebanon
Australia	Lesotho
Antigua	Macao
Aruba	Malta
Bahamas	Martinique
Belgium	Mexico
Botswana	Monaco
Bulgaria	Morocco
Canada	Panama
Columbia	Paraguay
Curacao	Portugal
Dominican Republic	
Ecuador	Puerto Rico
Egypt	Russia
England	St. Kitts
France	St. Maarten
Germany	Swaziland
Ghana	Syria
Gibraltar	Tangier
Haiti	Tasmania
Hong Kong	Turkey
Indonesia	United States
Italy	Uruguay
Jakarta	Yugoslavia
Kenya	

FOREIGN CASINOS

Many brochures aimed at foreign–bound travelers now boast of legalized gambling casinos. Often a visit to one of these casinos is part of the travel "package"—along with the air fare, hotel, etc. The list of countries that host casinos grows yearly, but the greatest concentration is in Europe.

Among the local rules you'll want to find out about from the country's tourist office in the United States: dress (it may not be as casual as gamblers from the United States are used to); language (English is usually spoken in all casinos); admission fees (they can vary quite a bit); entrance requirements (you will probably have to show your passport at the door); tipping, etc. Travelers' checks are usually accepted at most foreign casinos for conversion into chips, but the exchange rate there may be lower than the official rate.

For the most part, the gambling games in foreign casinos are the same as those in the United States. Blackjack and craps may not be offered, but roulette, baccarat, chemin-de-fer, and even slot machines are among the familiar sights. The smaller foreign casinos will have a smaller number of playing tables, though.

In anticipation of a big win, find out about restrictions concerning how much money you are allowed to take out of the country you will be visiting.

Aside from the foreign-based casinos, the gambling traveler will also find gambling facilities aboard most cruise ships. Pictured here are the slots aboard the Queen Elizabeth 2. (Courtesy of Cunard.)

MONTE CARLO

Reeking of gambling tradition, Monte Carlo is Europe's most famous casino. The name itself means "Charles' Mountain," after Prince Charles of Monaco, who built it on 350 acres of land overlooking the Mediterranean in 1850.

Monte Carlo became fashionable around the turn of the century, when the Prince of Wales (later Edward VII) became a regular visitor. And, despite a few financially lean periods, it has remained fashionable ever since. Glamorous visitors include royalty—Kaiser Wilhelm II, King Leopold II, Emperor Franz Josef, Czar Nicholas II, Prince Rainier (of course), among others—as well as the elite—Elsa Maxwell, André Citroën, F. Scott Fitzgerald, Winston Churchill, Aga Khan, Aristotle Onassis (who literally took over the place, via the Sea Bathing Society and Circle of Foreigners, which still owns the casino), and Maria Callas, to name but a few.

Today's gambling tourist will probably be disappointed by Monte Carlo. The gold leaf and crystal chandeliers shimmer and shine as always, but they and the big gamblers are found only in private gaming rooms. The tourists fill the smaller gambling rooms, known collectively as "The Kitchen." Tourists in Monaco looking for American style luxury can gamble at the casino in the Loew's Hotel.

Le Casino de Monte-Carlo.
(Monaco Government Tourist Office.)

KENO—JUST THE TICKET

Keno is a bingo-type game with one basic difference. In bingo, once you have purchased a card, you proceed to cover numbers as they are called; in keno, you choose the numbers you wish, and cover them first. You may choose one number or as many as you like up to fifteen. You must place a minimum bet but you may bet higher if you wish. Then you sit and wait to see if the numbers you covered are called. It is possible, if your bet is high, and the numbers you choose are correct, to win up to $25,000. That's the biggest single payoff in the casino—and the least probable.

The keno lounge is the management's favorite spot. There, the house conducts its business with around a 25 percent edge. Therefore, it can splurge on deep carpets, comfortable chairs, pretty girls and in some cases, free drinks. The girls will help you make out a ticket, carry it and your bet to the counter, bring you a receipt and a drink, and in general, make your stay in the lounge comfortable. Since tipping is practically mandatory in the keno lounge, and winners tend to be generous tippers, the staff actually roots for you to win.

HOW TO PLAY KENO

Obtain a ticket before the game starts, and choose your numbers by marking them off on the ticket. The minimum bet is 70¢. (If you mark

The game of keno.

one number, it is called a one-spot ticket; two numbers, a two-spot ticket; and so on.) You may choose up to 15 numbers, and still bet only 70¢. The catch is that the more numbers you pick, the more you have to get correct before you can win any money.

A popular keno ticket is the 8-spot ticket, on which a bet of $3.50 is placed. On this ticket you begin to win once five of the eight numbers you picked are correct.

The keno *writer* validates your ticket and gives you a copy. Then you sit back and wait while a machine randomly picks 20 out of 80 numbered balls and flashes the numbers on a screen.

The chances of selecting one of the winning numbers are 1 in 4. (For every correct number there are three incorrect.) This translates into 3 to 1 odds. If you play one number and bet 70¢, and it is a winning number, you will receive $2.10 (your wager of 70¢ plus $1.40). Winning $1.40 for a 70¢ bet is 2 to 1 odds. The difference between your odds of winning (3 to 1) and payoff odds (2 to 1) gives the house its 25 percent edge.

Keno is touted as the only game in the casino to offer the big, instantaneous, $25,000 payoff. All a bettor has to do to be eligible for this $25,000 prize is to pick eight numbers, bet $3.50, and get all eight correct. However, the rules also state that the house will pay $25,000 *in total* for that game. If there are other winners besides the one who hit the jackpot, the $25,000 is shared by all. If there are a lot of little winners, your $25,000 jackpot is reduced by the amount of the little payoffs. If there are several big winners, they are still paid out first, so the pot can all but disappear.

The odds against your winning the jackpot are immense. The chance of hitting eight out of eight and collecting $25,000 is 1 in 74,000. The likelihood of picking ten out of ten is 1 in 9 million.

Keno Betting

If you mark one number and bet 70¢, and that number is one of the twenty winning numbers, you collect $2.10. If you pick eight numbers and all eight are winners, you can win $25,000 if you bet $3.50.

Ticket	Number correct	Payoff for	
		70¢	$3.50
One spot	0	0	0
	1	2.10	10.50
Eight spot	0–4	0	0
	5	6.00	30.00
	6	60.00	300.00
	7	1,150.00	5,750.00
	8	12,500.00	25,000.00
Fifteen spot	0–5	0	0
	6	1.00	5.00
	7	5.00	25.00
	8	15.00	75.00
	9	75.00	375.00
	10	200.00	1,000.00
	11	1,500.00	7,500.00
	12	5,000.00	25,000.00
	13	15,000.00	25,000.00
	14	20,000.00	25,000.00
	15	25,000.00	25,000.00

Casino Cards

Gambling can fray your nerves and wear your patience, but imagine what it does to all those playing cards. Since Nevada has a total of about 2,500 tables devoted to card games, it should come as no surprise that it's a card–supplier's idea of heaven. One club alone—Harold's in Reno—wears out 10,000 decks of cards in one month. That means it replaces a worn deck every 39 minutes.

Las Vegas is one of the most respectable towns I've ever known; people are so preoccupied with gambling they've no time for the major vices.

(Noel Coward)

Way Tickets / Once the single number bets become boring, the keno player advances to the "way tickets." Here, numbers are grouped, and the ways of winning and the cost of the ticket begin to get complicated. It's a way of combining several tickets as one—a device to increase your winning possibilities on one ticket, and save you the expense of buying several tickets. For example, if you select twelve numbers and arrange them in four groups of three each, the keno man at the desk decides that what you have done, in reality, is create four nine-spot tickets, since each group of three numbers can turn up in nine different combinations. Therefore, your minimum bet is four times 70 ¢, or $2.80. The amount you can win varies with the total number of correct picks out of your total number of selections. The least is four out of nine, and would pay 30 ¢. The most you could have correct on one ticket is nine, which would pay $12,500. You would need all twelve correct to qualify for the $25,000.

Combination Tickets / The seasoned keno player can spend hours devising a complicated combination ticket. The keno writer or desk man will work with the player on one of these because of the challenges of coming up with the day's most complicated ticket.

The cost of these tickets and the payoff varies with each ticket. It is a matter of pride for the player to have invented the combination, and to have it accepted by the house.

Talk about luck!

1	●	●	●	5	6	7	8	9	10
11	12	13	14	15	●	17	18	19	20
21	22	23	24	●	26	27	28	29	30
31	32	33	●	35	36	37	38	39	40
41	42	43	44	45	●	●	●	49	50
51	52	53	54	55	56	57	58	59	●
61	62	63	64	65	66	67	68	●	70
71	72	73	74	75	76	77	●	79	80

*On this ticket the player has marked twelve numbers, grouped into four groups of three each
. . . which are in turn combined into four groups of nine each. Betting the minimum of 70¢
per group of nine, the total bet is $2.80.*

1.	2	3	④	16	㉕	34	46	㊼	㊽
2.	2	3	④	16	㉕	34	㊀	69	㊆
3.	2	3	④	46	㊼	㊽	㊀	69	㊆
4.	16	25	34	46	㊼	㊽	㊀	69	㊆

*Let us assume that six of the selected numbers are picked (4, 25, 47, 48, 60, 78). The player
would have the following:*

Ticket 1 wins 4 of 9 and collects . . . . $ .30
Ticket 2 wins 4 of 9 and collects . . . . $ .30
Ticket 3 wins 5 of 9 and collects $2.30
Ticket 4 wins 4 of 9 and collects . . . . $ .30
Total win $3.20

Junkets

Junketeers are people who organize gambling sprees, called *junkets*. (Some junketeers are employed by the casinos.) The chartered-plane fare, hotel, even meals and entertainment are paid for by the casino.
But, as you know, there's no such thing as a free lunch, and the gambler does eventually pay by gambling thousands of dollars.

Unless the gambler has established a line of credit with the casino, he must put up *front money*, in cash or a certified check, and deposit it in the casino cashier's cage. When he's ready to gamble, he approaches the playing table where he wants to gamble, and requests a specific amount of money in chips. He is given the chips and signs a *marker* (I.O.U.) for the amount. This may be repeated as often as the gambler wishes, until he reaches his credit line (or the amount of the front money). When he leaves, he settles up with the cashier. By the way, you don't have to lose all your front money on a junket but you do have to gamble with that amount. There are no written rules, but anyone who just goes along for the free ride will find they will be labeled *D.N.I.* (Do Not Invite) for the next junket.

SUGGESTED READING

Gambling—its who's, why's, where's, and how-to's—is a subject that could scarcely be exhausted in a single lifetime, let alone one single volume. For those who wish to dig deeper into this fascinating subject, or one particular facet of it, the following sources of additional information are suggested, many of which were used in researching this book.

PAST AND PRESENT,
FUN AND FLAVOR,
FACT AND FICTION

Bergler, Edmund. *The Psychology of Gambling*. New York: International Universities Press, 1970.

Bradshaw, John. *Fast Company*. New York: Harper's Magazine Press, 1975.

Browlaski, Harry. *Easy Money: Being the Experiences of a Reformed Gambler*. Searchlight Press, 1911.

Chafetz, Henry. *Play the Devil*. New York: Clarkson N. Potter, 1960.

David, F. N. *Games, Gods, and Gambling*. Charles Griffin and Co., 1962.

Devol, George H. *Forty Years a Gambler on the Mississippi*. 1892. Reprint. New York: Johnson Reprint Corporation, 1968.

Drzazga, John. *Wheels of Fortune*. Springfield, Ill.: Charles C. Thomas, 1963.

Hargrave, Catherine Perry. *A History of Playing Cards*. 1930. Reprint. New York: Dover Publications, Inc., 1966.

Hutcheons, John K. *The Gambler's Bedside Book*. New York: Taplinger, 1977.

Jacoby, Oswald and Moorehead, Albert. *The Fireside Book of Cards*. New York: Simon and Schuster, 1957.

Jimmy the Greek. *Jimmy the Greek*. Chicago: Playboy Press, 1975.

Jones, Philip J. *Gambling Yesterday and Today*. Vermont: David and Charles Inc., 1973.

Longstreet, Stephen. *Win or Lose: The Social History of Gambling in America*. Indianapolis: Bobbs-Merrill, 1977.

Messick, Hank and Goldblatt, Burt. *The Only Game in Town: An Illustrated History of Gambling*. New York: Thomas Y. Crowell Company, 1976.

Potter, Stephen. *The Theory and Practice of Gamesmanship*. New York: Bantam Books, 1965.

Puzo, Mario. *Las Vegas*. New York: Grosset & Dunlap, Inc., 1977.

Reid, Ed and Demaris, Ovid. *The Green Felt Jungle*. New York: Pocket Books, 1963.

Rouge et Noir. *The Gambling World*. 1898. Reprint. Detroit: Gale Research Co., 1968.

Steinmetz, Andrew. *Gaming Table: Its Votaries and Victories, in All Times and Countries, Especially in England and France*. 2 vols. 1870. Reprint. Montclair, N.J.: Patterson Smith Publishing Corp., 1969.

Todhunter, Isaac. *A History of the Mathematical Theory of Probability*. Chelsea Publishing Co., 1949.

GAMBLING AND GAMBLING GAMES IN GENERAL

Ainslie, Tom. *Ainslie's Complete Hoyle.* New York: Simon and Schuster, 1975.

Arnold, Peter. *The Book of Gambling.* New York: Hamlyn, 1974.

Carroll, David. *Playboy's Illustrated Treasury of Gambling.* New York: Crown Publishers, Inc., 1977.

Frey, Richard. *According to Hoyle.* New York: Fawcett, 1970.

Goodman, Michael. *Your Best Bet.* Chatsworth, California: Brooke House Publishers, Inc., 1975.

Goren, Charles. *Go With the Odds.* New York: Macmillan Publishing Co., Inc., 1969.

Hyams, Joe and Riddle, A. *A Weekend Gambler's Handbook.* New York: Random House, 1963.

Jacoby, Oswald. *Oswald Jacoby on Gambling.* New York: Hart Publishing Co., 1974.

McQuaid, Clement. *Gambler's Digest.* Chicago: Follett, 1971.

Newman, David. *Esquire's Book of Gambling.* New York: Harper and Row, 1962.

Scarne, John. *Scarne's New Complete Guide to Gambling.* New York: Simon and Schuster, 1974.

Thackeray, Ted Jr. *Gambling Secrets of Nick the Greek.* Skokie, Ill.: Rand McNally & Company, 1968.

Wykes, Alan. *The Complete Illustrated Guide to Gambling.* New York: Doubleday & Co., Inc., 1968.

Periodicals:

Gambling Times (published monthly). Available from Gambling Times, 839 North Highland Ave., Hollywood, CA 90038.

Casino & Sports (published bi-monthly). Available from Gambler's Book Club, 630 South 11th Street, Box 4115, Las Vegas, Nevada 89106.

(Note: The Gambler's Book Club publishes an extensive list of gambling books available from them by mail order. Write to the above address.)

CARD GAMES

Cohen, Leo E. and Scharff, Robert. *Cohen's Complete Book of Gin Rummy.* New York: Grosset & Dunlap, Inc., 1973.

Crawford, John R. *How to Be a Consistent Winner in the Most Popular Card Games.* New York: Doubleday & Co., Inc., 1953.

Dowling, Allen. *The Raw, Rowdy World of Poker.* Cranberry, N.J.: A.S. Barnes and Co. Inc., 1973.

Gibson, Walter B. *Hoyle's Modern Encyclopedia of Card Games.* New York: Dolphin Books, 1974.

Mar, Timothy T. *Face Reading: The Chinese Art of Physiognomy.* New York: Signet, 1974.

Roddy, Irv. *Friday Night Poker.* New York: Simon and Schuster, 1961.

Steig, Irwin. *Common Sense in Poker.* New York: Cornerstone Library, Inc., 1963.

Thorp, Edward O. *Beat the Dealer: A Winning Strategy for the Game of Twenty-One.* Rev. ed. New York: Random House, 1966.

U.S. Playing Card Company. *Official Rules of Card Games.* U.S. Printing Co., 1968.

Zadeh, Norman. *Winning Poker Systems.* Englewood Cliffs, N.J.: Prentice-Hall, Inc., 1974.

DICE, BINGO, LOTTERIES, SWEEPSTAKES

Feinman, Jeffrey. *How to WIN! Sweepstakes, Contests, Lotteries and Bingo.* Chicago: Playboy Press, 1976.

Frey, Skip. *Complete Book of Dice Games.* New York: Hart Publishing Co., Inc., 1975.

Jacoby, Oswald and Crawford, John. *The Backgammon Book.* New York: Viking Press, 1970.

Holland, Tim. *Beginning Backgammon.* New York: Crown Publishers, Inc., 1975.

————. *Better Backgammon.* New York: David McKay Co., Inc., 1974.

Scarne, John. *Scarne on Dice.* Harrisburg, Pa.: Stackpole Books, 1974.

HORSE RACING

Ader, Paul. *How to Make a Million at the Track.* Chicago: Contemporary Books, Inc., 1977.

Ainslie, Tom. *Ainslie's Complete Guide to Thoroughbred Racing.* Trident, 1968.

Alfange, Dean. *The U.S. Horseracing Industry.* New York: Kensington Pub. Corp., 1976.

Breyer, Andrew. *Picking Winners: A Horseplayer's Guide.* Boston: Houghton Mifflin Company, 1978.

Cohen, Ira S., and Stephens, George D. *Scientific Handicapping: Tested Ways to Win at the Race Track.* Englewood Cliffs, N.J.: Prentice-Hall, Inc., 1972.

Dash, Norman. *Great Betting Systems.* Los Angeles: Price/Stern/Sloan Publishers, Inc., 1968.

Flanagan, Tom. *Beat the Races.* New York: Arc Books, 1973.

Lewin, Sam. *The Education of a Horseplayer.* New York: Hawthorn Books, Inc., 1969.

Meadow, Barry. *Success at the Harness Races.* Secaucus, N.J.: Citadel Press, 1970.

Osborne, Walter. *The Thoroughbred World.* New York: World Publishing Co., 1971.

Reynolds, Randolph. *The New Handicapper's Manual: A Guide to Making Money at the Races.* Pagurian, 1975.

Robertson, W. H. P. *The History of Thoroughbred Racing in America.* Englewood Cliffs, N.J.: Prentice-Hall, Inc., 1964.

Scott, Marvin. *The Racing Game.* Chicago: Aldine Publishing Company, 1968.

Thoroughbred Racing Association. *Directory and Record Book.*

Tilley, Chuck. *This Is Horseracing.* Miami, Fla.: E. A. Seemann Publishing, 1974.

Veeck, Bill. *Thirty Tons a Day.* New York: Viking Press, 1972.

Periodicals:

<u>Systems & Methods</u> (published bimonthly). Available from Gambler's Book Club, 630 South 11th Street, Box 4115, Las Vegas, Nevada 89106.

SPORTS BETTING

Friedman, Arthur, with Cohen, Joel H. *The World of Sports Statistics.* New York: Atheneum Publishers, 1978.

Olshan, Mort. *Winning Theories of Sports Handicapping.* New York: Simon and Schuster, 1975.

Strine, Gerald, and Isaacs, Neil D. *Covering the Spread: How to Bet Pro Football.* New York: Random House, 1978.

Sturgeon, Kelso, and Sports Action Editors. *Guide to Sports Betting.* New York: Harper & Row, 1974.

CASINO GAMBLING

Adams, Harland B. *Guide to Legal Gambling.* New York: Funk and Wagnalls, Inc., 1969.

Andersen, Ian. *Turning the Tables on Las Vegas.* New York: Vanguard Press, Inc., 1976.

Barnhart, Russell. *Casino Gambling: Why You Win/Why You Lose.* New York: E. P. Dutton, 1977.

Graham, Virginia, and Tulcea-Ionescu, C. *A Book on Casino Gambling Written by a Mathematician and a Computer Expert.* New York: Van Nostrand Reinhold Company, 1976.

Nolan, Walter I. *The Facts of Baccarat.* Las Vegas, Nevada: Gambler's Book Club, 1976.

———. *The Facts of Blackjack.* Las Vegas, Nevada: Gambler's Book Club, 1976.

———. *The Facts of Craps.* Las Vegas, Nevada: Gambler's Book Club, 1976.

———. *The Facts of Keno.* Las Vegas, Nevada: Gambler's Book Club, 1974.

———. *The Facts of Roulette.* Las Vegas, Nevada: Gambler's Book Club, 1970.

———. *The Facts of Slots.* Las Vegas, Nevada: Gambler's Book Club, 1970.

Scharff, Robert. *The Las Vegas Experts' Guide to Craps, Blackjack, Card Games.* New York: Grosset & Dunlap, Inc., 1970.

Stuart, Lyle. *Casino Gambling for the Winner.* Secaucus, N.J.: Lyle Stuart, Inc., 1978.

Acey-deucey, 95
Arcaro, Eddie, 187
Around the corner gin, 119
Atlantic City, 17
Averages, law of (*see also* Probability theory), 22

Baccarat, 257-60, 266
  baccarat-en-banque, 257, 259
  chemin-de-fer, 257, 259, 266
  Nevada-style, 257-59
Backgammon, 60
  basics, 60-62
  doubling cube, 60, 62, 65-66
  history, 62
  how to, 62-*63*
  luck vs. skill, 20, 60, 61
  odds, using, 64
  one-board (chouette), 65
  score keeping, 66
  stakes, playing for, 60, 62, 65-66
  tournaments, 64, *66*
Balasco, Bodine Jackson, 19, 38
Bank craps (casino craps), 48, 253-54, 266
  bets, 254-56
  big 6 or 8, 256
  buy, 255
  hard way, 256
  odds, 255
  place, 255
  proposition, 256
  seven, 256
  system playing, 30-31
Baseball, 233, 241
  betting, 234-36
  handicapping, 217, 233-34
Basketball, 231, 241
  betting, 231
  college, 230, 231
  handicapping, 217, 230-31
Bergler, Edmund, 7
Betting and bets, *see* Gambling and gamblers; games, specific subjects
Betting cards or pools, 235
Bingo, 20, 121, 124
  basics, 122-23
  how to play, 124
  laws regulating, 121, 122
  night, setting up, 122
Bingo lottery, state, 134
Biorhythm theory, 32-33
"Black" Sox scandal, 235
Blackjack, 100, 266
  basics, 101
  betting limits, 101
  bonus payments, 104
  casino, *see* Blackjack, casino
  dealer's advantage, 104
  history, 100
  how to play, 101-6
  misdeals, 106
  pairs, getting, 105
  player's advantage, 104-5
  two-card total, probability of occurrence, 104

Blackjack, casino, 16, 100, 266
  betting, 248-51
    systems, 252
  card counting, 248, 251
  dealing cards, 248, *249*
  house advantage, 252
Blanc, Francois, 38-39
Bluff, 70
Bolita (*see also* Numbers), 151, 156
Bones, *see* Dice; Dice games
Bookies (bookmakers), 214, 227, 232
  amount, total, bet with, 5, 227
  baseball betting, 234-36
  basketball, college, 231
  betting lines and odds, 219
  boxing bets, 238
  England, 15
  finding and selecting, 226-27
  football betting, 219, 223-27, 228
  horse race betting, 185, 204
  percentage or edge, 28
Bowie, "Gentlemen Jim," 19
Boxing, 237
  betting, 238
  handicapping, 238
Bridge, 108-9
  gambling at, 109
  superstitions, 31
  types of, 108
Browlaski, Harry, 3
Brummell, George Ryan (Beau), 29
Bug (*see also* Numbers), 151

Card games (*see also* Cards; names of games), *13*, 15, 41, 70-119
  cheating or hustling, 18, 58-59, 96-99
  history, *11*, 13-15, 18-19, 77, 90, 95
  kitty, 95
  luck vs. skill, 20
  odds, computing, 28
  rules, standard, 41
  superstitions, 30-31
Card sharps, *see* Hustlers or cheats
cards (*see also* Card games)
  collecting as hobby, *67*
  combinations possible in standard deck, 101
  crimped, 98
  cutting to cheat, 99
  death, card of, 69
  history, *12*, 13, 14, 15, 68-*69*
  hold-outs (bugs) for, 18
  marked, 18, 96, 96-98
  mechanic's grip for manipulating, 99
  seconds, dealing, 99
  shuffling, 76, 98
  stacking a deck, 98-99
  standard, 41
  tarot, 14
  uses other than games, 14, *68*, *69*
Carnival games, and cheating at (*see also* names of games), 125-29
Casino gambling (*see also* names of games), 8, 9, 244-71
  cards, consumption of, 270

Casino gambling (*cont'd*)
  betting
    chips, 245-59
    house limits, 32
    house percentage or edge, 28, 245
    systems, 30-32
  cheating, 245
  history, *14*, 15-19
  junkets, 271
  legalization, 15, 17
  luck vs. skill, 244
  odds, 245
  personnel, casino, schools for, 256
  house rules, 244
  places and houses, notable, 15, 16, 17, 124, 219, 245, 246, *247*, 260, 264, 266-67, 270
Cat game, 128
Cauthen, Steve, 174
Chain letters, 157-58
Chance, *see* Luck; Odds; names of games
Cheating, *see* Hustlers or cheats; Swindles and scandals; names of games
Chemin-de-fer, 257, 259, 266
Chouette, 65
Clothespin game, 127
Coburn, D. L., 116
Coins, tossing, 20, 22, 26-27
  cheating, 59
Commission on the Review of the National Policy toward Gambling, 5
Compleat Gamester, The, *13*, 15
Contest Hotline, 150
Countdown, 18
Craps, 48
  bets, 49-51
    fading, 49
    hard way, 50
    point, 50
    point numbers, table of, 50
    proposition, 51
    side, 50-51, 57
  casino, *see* Bank craps
  cheating or hustling, 56-57
  come outs, 49-50
  history, 51, 54-55
  how to play, 49-51, 56
  odds
    figuring, 52-*53*
    laying in correct, 57
  point numbers, table of, 50
  stake, 49
  terms defined, 49-50
Crawford, John R., 89
Cups and balls, 58

Daily Racing Form, 178, 184
Dandolos, Nicholas Andrea, *see* Nick the Greek
Darrow, Clarence, 5
Dealer's choice poker, 91
  cards dealt, number and order of, 94-95
  mutual cards, 95-96
  ranks of cards, 94
  wild cards, 91-94

Death, card of, 69
Devol, George, 18, 37, 38
Dice, 17, 54, 255
    beveled, 57
    flats, 57
    gaffed, 56-57
    loaded, 17, 56-57
    manipulation of honest, 57
    mismarked or tops, 56
    percentage, 56
    shapes, 57
Dice games (*see also* names of games), 48-66, 253-55
    cheating or hustling (*see also* Dice), 17, 54, 56-57
    history, 12-13, 54-55, 255
    luck vs. chance, 20, 48
    probability theory and, 22, 23, 24-25
Dog racing, 210-11
Dostoevsky, Feodor, 7, 41
Dovetail or riffle shuffle, *76*
Draw poker, 70
    betting limits, 78-79, 85
    bluffing, 84
    hands
        average winning, 86
        probability of improving, 81-82
    high-low, 94
    how to play, 80-81
    jackpots, or jacks or better, 83
    tight/loose playing, 90
Dumont, Eleanor (Madame Moustache), 16, 103

Eisenberg, Billy, 60, 61, *66*
Etiquette, card-playing, 117

Faro, casino, 16, 18
Felberbaum, Moishe (Chico), 61
Fey, Charles, 261
Football, 220, 241
    betting, 223-27, 228
    college, 229
    handicapping, 220-23, 229
        power rating systems, 228-29
Franklin, Benjamin, 68, 137
Freud, Sigmund, 7, 32

Galileo Galilei, 24-25
Gamblers Anonymous, 9
Gambler's fallacy, 22
Gambling and gamblers, (*see also* names of games, subjects), 5-6
    amateur, serious, 8-9
    amounts wagered (handles), 5-6, *7*, 16, 138, 151, 227
    characteristics and motivations, 5-7, 94
    compulsive, 3, 7, 9, 11, 94
    even-up proposition or even-money bet, 27
    famous gamblers (*see also* names), 12-13, 15, 18, 29, 31, 34-42, 102, 103
    favorites or "safe" bets, 26, 28
    illegal, 5, 144-45, 151-59, 214, 227, 232, 262

Gambling and gamblers (*cont'd*)
    junkets, 271
    laws regulating, 5-6, 15, 17, 19, 121, 122
    legalization issue, 5-6, 121, 143, 232
    longshot betting, 28
    luck vs. skill (*see also* Luck), 20-21
    prevalence of, 3-4, 5, *6*
    professional, 9
    recreational, 8
    systems, 30-33, 206-8
    superstitions, 29-31, 151-53
    taxes, 4, 5, 21, 141, 142-43, 145, 146, 261
    unusual and/or bizarre bets, 15, 36, 40
Gambling houses, *see* Casino gambling
Gates, John W. ("Bet-a-Million"), 36, 193
Gin rummy (gin), 110
    around the corner, 119
    bluffing, 116
    discarding, 115-16
    history, 110
    Hollywood, 117-18
    how to play, 111-16
    knocking or going gin, 114-15
    odds, 115
    Oklahoma, 118
    partnership, 118-19
    scoring, 113-14
    for three players, 119
Goldberg, Allan, 96
Golf, 107
    hustlers, 107
Goren, Charles, 109
Greyhound racing, 210
    betting on, 210, 211
    rabbit, mechanical, 211

Handicapping, *see* Odds; Sport wagering; specific sports
Harness racing (*see also* Horse races), 170, 171, 175
Hayano, David M., 94
Hazard, *48*, 55, 255
Heckethorn, Charles William ("Rouge et Noir"), 30-31
Hickok, "Wild Bill," 31
Hockey, 239, 241
    betting, 240
    handicapping, 239-40
Hollywood gin, 117-18
Hoop-tossing games, 127-28
Horse races, 168-69
    allowance, 172, 188-91
    betting on or backing, 199, 209
        big Q, 205
        bookies, 185, 204
        combination, 205
        daily double, 205
        division of bet money, 204
        exacta, 205
        on favorite, 26, 28, 206-8
        luck vs. skill, 20
        odds and payout, 179, 199
        off-track, 6, 203, 204, 232
        pari-mutuel system, 199, 209
        payoffs, record, 178

Horse races: betting (*cont'd*)
        place bet, 179, 205
        quinella, 205
        show bet, 179, 205
        systems, 206-8
        tote board, 179, 199, 200-1
        triple, 205
        windows, at track, 178-79, 204-5
    claiming, 172, 173, 188
    flats (thoroughbred), 170-71
    handicap, 173, 180-81
    handicapping (*see also* Horse races, betting on or backing), 183, 196-98
        biorhythms, 32-33
        comment line, 193-94
        distance, points of call, fractional times, weight, 191-93
        information sources, 183-85
        jockeys, information on, 184
        morning line, 183
        mud mark, 186
        number of race, 185
        race date, 185
        race, type and class of, 188-90
        speed rating and track variant, 191
        touts and tout sheets, 183
        track, 185
        track condition, 186
    harness racing, 170, 171, 175
    history, 12, 170, 171
    horses
        breeds, and breeding, 170-71, 175, 188, 190
        buying, 189
        famous, 174-75, 188
        gallop, 194
        ownership, world of, 190
        speed horses and stretch runners, 192-93
        trainers, 189, 190
        mud mark, 186
    information sources, 178, 183-84
    jockeys, 174, 184, 187, 191, 202
    maidens, 173
    match, 173
    non-claiming, 172-73
    notable, 172, 174, 175, 180-81
    quarter horse, 170, 171
    stakes races, 172-73, 180-81
    thoroughbred (flats), 170-71
    track
        betting, *see* Horse races, betting on or backing
        going to, 178-79
        handicapping and, 185, 186, 191
Hoyle, Edmond, 15, 41, 62
Hustlers or cheats (*see also* Swindles and scandals; names of games)
    jargon, 129
    devices and tricks of, 18, 56-59, 96-99, 125-29, 235
    famous, 37, 40, 42

Ice hockey, *see* Hockey
Independent events, principle of (probability theory), 22-25, 32

Irish Hospitals Sweepstakes, 144-45
Ivers, Alice, *see* Poker Alice

Jaggers, Joseph, 265
Jefferson, Thomas, 137
Jackpots, or jacks or better, 83
Jareki, Richard, 32
Jones, William (Canada Bill), 20
Junkets, 271

Katz, Richard, *66*
Keno, 18, 269
  how to play, 268-71
  tickets
    combination, 270-71
    way, 270
Kentucky Derby, 172, 173
Kitty, 95

Labouchere System, 30-31
Ladbroke's, 15, 245
Laforgue, Rene, 7
Las Vegas, 15, *17*, 124, 219, 246, *247*, 260, 261
Longden, Johnny, 187
Lotteries, private (*see also* specific lotteries), 136-37, 143
  numbers, 151-57
  sweepstakes, 144-50
Lotteries, state, 8, 12, 17, 20, 132, 133, 134
  bingo, 134
  chances of winning, 139-41
  draw, 134-35
  debate on, 143
  history, *133*, 136-38, *142*
  instant, 135
  numbers, 135
  prize, largest, 135
  profits from, 139
  scandals and swindles, 136, 143
  taxes, 141, 142-43
  winners, stories of, 134, 141
  winnings, claiming, 143
Luck
  vs. skill, 20-21, 23, 132, 244
  probability theory and, 22-28
  superstitions concerning, 28-31

Magriel, Paul, 61, 64
Mah-jongg, 120
Martin, Bob ("Mr. Oddsmaker"), 219
Martingale System, 32
Maturity of chances (*see also* Probability theory), 22
McNeil, Charles K., 215
Mills, Hubert, 261
"Minnesota Fats," "The Fat Man" (Rudolph Walter Wanderone, Jr.), 40
Money store game, 125
Monte, 16, 18
  cheating or hustling, 58-59
  three-card, Coney Island style, *59*
  three-card, Wild West style, *59*
Monte Carlo, 39, 265, 267
Mouse game, 126

Moustache, Madame (Eleanor Dumont), 16, 103
Mr. Hoyle's Games, 15
Muybridge, Eadweard, 194

Negro numbers, *see* Numbers
Neighborhood games (*see also* names of games), 46-47
  backgammon, 60-66
  bingo, 121-24
  blackjack, 100-6
  bridge, 108-9
  carnival games, 125-29
  chouette, 65
  craps, 48-57
  gin rummy (gin), 100-19
  golf, 107
  mah-jongg, 120
  poker, 70-96
  poker dice, 57
Nick the Greek (Nicholas Andrea Dandolos), 34-35, 42, 84, 89
Numbers, 132, 155, 232
  how to play, 155-57
  lotteries, legal, 135
  odds, 151
  operations, network, 152-54, 159
  picking numbers, superstition, and, 151-53

Oblenski, Prince Alexis, 62
Occultism and superstitions, 29-31, 151-53, 162, 163
Odds (*see also* names of games)
  house percentage or edge, 28
  probability theory and, 26-28
Oklahoma gin, 118
Oller, Joseph, 209
One-ball game, 127
Overhand shuffle, *76*

Paper gambles (*see also* specific subjects), 132
  chain letters, 157-58
  lotteries, 8, 12, 17, 20, 132-43
  numbers, 132, 151-57
  punchboards (push cards), 158-59
  stock market, 132, 160-64
  sweepstakes, 20, 132, 144-50
Partnership gin rummy, 118-19
Pascal, Blaise, *24*, 25
Penny fall game, 128
Pigeon (*see also* Hustlers or cheats), 58
Poker, 70
  acey-deucey, 95
  around the world, 95
  basics, 71-72
  betting, 75-77
    calling a bet, 76
    checking, 75, 76
    dropping or folding, 75-76
    limits, 78-79
    opening the pot, 75
    raising, 76, 79
    sandbagging, 76-77
  bluffing, 76, *77*, 84, 96
  casino, 16, 18, 260

Poker (*cont'd*)
  cheating or hustling, 82, 96, 98
  clubs, 78, 80
  criss-cross, 95-96
  dealer's choice, 91-96
  deck, 71
  draw, 70, 78-79, 80-84, 86, 90
  ethics, 84
  faces, characteristics and, 92-93
  hands
    flush, *73*
    four of a kind, *72*
    full house, *73*
    high card (no pair), *74*
    highest, probable original, 86
    improving, 81
    ranking, 71-74
    royal flush, *72*
    straight, *73*
    straight flush, *72*
    three of a kind, *74*
    two pair (a pair), *74*
  high-low, 94, 95
  history and anecdotes, 15, 77, 78, 89, 90, 95
  how to play, 75-77
  lowball, 94
  luck vs. skill, 20, 22, 23, 70
  pass the garbage, 96
  penny ante, 79
  players, profile of, 94
  pot, 71, 75, 79
  psychology and, 70, 71, 84, 92-93
  roll your own, 95
  shuffling cards, 75, 76
  strip, 88
  stud, 70, 84-88, 91-94
  superstitions, 31
  table stakes, 79, 96
  tight/loose playing, 89-90
  two-card, 94-95
  wild cards, 91-94, 95
  winning consistently, "rules" for, 89
Poker Alice (Alice Ivers), 16, 41-42
Poker dice, 57
Policy numbers, *see* Numbers
Pools, 235
Popular Bridge, 109
Private games, *see* Neighborhood games
Probability theory, 22-25, 32
  odds, computing, and, 26-28
  poker hands, ranking of, and, 71-74
Puerto Rican (*see also* Numbers), 151
Punchboards (push cards), 158-59

Queen, Madame (Stephanie St. Claire), 159

Reik, Theodore, 7
Resorts International, 17
Riffle or dovetail shuffle, *76*
Riverboat gamblers, 15, 18-19, 37, 38, 55
Roberts, Brian, 90
Roulette, 16, 18, 20, 245, 263-64, 266
  history, 263
  how to play, 265

Roulette (*cont'd*)
    odds, computing, 27
    system playing, 30-31, 32, 265
Rowan, Hughie, 41
Rules, first standard (*see also* names of
        games), 41

Scarne, John, 126, 252
Schultz, Dutch (Arthur Flegenheimer), 159
Scheinwold, Alfred, 108
San Francisco, early days of, 16
Shell game, 18, 19, 58, 59
Sheridan, Danny, 222
Skills (*see also* Hustlers or cheats), 58-59
Shoemaker, Willie, 187
Shuffling, 76
    to cheat, 99
Skill
    betting on feats of, 59
    vs. luck (*see also* Luck), 20-21, 23
Slot machines (slots), 18, 261-62, 266
    illegal, 262
    machines, mechanics of, 262
    payouts, 261
    taxes on machines, 261
Snyder, Jimmy "The Greek," 219
Soccer, 236
Sports wagering (*see also* Dog racing; Horse
        races; names of sports), 8-9, 213-41
    betting cards or pools, 235
    big eight or over/under, 235
    bookies, 219, 224-27, 234-36
    cheating and hustling, 231, 235
    gimmick bets, 235

Sports wagering (*cont'd*)
    homers, 235
    information sources, 217-18, 226
    luck vs. skill, 20
    point spreads or betting lines, 215-16,
        220-21, 223-26, 228-29, 231
    power lines or rating systems, 217, 219,
        228-29
    rum pools, 235
    six hit pools, 235
    sports lines, 219
Squeeze spindles, 18
Stock market, 132, 160
    history, 162-63
    how it works, 160-61
    occultism and, 162, 163
    tips on investing, 164
    swindles, 162
Straight poker, 70
Strip poker, 88
Stud poker, 70
    bluffing, 84
    five and dime, 91
    five-card, 85-86, 95
    hands, average winning, 86
    high-low seven-card, 94
    how to play, 85-88
    Mexican, or flip or peep-and-turn, 91-94
    seven-card, 86-88, 91, 94
    wild card, 91-94
Sucker (*see also* Hustlers or cheats), 58
Sutton, Glenn, 224-25
Sweepstakes, 20, 132, 146-48
    chances of winning, 148-50
    information source, 150

Sweepstakes (*cont'd*)
    Irish, 144-45
    taxes, 145, 146
Swindles and scandals (*see also* Hustlers or
        cheats)
    chain letters, 157-58
    lotteries, 136, 143
    punchboards (push cards), 158-59
    stock market, 162-63

Tarot, 14
Taxation, 4, 5, 21, *69*, 142-43, 145, 146, 261
Television game shows, 21
Thanatopsis Literary and Inside Straight
        Club, 78
Thompson, Ty ("Titanic") (Alvin Clarence
        Thomas), 9, 42
Thorp, Edward O., 252
Three-shell game, 58
Thurnblad, Arthur, 40
Turf Guide, 183
Twenty one, *see* Blackjack, casino

Vanderbilt, Harold S., 108
Vestal, Madame (Belle Siddons), 16, 102

Wanderone, Rudolph Walter, Jr. ("The Fat
        Man"), *see* "Minnesota Fats"
Wheel (*see also* numbers), 151
Wheel of fortune, 20, 126
Wild West, 5, 15, 96
Whole World Lottery Guide, 141
Wrestling, 238